In The Wings

My Life with Roger McGuinn and The Byrds

Ianthe McGuinn

NEW HAVEN PUBLISHING LTD

In the Wings

First Edition
Published 2017
NEW HAVEN PUBLISHING LTD
www.newhavenpublishingltd.com
newhavenpublishing@gmail.com

Front Cover Photo©Cyril Maitland
Back cover Photos©Courtesy of the Author
Cover design©Pete Cunliffe
pcunliffe@blueyonder.co.uk

In the Wings is a compelling tale of a woman's struggle to maintain a marriage with a celebrity rock 'n' roll band leader who becomes wasted on the way, and her ultimate redemption raising two children as a single mother amidst the conflicts of Sixties excess. I followed Ianthe's story with enthusiasm. Her victory was my hope with every turn of the page. Inspirational.

-   Jesse Lee Kincaid
    Rising Sons

Table of Contents

Destiny Train   5

Prologue Arizona Snapshots   7

1963-64 – Limitless Possibilities   33

1965 – Forging New Adventures   48

1966 – Prejudice vs. Fifth Dimension, Baby   89

1967 – Change is Now   109

1968 – Tromping Muddy Pastures with Rolling Stones   123

1969 – Juggling Chaos and Second Child   140

1970 – Three is a Crowd   151

1971 – Earthquake: God's Answer — Pick Up, Dust Off   171

1972-75 – Rebuilding (A Family sans Father)   191

1976-89 – The Ties that Bind   221

Epilogue Forgiveness   232

Afterword   234

Destiny Train

We are all given choices. Decisions must be made, goals must be set. How options affect our lives has always fascinated me. Riding in a train through the Italian countryside in 1968, we passed a small brick cottage. A young woman stood in the open doorway. It was summer. She wore a white shirt and pale blue skirt. Her left arm rested against the doorframe. She watched the train as we passed. I imagined it was something she did as a daily ritual, longing to be a passenger in a train that would take her away, dreaming of exotic places. What had been her destiny? She probably married a boy from the same village and had a brood of wild-haired children. I could have been that woman. It was me in the train, though, going from Rome to Calais. I was there with my husband, the man I loved. He was a member of the Byrds, a rock and roll band popular in the Sixties. They were on a European tour.

We had met in Los Angeles in late 1964. He was a struggling musician and I was a student and part-time waitress at the Ash Grove, a coffee house that featured traditional folk music. I was in love the moment I saw him. He had a halo around his golden hair. That was enough of a message for me.

He came in, sat in the back of the room, and listened to the music, quiet, pensive. I brought him coffee and plates of spaghetti. We used my evening's tips to fill the gas tank of an old Renault I had just bought. We'd drive around Los Angeles with other members of the band squeezed into the back seat. They were heady times.

In the summer of 1965, the Byrds' first record hit the charts. Girlfriends became history as the band's wallets were filled and groupies clamored for their attention. Jim and I managed to survive the turbulence of the changes and got married after our son, Patrick, was born in 1966. How we both made the choices that brought us to that moment in time is a mystery. Fate evolved and we connected.

We really don't know what guides us through life. Sometimes we live our lives ignoring messages and missing events. Overwhelmed by the acts of daily living we forget *the Now*. Stop... listen to your heart and body. Weigh your spirit. They hold the answer and the key.

(from a journal entry, November 8, 1995)

A musician will never go hungry as long as he finds a nice waitress.

—Johnny Cash

Prologue
Arizona Snapshots: 1942-1963

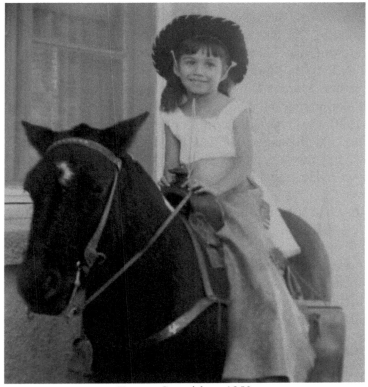

Tucson Cowgirl, ca 1950

Arizona was part of the New Mexico Territory when my family settled in the region. Gold and silver finds in the Chiricahua Mountains lured young men, including Wyatt Earp. Grandfather Quireno Montoya constructed his stone house in those rugged hills between Dos Cabezas and Mascot. The nearest city was Wilcox where a train station had been built in 1880. He was originally from Santa Fe, New Mexico. He had stern, handsome features, his Spanish heritage evident. Seeing old photos of him, it is certain you did not want to be on his bad side.

Mother, Esperanza Montoya, was born at home in 1915, three years after Arizona gained statehood. 'Esperanza' means 'Hope' in Spanish. By then her father had become night watchman at the Mascot mine. She was the second to youngest of twelve children. Her mother, Dolores, was a midwife and essential to the community. I was named after her. My grandparents were true pioneers of the old American West. Because of Mother's history, character and determination, she was featured in a popular nonfiction book about Mexican-American women titled *Songs My Mother Sang to Me* written by Patricia Martin in 1992.

My father, Marcus DeLeon, was debonair, sophisticated and well dressed, compared to the boys Mother knew in Globe, Arizona. They met in 1930. He drove a Lincoln Zephyr his mother bought him. Dad had a stylish presence that was irresistible to Mom's small town reserve. They met at a dance. He whispered in her ear that she would be his wife. He had instantly fallen in love with her shy, sweet goodness.

Mother had a beautiful face, wavy brown hair and an hourglass figure; some said she resembled Kay Francis, a 1930s actress. Esperanza was only fifteen when she met Marcus. It was a whirlwind romance. They had to lie about her age to marry.

I was the fourth child, born November 3, 1942 during World War II. By then Dad was working for a copper mine in Ray, Arizona, an essential worker for the war. My siblings, Bernice, then nine, Marcus, eight years old, and Hugo, seven, were not sure what to make of me because I cried all the time, only stopping when Mother was in my line of vision.

When I was a toddler, my parents grew unhappy. A failing business venture led to Dad's excessive drinking. The death of Grandma Dolores and my unexpected arrival complicated the relationship. My parents divorced in 1945. Mother took her kids to the dusty town of Tucson, Arizona, where her sisters lived and where I grew up.

I was too young to remember my parents being together. I would later see my father on summer visits to Miami, Arizona, where he lived in close proximity to his mother and sister. His mother, Rumalda, owned a Mexican restaurant and boarding house there, which had been a staple of the community, and helped the family survive during the Great Depression. My Aunt Elojia eventually took over the business.

My earliest childhood memory was of a big house in Tucson divided into three apartments, where my aunts lived above and below us. I lived with my mother and three older siblings. The Santa Cruz River was on the west side of the complex and along the banks were rows of cottonwood and tamarix trees.

During the summer monsoon season, the river was full and ran wildly. We could hear the roar of water and the croaking of frogs. My uncle Manuel had a fenced-off area where he raised rabbits. He occasionally used them for food. I remember rabbit pelts on the roof of the pen, salted and laid out to dry. He worked for the Southern Pacific Railroad.

Attached to Manuel's house was a cellar, probably used by bootleggers in the Prohibition days. The floor was packed dirt. In the corners of the cellar were large bullfrogs, or Colorado River toads, as big as salad plates, lying still in the cool earth, their yellow eyes reflecting in the light. Manuel had baskets of dry goods on the shelves: onions, potatoes and other root vegetables. He had a small leftover Victory Garden where he grew corn, melon, carrots and radishes.

Since my mother worked, my aunt Sarah, Manuel's wife, took care of me in the morning when my older siblings left for school. She gave me breakfast, usually a bowl of Cream of Wheat or oatmeal. Sarah prepared a large bowl for me—too large to finish. "You're not leaving the table until you finish your breakfast," she scolded. By that time, the cereal had turned cold and lumpy, and I'd stare into it, knowing I couldn't finish.

She forced me to sit and squirm, until Uncle Manuel came to my rescue and said, "Now, Sarah. Let Dolores go out and play. You can't force a child to eat."

"She's going to see that cereal for lunch!" she'd threaten.

"Don't stand next to that broomstick, Dolores," Uncle warned. "Your aunt is going to think you're the broom and start sweeping with you. Maybe you should have eaten that cereal!"

When Manuel came home from work, he'd always saved his dessert— a cookie, a piece of cake—for me. He'd let me open his tin lunch box to see what was there, and I thought it was like opening

9

a treasure chest. He was a loving uncle and we spent many mornings listening to the radio soap operas, *Helen Trent, Our Gal Sunday* and *Young Doctor Malone.*

Next to the house was a huge building that had once been a ballroom. It had been converted into a factory called The Milk Print. They made plastic bags and little bags of dye filled with pale margarine, and a dye capsule, to combine the margarine, for that particular brand. My mother worked there part-time to support us.

Sometimes we kids snuck into a large rear storage room at the Milk Print that was not in use. It was filled with old soda fountain tables and chairs, and a closet with New Year's Eve costumes: paper top hats, gentlemen's canes, party masks and streamers. We played with them, and no one noticed or seemed to care.

The triplex we lived in was behind a family restaurant called the Chicken Castle on Congress Street in downtown Tucson. My mother also worked there in the kitchen briefly, before she worked at the margarine plant. I remember waiting for her, on a porch swing in the back of the restaurant. I often fell asleep waiting. Hugo would sometimes wait with me. In those days, people didn't lock their doors, or worry about child abduction, and thought nothing of children, alone, waiting quietly.

I remember with tears in my eyes the innocence I felt knowing this was my home, my people. I owned it all — it was everything. The poverty that I eventually came to realize I was a part of never affected me. In those times, the birds sang every spring, and blades of grass popped up between the cracks of the concrete walk where I skipped. On more thoughtful days I kicked stones that singularly met the toe of my shoe.

Life seemed glorious, with the bluest of skies and white puffs of clouds that floated by, and a smell of honeysuckle that tickled my brain. God was good and sweet and oh, how I longed to be good and sweet and somehow deserve all this. After a rain, there were tadpoles, and in the soon dry riverbeds, where the earth curled, we made plates and dined with pretty pieces of broken glass we collected.

Across the river on the other bank, an old Mexican man named Lucero had started sculpting the Saints and Jesus into life-size tableaus of the Last Supper and Jesus on the cross. My two brothers and my cousin, Henry, helped him raise the cross. Lucero had fought in World War I and made a promise to the Virgin Mary, as he lay injured on the battlefield, that if he survived the war he would dedicate the rest of his life to making religious sculptures in tribute to God.

Lucero lived under the bridge in a plywood shack, his only shelter. As a small girl, I went to see him as he worked on his sculptures. He was very quiet, but a bit more talkative with my brothers. Nothing was going to deter Lucero from making the statues. His method was to gather river clay, packing it tight over objects he'd find, putting chicken wire around certain shapes, and then covering the form with white plaster, where he'd add more detail. The process was fascinating. The area, now known as the Garden of Gethsemane, still stands today. I go there on occasion.

I loved my mother very much. She was strict but affectionate, a disciplinarian who always kept an immaculate home. We thought she could do anything. Single mothers were a growing phenomenon in those days. She had four children to raise in a very tough, post-war Arizona.

She was a force in the kitchen, having worked as a young girl helping her mother, when miners boarded at their house. She could make any type of food, with excellent results. My earliest food memory of her delicious cooking was roast beef, mashed potatoes and string beans. "People think just because you're Mexican, you don't make standard, all-American food," she would say. Her repertoire was varied. My favorite dishes were her beef tacos, tamales and fried chicken. She could make every kind of pie, and she started working in a professional pie kitchen, in a downtown Tucson restaurant, Georgette's. This job provided the most stability for the family.

Around my fifth birthday in 1947, my mother met and later married Augustine Padilla, a kind, gentle man with dark good looks. The courage that he had to take on four children along with my mother was admirable, and showed how much he loved her. I have a vivid memory of my jealous father, Marcus, trying to win my mother back by punching poor Daddy Gus in the eye, almost blinding him. My uncles came to Gus' rescue, and pulled my raging father away.

My father Marcus had a violent temper, exacerbated by alcohol. Although he loved my mother, he made her suffer a great deal. Any time he appeared, we knew trouble would ensue. It just seemed to follow him. My siblings later shared stories of the pain and suffering he brought to the house, and the fear they lived in when he drank, when my parents were still married. He had a Jekyll-and-Hyde personality, which emerged after his first drink of liquor. I heard tales of brawls in bars triggered by a passing glance from a stranger he didn't like.

Despite this, I loved my father very much. I stuck by him, even as my other siblings distanced themselves as they grew older. I was always eager to visit my father during my childhood. Grandma Rumalda's restaurant left me with memories of plentiful, good food and stacks of Barq's soda. Miami was a small mining town that was still active, and it was always good to see my cousins who lived there, too.

Back in Tucson, Gus moved us to a small house off Sixth Avenue near the Santa Cruz Church, which was where they decided I should attend first grade. They wanted me to get a Catholic education. The nuns were very rigid. I walked to school in the morning and along the way I would meet my friend Carmen, and we'd walk together the remaining distance. One day, I left my lunch box at Carmen's. When lunchtime came, I told Sister Margaret, who became furious at me. As punishment, I had to sit in front of the lunch auditorium, watching everyone else eat. I was not only hungry but also deeply hurt. I remember the little faces ignoring me as I stared out at them. One of the bullies stared at me and chewed his food with his mouth open to mock me. I turned to look out the window for the rest of the lunch break.

To add insult to injury, when lunch was over, I was kept after school. I had to lay my head on the desk. After Sister Margaret left, a kind nun took me into their kitchen and gave me half a cheese sandwich. Never had something tasted so good before, as I sat at their table in the faculty kitchen. I began crying, confused by this strange torture, because my mother had never starved me before. I was finally sent home.

A walk in Downtown Tucson, ca 1949

As I made my way back, my brother Marcus was coming toward me on his bicycle.

"Mom sent me; she wants to know why you're so late."

I couldn't hold back my tears, and I told him the story of the forgotten lunch box and the cruel treatment by Sister Margaret.

I sat on the top tube of the bike, hanging onto the handlebars, crying all the way, as Marcus pedaled us home. That evening, my uncle Eddie, Mom's brother, came to visit, and heard the story. He was furious, and demanded that Mother withdraw me from that school immediately.

"Those nuns are wicked!" he exclaimed.

Within the week, I transferred to Carrillo Public Elementary School. Not long after, Gus moved us to a big house on Wood Street in the nearby Barrio El Hoyo. It was a working-class neighborhood, but the house offered more space. Mom discovered that there was no gas connection for her stove. She soon realized the entire neighborhood did not have natural gas service. Shocked, she started a petition everyone in the neighborhood signed. It was a happy day when Mom could start cooking her meals with her own stove, using natural gas. Gus worked at a furniture store in the shipping department. A new baby son, Larry, came along in 1949. I'd been the youngest, so of course being displaced was something I had to get used to. Larry was a baby boomer, and was going to be lavished with more privileges, as he was Daddy Gus' only son.

One day I took the baby for a ride in his buggy in the front yard. Larry was probably about two months old. It was a black leather buggy, with large wheels and a collapsing sun hood. I pushed the lumbering buggy around the yard, when suddenly the large wheel caught on a brick in the walkway. To my horror, the entire buggy flipped on its side, and baby Larry started wailing.

I cried out to my mother and started screaming, "The baby!" She ran from the porch where she'd been visiting with a friend. She lifted Larry from the tangled bedding and inspected him for any injuries, and he gradually quieted down. I expected Mom to punish me, but she took pity on me, and said, "He's okay. He's not hurt. Everything's okay." With her hand, she cradled me toward her leg, while holding Larry in her other arm. I knew mother loved me.

My siblings and I, though not aware of it, had grown up without a lot of money or possessions. We never realized it, because there was always food on the table, and a warm bed. Mother would say, "They never turned the electricity off!" She always made sure the bills were paid.

Late one night, there was a knock at the door, when everyone was in bed. There stood my cousin Julio Montoya, in his military uniform, just off the train, and eager for one of Hope's hot meals. She was very happy to see him. The whole family woke up to greet him and spend time with him in the kitchen. Mom put on a pot of coffee, a plate of fruit turnovers in front of Julio, and some hot cocoa for us kids. We were enjoying his company when we heard another knock on the door. Mom went to the door to answer, still wearing her robe. In front of her stood a middle-aged man, wearing a crumpled fedora, obviously a drunk hobo. He must have seen the house lit up at that late hour.

"Please ma'am, can you offer some spare coins, and put them in my tambourine?" he asked, extending his tambourine, with a little shake.

"No, I'm not going to give you any money. You're just going to use it to get more drunk. If you want something to eat, that's different," she said sternly.

Her voice was so firm and threatening that the man stumbled back a little bit. He started shaking the tambourine, loudly.

"What are you doing? You're going to wake up the neighbors!" she scolded, stepping forward as he stepped back, losing grip on his tambourine. It dropped on the porch.

"Oh please ma'am," he said, stumbling down the stairs. "Please let me have my tambourine."

"I'll give you your tambourine!" she said, tossing it at him. He caught it and ran off into the dark night.

I was surprised at my mother's strength, because she'd changed, over the course of being married to my father, from a meek young woman to a commanding presence. She wasn't afraid of anyone, after standing up to my father. Even cousin Julio was impressed by my mom's display of fierceness. Daddy Gus called Mom 'Boss.'

She and Daddy Gus had been saving money, and Mother decided to open a restaurant. She named it El Saguaro, after the distinctive cactus that grows only in the Sonoran desert. The restaurant was located on Fourth Avenue, south of Twenty-Second Street. It was a lively restaurant with an array of Mexican and American cuisine. I spent time in the kitchen watching the Mexican women making tortillas, and Mom issuing orders in Spanish as she helped prepare food.

Spanish was a foreign language to me, but in this kitchen I learned the basics. My father Marcus had wanted his children to speak only English to be more 'American,' so none of us actually knew Spanish. We all gradually learned it, since our mother spoke to Gus' family only in Spanish.

El Saguaro didn't last more than a year— Mom had two teenage sons who were left to their own devices while she was at work, and the responsibility of me and Larry was too much. Despite the community's enjoyment of the restaurant and its obvious success, my mom sold the business. Mom always said, "I'll open another one someday," but she never did.

After I entered first grade at Carrillo Elementary School, I enjoyed a full circle of friends and kind teachers. One faculty member, Marguerite Collier, an older woman, taught us the traditional Mexican folk dances that she knew. We practiced as she played records and coached us. "Step lively children! You're wearing a beautiful dress, you have to make it swirl when you dance! This isn't a dirge!" The children wore traditional dress when dancing, and the parents attended the performances once a year, usually in the spring.

At Christmas, she organized a traditional Nativity Pageant with schoolchildren and faculty members as chaperones for 'Las Posadas.' Two children, in costume as Mary and Joseph, would walk through the neighborhood as others chanted, "Who has room at the Inn? Who can give us a room? *Quien esta posada?*" while the procession continued to various homes. The annual event is still a tradition in Tucson.

We attended Catechism classes at San Cosme Church near the school. The older group of children were preparing for their first Holy Communion. The nuns of St. Augustine asked me to lead the children's Communion Ceremony wearing an angel's costume, along with another girl, one of my friends. She and I, being six years old, were too young to participate in Communion. The outfit was a long white satin dress with angel wings that attached in the back and a sparkling halo headband. I took the costume home to practice in. We rehearsed down the long aisle in the grand St. Augustine Cathedral, my friend and I leading the Communion group. Afterward, I'd come home from school, lay the outfit gently on my bed and admire it. This became an after school ritual for the next few days, even when I wasn't rehearsing. I loved the vision of this purity.

That Sunday, the ceremony took place, and it was an uplifting experience, leading the procession. I went home, still wearing the angel outfit. I'd become attached to it. On Monday afternoon when I came home from school, I walked into my room, to enjoy my ritual of admiring the angel dress. I opened the closet door and was startled to see the outfit missing. I panicked. I ran to the kitchen where my mom and sister were preparing dinner.

"My angel dress is gone!" I cried.

My older sister Bernice scoffed, "The nuns came and took it! You're not an angel anymore!"

My mom laughed. I started crying, "I want to be an angel!" Bernice laughed, "Now you're going to be a little devil instead!"

"Mom!" I cried, tears streaming down my cheeks.

"Bernice, don't tease her." Mom shook her head. Bernice laughed, reveling in my disappointment. I left them, pouting, stomping into the bedroom. It was another low blow from the nuns.

I was in the third grade when I woke from bed one morning with a terrible fever and sore throat. When Mom came to check on me, I was covered in a red rash. She thought it was measles. The room was spinning, I'd never felt so ill before. She took me to a doctor that morning and he diagnosed scarlet fever, which frightened my mother. Children could die from scarlet fever in those days, without antibiotics. The illness lasted over two weeks, and my right ear became infected, leading to a ruptured eardrum. I was kept out of school for three weeks. Marcus used to come in and tease me, lifting the corner of my bed and saying, "The bed is spinning! The bed is spinning!" I screamed with fear: "Mom! Help! The bed is spinning!"

This was a miserable time for me. Because of my continuing ear problem, I had to see an ear-nose-throat doctor, Dr. Saylor. I had to visit him once a week and get a shot of penicillin in the buttock. My sister Bernice accompanied me to this weekly appointment. I cried after each time I received the injection, so in pain and upset that I didn't have any desire for the lollipop the nurse gave me. Bernice would take the lollipop from me, and enjoy it for herself. What an odd sight: fifteen year old Bernice sucking on the lollipop as we walked hand-in-hand down the sidewalk, me crying in pain.

One sweet gesture during this time was a stack of letters with get-well wishes from my classmates. I read each one, and felt eager to get healthy again and return to school. I loved attending school at Carrillo.

When I returned, I was joyfully bouncing around at school with my friends, when one afternoon I sprained my ankle. It was difficult to walk. My mother arranged for me to visit a family friend, Mr. Valenzuela, a quiet older man who had worked as a horse wrangler on a cattle ranch.

Bernice and I took a bus to the south side of town, getting off at Thirty-Third Street. I limped the whole way, with my ankle swelling painfully. Mr. Valenzuela sat me up on a table. He then rubbed liniment on my ankle, deeply massaging it. The pressure of his hands squeezing my ankle to realign the tissue was so painful I yelled, "Mama! Mama! Mother! Mother! Help!" The pain was excruciating. Skillfully, he pushed the tendon back into place, and wrapped my foot with a bandage. The ankle swelling soon went down. Bernice collected me and we left, thanking him. During the bus ride home, Bernice shook her head, laughing, "*'Mama! Mama! Mother! Mother!'* You're a mama's girl." Her teasing could be merciless.

On weekends, Bernice would say, "Mom, I'm taking Dolores to the movies." Mother gave her a dollar to spend on our afternoon together. In those days, theater admission was twenty cents. We'd go to the Lyric Theater, Bernice holding my hand as we approached. She'd seat me in the front of the theater, and tell me, "I'll be right back."

A quarter of the way into the movie, Bernice still hadn't returned. I'd get up to look for her, and she'd be in the back row of the theater, necking with her current boyfriend. She'd spot me, and her boyfriend would give me a nickel to get some candy. I saw many B-movies under these circumstances. Bernice told me not to tell Mom, and I didn't. However, whenever Bernice got on my nerves, I'd call out, "Oh, *Mom*...!" Bernice would flash me a dirty look.

Mother became impatient with Bernice, as did Daddy Gus, but he rarely got involved. Bernice was becoming too much to manage. When she wanted to go out, and Mother refused to let her go, Bernice cried, "I'm gonna kill myself! I'm gonna kill myself! I'm going to drink this bleach and I'm going to die! Then you'll be sorry!"

"Aw, go ahead and do it!" Mother called out, exhausted by Bernice's antics.

"Mom! Bernice is going to die!" I cried.

"Bernice has been watching too many movies." Mom shook her head, exasperated.

Bernice grew tired of the boundaries— she eloped at the age of sixteen. Just like Mother, she had to pretend to be older to get married. She wed a young serviceman from New Mexico who was stationed at Davis-Monthan Air Force Base in Tucson. Bernice moved to Albuquerque with her new husband's family, and would soon be having children of her own.

Mother was initially furious at Bernice, but she felt this marriage might help her settle down. Bernice had caused strife within the household, since she refused to obey Mother's demands to come in early, or keep our room tidy or help around the house. She was a true 1950s rebel. I had wondered what it meant when Bernice packed her bag that night and slipped out the bedroom window. Mother cried a lot the next day; it felt terrible to see her suffer. After my sister left, the house was a lot calmer. Marcus and Hugo were starting to experience their own rebellious nature. Both of them had taken up musical instruments: Marcus the saxophone, and Hugo the violin. I remember Hugo practicing a squeaky 'Twinkle, Twinkle Little Star' many an afternoon.

The civility of playing music calmly was short-lived. Sometimes they'd get into fisticuffs in the living room, and tumble into a pile. I'd jumped on top and start pounding my fist on the shoulder of whoever was on top. Then they'd flip and I'd climb on top again, to punch the shoulder of the new person on top. I tried not to take sides.

Hugo was quiet most of the time, different from the earlier stories I'd heard when they were all living with Dad. Once Hugo donned a cape and, thinking he was Captain Marvel, leaped off the roof of a storage shed, yelling, "Shazam!" Luckily, he didn't get hurt. He took a lot of flack from Dad in those early days. He had a mind of his own, and was always daring and mischievous, despite his quiet exterior.

Mother and Gus decided to move from Barrio El Hoyo, this time to a suburban area on the south side of Tucson. They'd been looking for some time, but in those days, Mexicans and Blacks could only live in certain parts of town. Jews were not allowed in the WASP country clubs. Arizona has had a long history of conservatism.

Marcus and Hugo joined the US Air Force in their late teens. Mother was very upset. She couldn't believe how quickly they'd grown into men, and missed their presence around the household. Now, it was just me and Larry. Marcus was stationed in England, and

Hugo in Germany. She mailed them care packages for Christmas, filled with homemade cookies and candy. They wrote letters to Mother and me. Once, for Christmas, Marcus shipped us a box of beautifully wrapped presents from London, which seemed very exotic. I missed my brothers.

When I was in the fifth grade I attended C. E. Rose Elementary School, and I had a teacher by the name of Robert Stanley who played the guitar. He opened my world to folk music. The class sang along to 'Old Smokey,' 'John Henry,' 'Goodnight Irene and 'Old Black Joe.' Sometimes Mr. Stanley read different stories that depicted social inequity: *Tom Sawyer* and *Huckleberry Finn*. The classes were lively with enthusiastic participation.

Going into middle school was a big change. Wakefield Junior High had a large campus, partially integrated with whites and Mexicans. I knew a few students from previous years, but puberty had hit. We had a gym class, and the girls had to wear gym outfits. Showers were mandatory after gym class. It was strange to see my peers nude, in different stages of physical maturity. My mother never discussed menstruation with me. I learned about it from the all-female health class that I attended. Luckily, I was a late-bloomer, so I knew what to expect when the time came.

As my brother Larry grew older, I took him on Saturday mornings to the Fox Theater in downtown Tucson. There we attended *The Mickey Mouse Club*. They usually showed six cartoons, a *Flash Gordon* serial, and a full-length feature. Larry and I walked out in the bright sun around noon, and made our way to Georgette's. We'd go in the back door where Mom was working, getting ready for the lunch crowd. She baked pies in the morning, and then she'd help the owner at the steam table for the lunch rush.

She'd ask us what we wanted for lunch. We'd get a hamburger, fries and a malt milkshake. Sometimes she'd give us fried shrimp or fried scallops as a treat, and we'd sit and eat at a small table that was near the back office. There were two chefs: one was Greek, and the other, named Tommy, was from New York City. They were very friendly and chatty with us. They wore large white chef hats. I'll never forget the smell of the cooking grease that would cling to Mother's clothes when she came home.

There was a baseball team in town for spring training in 1955. Georgette's had a large downstairs banquet room, and the team had reserved the space and ordered a buffet meal, setting the time for one in the afternoon. At twelve-forty, a young black man came in and sat at the counter. The waitress said to him, "Sorry, we do not serve any Negroes here." He politely started to leave.

Suddenly the baseball team barged in, hungry and ready to eat their meal. The black man was part of the team, and he'd arrived first. The team manager found out that Georgette's wouldn't serve him. All of the banquet food went to waste when the team refused to eat there in protest. This was one instance of the segregation at the time.

At night, I listened to radio shows before bed. I'll always remember Orson Welles' booming voice. As a family, we'd sit and listen to *The Shadow*, *Amos and Andy*, *The Jack Benny Show* and *Fibber Magee and Molly*. On Saturday mornings, there were shows like *Lassie* and *Let's Pretend*. My imagination was fueled by the interesting stories that I'd hear and the fairy tales that always included the phrase: 'East of the sun and west of the Moon.'

In 1956, when I was in the eighth grade, two songs came out: 'Rock Around the Clock' and 'Heartbreak Hotel.' This new sound, rock 'n' roll, was infectious and exuberant. Everyone my age felt this excitement. Previously, crooners were the norm, in addition to innocuous fluff like 'How Much Is That Doggie in the Window.' Rock 'n' roll captured the rebellious feeling of the time. There was a general air of wanting to break from conformity and I was part of it.

Larry had been whining for a television set, and Daddy Gus finally conceded, bringing home a large wood console with a small black and white picture. We were one of the last people in the neighborhood to buy a TV. Now, Larry glued himself to the set, and didn't have to go to the neighbors to see westerns or *Howdy Doody*.

I enrolled in Pueblo High School in 1958. This was a fully-integrated school, with whites, blacks and Mexicans. My friends Josie and Bertha, two Latinas, had carried over from junior high to the first semester of our freshman year. Josie was my neighbor. She and I were alike in many respects: Latina, but not traditional in our outlook. On weekends, we'd go hiking and spend time talking about our classmates and different kinds of music. She and her sister lived with their grandmother. After school, Josie and I rushed home to

21

catch Dick Clark's *American Bandstand*. We scrutinized the East Coast fashions and dancing styles, hearing the latest hit songs by the Everly Brothers, Bobby Vinton and Frankie Lymon and the Teenagers.

In my sophomore year, I joined the school newspaper as a cub reporter. I wrote several articles for the paper. One of them was critical about a group of Varsity youths who stood in a row against the back wall, loitering during change of classes, hovering as everyone passed by in the hall. I encouraged the girls to try to take their spot, to displace these youths from eyeing everyone. I found the Varsity boys annoying. My piece in the paper caused resentment, but I had my supporters who thought it was a funny article.

Josie had met a young man at the University of Arizona who belonged to a fraternity. He had a friend, Jim Graves, and Josie asked me if I wanted to join them on a double date. He was three years older than me. Jim was tall and thin, fine featured with a crew cut. He drove a 1955 red Chevrolet. We all went to a fraternity party, after a U of A football game. I didn't tell Mother about this. It was a thrill to be among older boys. Everyone was full of vitality, sophistication and new ideas. High school was childish compared to the college scene.

The following weekend, the fraternity had a barbecue cookout in nearby Sabino Canyon. The guys brought a keg of beer. It was my first time drinking beer. It had a terrible taste. I remember the lads singing 'Tom Dooley' while one of them played guitar. I'd accompanied Jim at these and future parties. We were unofficially dating. That night, I arrived home late from the barbecue, at one in the morning.

Marcus had returned from his military service, and he was waiting up with my mother when Jim dropped me off. Marcus asked solemnly, "Who is the guy with the red Chevy?" Feeling a pang of guilt and fear of discovery, I muttered, "Just a boy I met." I could see that Mother was concerned that I'd follow in Bernice's footsteps. Marcus was living at home now, and he became concerned about my conduct. One afternoon, he even went on a search at the University to find the red car that had dropped me off.

When Jim called me at the house a few days later, Marcus intercepted the phone. "Who is this?" Marcus asked. Jim wanted to come over to the house and speak to my mother. Marcus agreed. Jim arrived, sat in our living room and asked my mother for permission to date me. His proper approach went over well with my mother, so she gave consent. Jim and I continued to date, but when the summer rolled around, he went back home to Maryland. He and I corresponded that summer, but something I wrote upset him so much he replied saying that I was immature and that he no longer wanted to see me.

Marcus, culturally enriched by his experiences overseas, had a collection of jazz LPs: Gerry Mulligan, Miles Davis, Dave Brubeck and Tito Puente. Jazz filled our home with new sounds, and I could sense Marcus' restless nature. He bought a Triumph motorcycle and spent weekend days with friends, riding out in the desert. Sometimes I'd ride with him on the jump seat, both of us without helmets. Marcus had decided to return to school on the G.I. Bill.

When Hugo completed his military service and returned home, his love for East Coast jazz was evident. His record collection included Charlie Parker, Dizzy Gillespie and Lester Young. He also had a rhythm and blues compilation that included songs later re-recorded by more mainstream artists. 'Dance with Me Henry' and 'Tutti Frutti': Pat Boone did clean-cut versions of those two songs, originally performed by black artists. Our old RCA console was getting a lot of use. Mother enjoyed all the new sounds, and having her sons back from military duty, although their music competed with her beloved Mariachis.

That fall, I met Jon Kamman, a handsome and bespectacled fellow student. We had an English class together. One afternoon he was walking by our house when I was outside watering plants, and he said hello. We chatted for a while out front, and I realized how charming and intelligent he was. We had a mutual crush that deepened each day as he walked me home from school. Marcus had taught me to play chess, and Jonny and I played it a lot together. We double dated with another couple, Jack Murietta and Nancy Lynch. The four of us attended the junior prom together. This was a very innocent time. Jonny was kind, sweet, considerate, and we both felt a lot of attraction for each other. We'd go to the drive-in movies, and I'd neck in the front seat with Jonny. He drove his mom's Buick. We were going steady.

Jonny was very loving. We were getting more serious, but it was an innocent teenage love: I was still a virgin. Jonny's mother was divorced. She did not like me, and thought that my romance with Jonny would be short-lived. He relayed to me her skeptical attitude that our petting might go too far.

I was seventeen when the school paper assigned me the job of student correspondent for Tucson's morning newspaper, *Arizona Daily Star*. This was to become a touchstone for me. I realized I wanted to have a career in journalism. Tucson, Arizona was not known for its opportunities. Salesgirl or waitress were the choices for a Latina high school graduate in the late 1950s. I decided I wanted to be a journalist in Los Angeles: it was a big city that ignored one's ethnic background, or so I thought.

In my senior year, I became the editor of the high school newspaper, *El Guerrero*. I wrote an article about the prom: I didn't feel that formal wear had to be a necessity, since a lot of the kids could not afford the rental or purchase. There was an immense backlash against my article. I felt stunned that even the financially-challenged students were not more sympathetic. Sherilyn January and I were good friends, and she was the assistant editor of the paper. She said about the article, "Conflict is good. It makes people think." She was a very observant, smart kid. There was a question as to whether communism should be taught in schools. Sherilyn said, "Of course it should. How will anyone know whether they are for or against something if they don't know what it represents?" One of her humorous anecdotes was, "The reason kids run away from home now is because of the ten-cent hamburger."

I learned about financial reality and fashion in Tucson, when I took a part-time weekend job at Lerner, a women's apparel store. I earned fifty cents an hour, which was low even in those days. Discounts were offered to employees. Despite the pay, I increased my wardrobe and had a small budget for attending films and music events.

That October, Tito Puente's Latin Orchestra came to Tucson, performing at the Ramada Inn downtown. I'd become familiar with their music from Marcus' vinyl records. I encouraged Josie and Sherri to join me at the show. It was an evening performance on a Friday night.

We drove in Sherri's MG convertible to the Ramada Inn, and found a table up close to the stage. We ordered Cokes. We admired the large stage set up for the twelve-piece band, with podium partitions emblazoned with 'Tito Puente Orchestra.' The band took the stage, and their music immediately stirred up the audience to dance. There were a large number of people in attendance of all ages. We were the youngest ones there. Young men approached us, and asked all three of us to dance to the joyful, spirited salsa music.

After the first set, the band took a break and the flute player, whose name I later learned was Peter Fanelli, and his friend walked past our table. He looked me in the eye and said, "She's the cutest girl in here," within earshot as he passed by us. Josie, Sherri and I laughed at the flirtation. He was a mature, suave, handsome man with Italian good looks and an air of East Coast sophistication, wearing black horn-rim glasses.

During the next set, I noticed Peter was smiling, keeping his eye on me. I was flattered, and smiled back from the table. The music was compelling and seductive, full of sensual energy. It was a heady feeling. When the show ended, Sherri and Josie were preparing to leave. Peter crossed the stage as the other musicians were packing up and took me aside, asking, "Can you join me for breakfast tomorrow? We're going to Phoenix in the afternoon. Room 204." I nodded.

I felt a tremendous rush of warmth and excitement at the thought of spending time alone with Peter. I didn't keep this invitation secret for long. "What did he ask you?" Sherri said as we got into her car.

"He asked if I wanted to join him for breakfast." The girls squealed with delight. "What are you going to do?" Sherri asked.

"Well, do you think you can give me a ride in the morning?"

"Of course!" she said.

At home, I decided what I'd wear the next day. I chose a striped, silk, boat-neck dress, with ballet flats. I was thrilled to think about what Peter and I would talk about. I had a lot of questions about the East Coast, because Sherri and I had seen *Breakfast at Tiffany's*, and had become fascinated by New York City. 'Moon River' was becoming a hit, and Sherri called me her 'Huckleberry friend.' We always dreamed of going to New York together. We'd stay up late Friday nights to watch *The Jack Parr Show*. Peter was significantly older than I was, and seemed very cosmopolitan.

The following morning, Sherri picked me up at nine o'clock. We drove to the motel and she said excitedly, "Aren't you glad I made you get a diaphragm?" She had been dating a foreign student from Brazil who attended the U of A, and was taking no chances in getting pregnant. She had encouraged me to make an appointment with her doctor for a fitting, which I did. This would be the first time I would use it.

We arrived at the Ramada Inn. Sherri wished me luck. I walked into the empty restaurant. I mustered up my courage, walked up the stairway to the second floor, and gingerly knocked on the door. Peter answered the door in a crisp, white, untucked dress shirt hanging over Herringbone black and white slacks. "Wow, you are early," he said, as he took my hand and pulled me gently toward him, sliding my purse out of my hand and closing the door behind me.

"You're much sweeter than I remember you." He enfolded me in his arms and began kissing my neck, my face and finally my lips. He had just shaved and his aftershave was a scent of Jean Naté. I had to catch my breath. I was overcome with excitement, and a passion quite new to me. My body trembled as he sat on the edge of the unmade bed and began to unbutton the front of my dress. Removing the dress along with the light trench coat I was wearing, he easily managed to slide them off me. I stood in my slip. He picked me up and lay me on the bed. One shoe fell off my foot as I slowly kicked the other off.

He looked down at me smiling as he unbuttoned his shirt, placing it on the back of a chair and slipping off his pants. We began with tender kisses that exploded into uninhibited passion. He seemed to explore every part of my body as he stripped off my underwear. "I'm wearing a diaphragm," I murmured in his ear, as I bit it gently. This melted any reservation he might have had. His naked body pressed against me and he pushed inside me, finding resistance, but he successfully overcame it, much to the initial pain and pleasure I experienced. It was over quickly and he said, "Let's shower and go downstairs and grab a bite to eat."

He ran the shower and we got in together. I felt embarrassed and timid; I'd never showered with a man. "My dear, you are a beautiful young woman... don't be ashamed of your body." He began soaping my breasts as I tried to keep my hair from getting wet.

Downstairs we met up with his friend Shep. We ordered breakfast and other members of the band came down. Some were with girls, who had obviously spent the night: they still had their evening dresses on. Peter laid out a plan. The band had a gig that night in Phoenix, and they were traveling in a bus. He gave me the money to take a Greyhound to meet him there, since I couldn't join them. Tito did not allow anyone but members of the band on the tour bus.

I was more than excited. It was Saturday morning and I took a cab home, and asked the cab to wait. Mom was working and Larry was sitting in front of the television watching cartoons. I quietly went into my room and got another dress, some underwear, Capri pants and a blouse. As I was stuffing them in an overnight case, ten year old Larry came in and asked, "Where are you going?"

"I'm going to Sherri's. I'll be back later."

I ran to the waiting cab, which took me to the Greyhound bus depot, where I bought a ticket to Phoenix.

All the way during the two-hour trip, I thought about my actions, this unbridled surrender to someone I didn't know. I wondered what Jonny would think. I'd have to tell him when I returned. I was hoping I'd get back in time for school on Monday, for the editorial meeting. Then I worried about my poor mother, who was probably wondering about me at this point.

Peter told me to meet him at a motel on Jefferson Boulevard in Phoenix. The band was supposed to play at a club called, appropriately, El Calderon (the cauldron). Bernice was now divorced and lived in Phoenix, so I wasn't worried about being a stranger in the city. The bus pulled into the station, and I took a cab to the motel on Jefferson. I went to the front desk to ask what room Peter was in, when I saw him in the lobby. He had stayed there before, and the owners were behind the front desk, discussing magic tricks with him.

The owner was a performing magician, and his wife a hypnotist. Peter saw me and gave me a big hug. "Here she is!" he said. The front desk couple smiled at me. Suddenly I felt like a true adult, independent, and free to do as I pleased. We went to Peter's room, and made love all the afternoon, until it was time for him to get ready for his performance. We had dinner together at a bar and grill across the street from the motel. I had a bacon-lettuce-tomato sandwich and he had a club sandwich.

All of the other musicians were friendly and welcomed me. I was happy to see Tito Puente's performance at El Calderon that night. I was asked to dance, but I stayed at a front table and watched Peter play flute and smile at me encouragingly. I hadn't called Bernice, and I certainly hadn't called my mother, but I tried not to think about that. The band played pretty much the same sets as the night before.

After the show, Peter and I returned to the motel. We made love again, and he began to fall asleep. "I have an early wake up call. The band has to catch a flight to Frisco in the morning," he said. I closed my eyes and wondered what San Francisco was like.

In the morning, he asked, "Are you going back to Tucson?"

I was crestfallen and confused; I didn't know what to do. He offered to pay my return ticket home, and I accepted, embarrassed. "We're going to be in LA next weekend. Maybe you can come out. We'll be there a while. Tito's recording an album at some Hollywood studio. We'll be at the Lido Hotel. You can reach me there." He finished dressing. "Check-out is eleven. You can sleep in 'til then." He placed some cash on the night table.

He gathered his things and left the room, suitcase in hand. I felt alone, deserted and sad as I lay in bed. I awoke an hour later, and decided to call Bernice.

She answered. "Boy, is Mother mad at you. She's been calling all over for you. Where are you?" I told Bernice I was in Phoenix, and asked if I could come over. She said yes, so I quickly got dressed and took a cab to her house.

Bernice met me at the door, clearly irritated. I walked in with my small suitcase. Her young children, Mike and Cathy, were sitting at the breakfast table eating cereal. I sat down in the living room and told Bernice the whole story. Bernice listened quietly. Finally she said, "Mom's so mad, I don't think she wants you back. I think you're on your own now." Bernice's words were painful to hear. "Is it all right if I stay here for the week?" I asked. Bernice agreed. "Sure, you can babysit."

As the week passed, my thoughts drifted to a departure to Los Angeles. I counted the money I had, and it was just enough for a bus ticket. I called Sherri and told her that my mother was so angry she'd thrown me out of the house.

"Everyone's wondering when you're returning. We had the editorial meeting on Monday, and I'm the interim editor. Aren't you coming back to school?"

"I don't know what I'm doing. I've been invited to Los Angeles this weekend to meet Peter."

"Are you crazy?" Sherri asked. "Dolores, come back home while there's still a chance. Jonny asked me what happened to you. I haven't said anything."

At that moment, my Tucson life seemed irrelevant, part of the past. All I could think of was getting to LA and being with Peter. "I'll let you know what I'm going to do after I go to Los Angeles," I told Sherri.

"It may be too late by then," she said. "That newspaper isn't going to wait for you."

"I could care less about the newspaper," I said, still angry about the reaction to the prom article I'd written. It all seemed petty and childish. We said goodbye.

The week dragged. I did housework and took care of Bernice's kids. On Friday afternoon, I called the Lido Hotel, and the band still hadn't arrived. I wondered if Peter had told me the truth. I asked Bernice to loan me fifty dollars and borrowed some clothes from her. That night, I took the bus to Los Angeles, not knowing if Peter would be there. I had cousins in Los Angeles, so I thought the trip would do me good either way.

The bus pulled into the Hollywood stop. I stepped off and phoned the Lido Hotel. This time, the band had checked in. I asked for Peter's room, and they transferred me. It was seven in the morning. Peter answered the phone, half-asleep.

"Hi, it's Dolores," I said.

"Hey kiddo. Are you coming to LA?"

"I'm here," I muttered. "In Hollywood."

"Get yourself down here!" he said with happiness. "It's on Yucca near Hollywood Boulevard. I'm in room three-fifteen."

Elated, I hung up the phone and I walked to the hotel. Hollywood Boulevard, a quiet place in 1961, was just waking up, early on a Saturday morning. Some of the stores were just opening, and very few people were out. I got to the hotel, and found Peter's room, and knocked on the door. "It's open," he said from inside.

I walked in, and the shades were drawn. It was dark. Peter was in bed, naked. "Come and join me," he said. I slipped off my clothes and got under the sheets with him. "Wow, you're cold!" he said. "Let me warm you up."

That afternoon, we woke up for breakfast. Peter was happy to be with me. Tito's band was performing at the Hollywood Palladium that evening, a ballroom on Sunset Boulevard. After we spent the afternoon together, Peter had to dash for sound check. I changed into eveningwear and joined him, again seeing the familiar faces of the band members. Their lively Puerto Rican and Cuban New York accents echoed through the large hall as they playfully argued about the Yankees and travel conditions.

It was interesting to be behind the scenes and watch the musicians preparing for their show. It was a large on-stage set up of piano, horn and percussion, congas, timbale, vibes. It was good to forget my own problems for a while. That evening, as the ballroom filled, the audience arrived, all dressed up. The men wore suits and skinny ties, and the women, with bouffant hairdos and stiletto heels, wore tight cocktail dresses. The band put on a rousing set as usual, and there was very little room on the dance floor.

I sat with some women who were friends with the band, at a table on the side. I danced occasionally with someone who asked me.

That night, Peter and I returned to the hotel. When I asked him where he lived in New York, he grew quiet. "West Seventy-First Street," he said. I asked him if I could visit him there someday.

"Well," he said with a long pause, "I live with a girlfriend who's a stewardess. I don't think she'd appreciate it." I felt confused and betrayed. The uncertainty I may have had about becoming a part of his life was replaced with a clear vision of falling prey to the seduction of an older man. After that confession, Peter seemed to withdraw.

On Sunday, Peter and I walked on Hollywood Boulevard. It was another quiet day. He talked about being in the musicians' union in New York and playing for Broadway shows. I didn't feel that I had anything to contribute to the conversation, especially since my dreams of visiting him in New York were squelched.

The next morning, the band had prepared to record in a small studio in Hollywood. I went along. I sat in the waiting room with the band boy, a roadie in his twenties, Izzy. He was a chubby Puerto Rican kid. He had set up all the instruments in the studio and was awaiting orders. You could see into the recording studio through a little window. I saw Peter performing, playing the flute. I felt distance and a sense of uselessness. I knew my life could not go on like this. I decided to return to Phoenix that night.

Just ten days before, I was a high school senior, editor of our school newspaper, with a sweet boyfriend who respected me. This whirlwind affair with an older man had taken me all the way to Los Angeles. It was incomprehensible. I realized I had to back track. This was no future. When I told Peter I was returning to Arizona, he seemed relieved. He paid my bus ticket back to Phoenix.

I returned to Bernice's and stayed with her for the next month. One of the saddest days of my life was when Bernice and I had Thanksgiving dinner with her children at a Chinese restaurant. I missed my mother and her wonderful cooking. I missed my social network and my carefree student life.

My brother Marcus visited us in Phoenix and asked me to return to Tucson, because Mom had become distraught with worry about me. Marcus said my high school counselor, Ms. Urquides, had come to the house to speak to Mom, trying to encourage me to return to school because I would be compromising my future.

All signs pointed to Tucson, and I joined Marcus on the trip back. It was a quiet two-hour ride. We both knew that I had subjected myself to a variety of dangers and scrutiny, and my reputation as an innocent teenager was forever changed. There had been unfounded gossip at the high school that I was pregnant with Jonny's child, and had had to leave town.

Upon arrival, Mother was happy to see me, but she was reserved, and a new set of rules awaited me. I was grounded for as long as I would live with her. There was no returning to school until next year, so I started helping mom at the L&L restaurant in the kitchen when she prepared food, as a dishwasher, washing the large pots and pans. It was miserable work.

One afternoon, the editorial staff from school came in for hamburgers. I had spoken to Sherri on the phone, but I hadn't seen her since my return. I peeked out at all of the students together, and saw Sherri, now the editor of the paper, confident and holding court.

I realized what I'd given up and I felt a pang of regret. I saw my dreams fading. Luckily, I had the courage to return to school the next year, finish my studies and earn a diploma in 1962.

Sherri and I once again bonded. She had graduated, and was taking secretarial classes at Lambert business school. We spent some weekends together, and visited a small art cinema on Fifth Avenue near the U of A with her Brazilian boyfriend to see *Never On A Sunday*, and, later, *Black Orpheus*. I knew there was a bigger world out there, and we made plans to be a part of it. Our strategy was to move to Los Angeles.

Jonny, hurt about my abandoning him, had gotten together with Josie, and Josie had become pregnant. They were pressured to marry. I wondered if that could have been me, pregnant while in high school. I counted my blessings and was grateful to my mother for her forgiveness.

1963-64 - Limitless Possibilities

Taken by Chris Hillman on Woodrow Wilson Drive, 1965

Working the summer of 1963 as a waitress in Tucson, I earned enough to pay for the bus to LA. Ironically, Sherri became so qualified with her secretarial skills, she remained in Tucson working for AT & T. I arrived in Los Angeles, initially staying with my brother Marcus and his new wife, Barbara, and their small family, before I enrolled in Los Angeles City College.

That fall I met Nick Gerlach. He was taking drama and music classes. He was a brown-haired Jewish kid from central Los Angeles, who had a kind face. We'd met when he passed me on the sidewalk near the school, alongside his friend, and he shouted out, "Who's that fox?" with a wry smile.

I started laughing, and there was an immediate connection. We hung out between his music theory classes as students practiced piano scales or played 'Für Elise.' The music wafted through the huge trees that surrounded the sunny paths. I was now rooming with a girl I'd met in a modern dance class, Jane Nakamura. She was a Japanese girl from Hawaii. On our days off, we went to a Japanese movie theater near Pico. That's where I first saw *Seven Samurai*.

Nick invited me to dinner with his mother, Madelyn, one night. It was a special evening. She was dating a French explorer, Jean-Pierre, who had gone into the Congo, and brought back African artifacts that were going to be displayed at UCLA. He was missing an arm, which he said had been eaten by a lion. Madelyn had prepared beef brisket. She was scrutinizing me, to see if I was right for Nick. He seemed to think I was.

Living with Jane was short-lived, as Nick wanted me to move in with him. We found an apartment in Silverlake on a steep, ivy-filled street up in the hills, right off Hollywood Boulevard near the Havana Club.

Reality struck quickly. There were financial expenses Nick and I needed to meet. I quit school to work as a file clerk at Occidental Insurance Company in downtown Los Angeles. Nick worked as a Kosher-deli deliveryman. We struggled, but weekends would find us visiting Nick's Uncle Fred, who lived in Venice Beach. He was a twelve-string guitarist/folk singer who had played in Greenwich Village with Josh White, Guthrie, et al. He had recorded an album on the Folkways label. He and his wife, Barbara, invited us on Saturday nights. After supper, we'd play a round of poker. Fred smoked his cigar and commented on the latest happenings in New York City. "A guy named Bob Die-lan," he joked, "is making a name for himself in the Village."

We also babysat two young half-siblings for Nick's father John, a wonderful man who had fought in the Spanish Civil War alongside Ernest Hemingway. He prepared a delicious chicken fricassee in an iron skillet, with carrots, celery and onions, served over egg noodles. "It tastes better if the chicken has been stolen," he reminded us. I still make this dish, and named it 'Chicken Hemingway.'

There were evenings when we sang folk songs with my high school friend Sherri Danz and her new husband, Roger. We also had visits from Sidney Smith, Nick's high school friend. We listened to Modern Jazz Quartet, John Coltrane, Cannonball Adderley and Miles Davis on vinyl. Sidney, a handsome African American, played the alto sax, and he and Nick talked about music constantly. Nick liked to practice his guitar playing in the tiled bathroom, because he said the acoustics were great.

Occasionally, Sidney brought a joint for us to share. I had never smoked marijuana; it was exceedingly rare in those days, and difficult to procure. Once when we were smoking with Sidney, my older brother Marcus, now living in the Valley, arrived unannounced at the apartment. The smoke-filled room had a distinctive smell, and he knew immediately what was happening. He left right away, upset. Marijuana made me cheerful and giggly. Marijuana enhanced the music.

Nick and I would save our money and go to the Ash Grove, a folk club on Melrose Boulevard in West Hollywood, to hear Lightning Hopkins or the New Lost City Ramblers. This music was traditional, and the owner, Ed Pearl, prided himself in never booking 'commercial' folk artists that were prevalent at the time. We went frequently enough that I became friendly with Nancy Kubo, a Japanese girl who worked the box office. There was a strict cover policy, so she never got us in for free. Once she told me an amusing story about a skinny Jewish kid with an entourage of young people from New York City, who was incredulous when she refused to let them in without paying the cover charge.

The young man asked indignantly, "Don't you know who I am?"

Nancy smiled and shrugged her shoulders – she'd heard that one before.

The young man - Bob Dylan, he said his name was - scoffed as he asked to see the owner of the club. Ed Pearl himself came up front and asked Dylan to pay the cover charge of $1.25 if he wanted entry into the club. Ed Pearl insisted that he pay, and finally, one of the entourage shelled out the $1.25 to end the argument.

The day John F. Kennedy was assassinated I was sent home early from work. I met Nick at our apartment and we were both stunned. Nick and I held each other and wept. We could not finish our meal. Everything had shattered. We, like all of America, felt a profound sense of loss. That weekend, Nick's father visited us. We witnessed, via television, Harvey Oswald's killing. No one knew the answers to so many questions raised that year.

Our landlady, Mrs. Archie, was a crazy old woman from Australia who had had her deceased black border collie stuffed. It sat beside her piano as she played. She kept talking about Joan Sutherland, the opera diva, who must have inspired her as she pounded on the piano and wailed. One rainy night while Nick and I were in bed, the ceiling caved in on us. Plaster and water covered our bed. It was disgusting. Mrs. Archie accused us of malicious damage, and expressed concern about Sidney, our 'Negro friend' visiting her property. That sent us looking for another apartment, which we found in Echo Park, on a hill.

This new apartment was on the upstairs of a duplex unit. Nick found a new job at Will Wright's ice cream parlor in Beverly Hills, and he had me apply as well. I got the job as a waitress. Life was sweet, and there was a lot of free ice cream. On special nights, I broiled pork chops for dinner. We'd take the bus down Sunset Boulevard to Beverly Hills, and sometimes Nick's mother loaned us her gray Morris Minor to drive.

One night at the Ash Grove, Reverend Gary Davis was performing. We loved his show. He was a blind African-American musician known for playing blues guitar on a six-string that he called 'Miss Gibson.' He toured the folk music circuit and jokingly chanted, "All I hear about is John Hurt, Lizbeth Cotton, John Hurt, Lizbeth Cotton,"– they were his competitors. His music was very different from theirs; it had a forceful, rugged quality, full of whiskey, cigars, and smoky saloons. He concealed a stiletto knife in his coat pocket, because he'd been robbed.

We were talking with him after the show, when we learned he was going to crash on the couch in the artists' lounge at the Ash Grove, as he didn't have a place to stay. We were shocked, and offered him our guest room. He was grateful for the lodging, and stayed the whole weekend with us. He taught Nick to play 'Candy Man,' and addressed me as 'Miss Sam.' He had a healthy appetite, and because he was blind, Nick helped him with a bath. He hadn't bathed in some time. He enjoyed staying with us, and it was a tender goodbye after the last gig of his Ash Grove engagement.

Nick and I talked about marriage, and even had enough courage to talk to John, Nick's father, about it. John said, "Nico, why do you want to marry Dolores? She hasn't got a pot to piss in!" Nick replied, "We can make it work out."

That year I turned twenty-one, and got a job as a waitress at the Ash Grove. Nick had been thinking about trying to make a name for himself as a musician, and finally decided to drive to Cambridge, Massachusetts after Christmas, in an old Buick he'd bought from his Uncle Fred. He would be gone an unspecified amount of time, since he'd gotten a gig playing twelve-string guitar at Club 47 in Cambridge. People like the Muldaurs and the Baez Sisters performed there. In those days, people were very optimistic when driving American cars across the country. I was very sad he'd be gone so long, but Nick said, "You can come and visit."

At my modern dance class, I had met Karen Haynes, a Caucasian/African-American girl with beautiful brown eyes. She was exotic and statuesque. She pulled her hair back in a bun, which emphasized her lovely features. She, along with her friend Nina, a short, freckle-faced Jewish girl, moved into our Echo Park apartment to share expenses. Karen worked at Los Feliz Cinema on Vermont and Sunset Boulevard. She got Nina and me into the movies free. Nina dated a film school student from New York. Karen was dating a UCLA film student, David. We all went to the midnight movies at the Western Theater to see the latest art-house films.

Meanwhile, I worked serving pitchers of beer to folk music enthusiasts. The great thing about the job was that there was always a lively assortment of traditional folk musicians performing without pretense and full of ideals. Ed Pearl was a short, savvy man, who always kept an eye on the bottom line. He had a reputation for being 'left of Liberal.' He sent food to the Civil Rights Marchers in Selma, Alabama, and he booked singers from the Student Non-Violence Committee and the Chambers Brothers to perform at the Ash Grove.

The Ash Grove had a busy kitchen that served an array of bar food: cheese plates, sandwiches, wine in a basket-bottle, spaghetti with meatballs and all kinds of Italian desserts, made personally by our Trotsky chef, Roger, and Latino counterpart, Fernando, who cautioned me about befriending or becoming intimate with the musicians at the Ash Grove. People mostly came for the music. I was responsible for updating the signs posted outside, which Ed asked me to paint.

Nick and I spoke on the phone once a week and he told me how it was going there, on the wintry East Coast. He was having a great time, and said I should come out and join him for a short visit. He was sharing a room in a brownstone in Cambridge with a bunch of other young people, co-ed. I thought he might be having an affair with one of his housemates, but tried not to dwell on it. I booked a bus ticket for January 12. I told my boss Ed that I'd return in February, and he understood. He said my job was secure at the Ash Grove.

I boarded the bus that night, and three long days later, I was in Cambridge, snow falling on the ground. When I saw Nick I cried, and he gave me a big hug and kiss. He took me through the bustling town center of Harvard Square to get a submarine sandwich, a new eating experience. We caught up in the tiny sandwich shop, but I was chilled to the bone, being a girl from the southwest.

Next, a bath. We got to Nick's new home: a brownstone he shared with Taj Mahal, Taj's girlfriend Maud, and some other girls. I was struck by the impoverished surroundings. Plastic sheets covered the wood-framed windows to keep out the cold air. Old radiators hissed and the walls were grimy. The hot water in the claw foot bathtub trickled out of a tiny showerhead. It was euphoric to bathe. When it was time for bed, Nick and I shared a single bed. He held me gently, but I felt a distance between us, even though we were in each other's arms.

That weekend was filled with music at the Club 47. We saw Jim Kweskin's Jug Band and Mimi Farina. One of Nick's housemates, an African-American man, gave me a tin kazoo as a welcoming present. Nick and I performed in the subway together, Nick playing a Martin six-string guitar, me playing kazoo, and his friend singing. In the evening, we drove in the snow to a nearby town to see Taj Mahal play guitar. Nick had met Taj and they had become instant friends, deciding to perform as a duo together. When I heard Taj play guitar,

I was struck by his engaging stage presence and openness. I knew if he and Nick played together, they might find success.

On our way back to the brownstone, I slipped on black ice on the sidewalk and fell on my ass. Nick helped me up. I realized I wanted to go back to Los Angeles, pronto. I was not a cold weather person. I cut the visit short. Nick took me to the bus station the next day. It was clear that our romance had cooled down and I thought it was best to go home. He was understanding and probably felt the same way.

I boarded the bus the next day to return to Los Angeles. When I arrived home in Echo Park, Karen told me that the lease would soon expire, and we'd have to move. Nina had relocated already, and Karen eventually moved back in with her mother in Silverlake. Wanting to get on with my life after the East Coast visit, unsure of my future with Nick, I decided to return to school and take an art class at City College. I began looking for a new apartment near the campus. I worked the Ash Grove nights and weekends, and I attended the art class during the day, sketching still-lifes in charcoal, and learning the principles of drawing. My aspirations for journalism took a backseat. Nick and I spoke less often on the phone.

At the Ash Grove, Ed had children's concerts on Saturday and Sunday afternoons that featured artists like Oscar Brand. I worked extra days to earn money. Other weekends, Ed held seminars where people like Ry Cooder, David Lindley and David Cohen taught guitar, mandolin and blues guitar to aspiring musicians.

Ry Cooder, a handsome and intense teenager who played blues guitar, was one of Ed's protégés. Ed featured him regularly at the club. We became friendly during his stints. We'd discuss old blues musicians like Blind Lemon Jefferson and Robert Johnson. I talked about my interest in writing. "You should read Norman Mailer or Gore Vidal," he'd say. I remember thinking, "He's just a kid. If only he were five years older."

That spring, the New Lost City Ramblers came to LA to play the Ash Grove. I was working that night and it was a busy crowd. The band put on a fantastic show that got the audience going. Mike Seeger, whom I'd met on the first night of their three-day engagement, had a funny quip: "Drink up, folks. The more you drink, the better we sound!" So it was always a rowdy crowd. The night of their last show Mike invited me to have coffee with him.

After the band packed up and the club closed, Mike, who was quiet and polite offstage, patiently waited for me outside. He smiled when I approached. We drove in his rental car to Canter's, a classic Los Angeles delicatessen on Fairfax Avenue. It was a great late-night place to hang out. During our conversation together, he mentioned that I resembled his wife. I was taken aback, because I had no idea he was married and at that point his charm had seduced me. After coffee, Mike asked, "Is it all right if I drive you home?"

I felt a sudden welcome flirtation ensuing. After all, Nick was likely dating someone else back in Boston. I didn't see any harm in spending time with Mike. "Yes," I replied, smiling. We drove down Sunset Boulevard, in the cool night air. We arrived at the Echo Park apartment and climbed the stairs to the entry. Karen wasn't home yet. She was probably at the midnight cinema with her boyfriend. I was excited I'd be alone with Mike and I felt a rush of infatuation.

In the living room, Mike took off his jacket and laid it on a chair.

"Sweet little place you have here," he said.

Before I knew it, we were on the couch, kissing passionately. I felt alive, and he was gently sighing. I stood and took his hand, leading him into my bedroom. We kissed some more as we shed our clothes. He stayed the night with me, and we tenderly made love, all through the night. He was sweeter than any man I'd ever known at that time. The following morning, I woke up and started dressing. Mike was asleep, naked under the sheets. I thought he was a beautiful man, and that I would make us some breakfast.

Getting dressed, I turned to look out the bedroom window at the bright morning sun, when suddenly I saw Ed Pearl pulling up the driveway in his Mercedes. I'd completely forgotten that he'd planned to take me to work for a Sunday concert at the club. In a panic, I shook Mike. "Wake up! Ed's here! I'm supposed to work today!"

Mike bolted upright, stunned and confused, and gathered his clothes, awkwardly fumbling to dress.

Ed knocked on the door and I grabbed Mike's arm and shoved him into the small bathroom where Karen was just finishing up, after a shower, with a towel wrapped around her torso. She gave a quick shriek of surprise when she saw Mike, half-naked, dressing in the bathroom with her. I shut the bathroom door quickly.

Ed was now banging on the front door. "Dolores?"

"Wait – I'll be right out!" I quickly finished dressing, grabbed my handbag, and in a flurry ran down the stairs and out the door – leaving Mike and Karen alone in the bathroom together. She later told me how upsetting this incident was, but she and Mike became friends in spite of this.

I sat in the car with Ed, my heart racing as he drove to the club.

"Is everything all right?" he asked. I quickly nodded and smiled as best I could. Mike was married, so I was beginning to feel guilty. I'd never been with a married man before... I knew Mike would be discreet. And I certainly wouldn't tell anyone.

At the Ash Grove, my thoughts were about Mike and our night together, and I wondered whether we'd continue to have a friendship. As it turned out, we remained warm friends over many years. He was a true gentleman.

Across the campus of City College, I found a studio apartment. Echo Park was a memory. Karen moved in with her mom. I continued to attend art classes. Ed had been deducting money from my paychecks in order to accumulate enough money to purchase his 1957, maroon, four-door Renault. So now, I had a proper set of wheels. Around this time, I started seeing a friend of a fiddle player, Richard Greene. Richard was dating Sandy Getz, who managed the Ash Grove. Richard joked with me, saying, "Dolores is the femme fatale of the Ash Grove," – and I began to believe it. The reason his friend made such an impression on me is that he introduced me to Vivaldi's *Four Seasons*, Mozart, and Villa Lobos.

I received a phone call from Nick. He was returning to Los Angeles. I wasn't sure how to respond. He was planning to stay with his mother in West Hollywood. I thought to myself, I would see how I felt when I saw him. About a week later, Nick came over to my studio and we had tea. He was happy to see me, but he seemed different: older and distant, with a newfound purpose of succeeding as a musician with Taj, who was set to arrive in LA shortly. Nick and I had never really ended our relationship properly, so there were still many unresolved feelings. However, it soon became clear that we no longer shared the intimate spark we once had.

One night at the Ash Grove, a few days later, Rambling Jack Elliot was playing a weekend engagement. He had a reputation for being a flirt and a ladies' man, and he certainly flirted with me. The flirtation became mutual, and he joked, "Your place or mine?" He told me he was staying with friends in Topanga Canyon. "My place is closer," I told him.

After the show we jumped into my Renault and sped home to my studio apartment. We were both happily intoxicated on beer, and it was a playful romp, as I'm sure he'd experienced many times before, and many times after. Afterward, he had to get back to Topanga Canyon, so we dressed and I drove him down Melrose to return to the Ash Grove.

As we neared La Brea, I looked at the oncoming traffic coming from the opposite lane, and who should I spot in his mother's Morris Minor, but Nick. I was horrified that he might recognize me, and I believe out of the corner of his eye he did, because I saw in the rearview mirror that his car was making a U-turn to follow me.

"Oh no, that's Nick, my boyfriend!"

Rambling Jack sobered up and said, "My God, woman!" as we sped down Melrose and made a sharp turn to get Nick off our tail. We reached the Ash Grove, a bit shaken. I never wanted to see Jack Elliot again. He got out of the car and tipped his hat, saying "Thanks for a lovely evening." I sped back to the studio, in the event that Nick might be there. He wasn't. I tried to relax and got ready for bed, but I felt a rising sense of shame and disgust at my behavior.

A few hours later, there was a banging on the door. It was Nick. I let him in. "Were you driving with some dude earlier tonight?"

I lied, "No." Deny, deny, deny.

"I'm sure that was you, in that car, with someone." Nick was furious. He was realizing too much had gone down since he'd left for Cambridge. He was sullen and decided to leave. I felt terrible. I was angry at myself, falling for Rambling Jack's line. And Nick's feelings were hurt. He left without saying anything. I pretty much thought the relationship was beyond repair.

Despite this, I carried the kazoo that Nick's Cambridge friend had given me, at all times, almost like a talisman. During that holiday season, Brownie Magee and Sonny Terry were booked for a show. They really entertained the audience with their rambunctious blues. Sonny called out, "We need a kazoo player! Is there anyone in the house?" Nancy said, "Dolores, you have a kazoo, don't you?" I was serving beer and said, "I sure do!"

Nancy said, "Go up there!"

Almost as a joke, I ran up on stage, after Ed Pearl's approving nod, with my kazoo. Brownie and Sonny performed a song and said, "Go, girl! Right now!" at which point I tooted into the microphone what kazoo I could play. It was a thrilling moment, and it made my sadness disappear. This was Brownie and Sonny's last number, and the audience roared with adoration when the song finished. I stumbled off the stage with shyness and exhilaration, after they'd told me to take a bow. They played an encore, without me of course.

One autumn night at the Ash Grove, Kathy & Carol, a folk duo who sang beautiful harmonies, were booked as an opening act. Chris Hillman and Jim McGuinn walked into the seating area. I saw these two handsome young men and thought they had an ethereal quality. They were both lean and well dressed, with much longer hair than was standard for the time, their stylishness resembling the Beatles in many ways. At the same time, there was a scruffy, bohemian quality about them. They'd been living on the edge.

I walked up to their table and asked them what they wanted. "Two Cokes," Chris Hillman replied. Jim was absorbed in the ambience of the Ash Grove. I went back to work, attending to other patrons who were watching the show. I stood by the server station, gazing out at the audience and watching the show, and these two lads. A shaft of stage light caught Jim's blond hair and it glowed like a halo around his head. This is when I became fascinated by his angelic quality; I'd never met or seen a man like him before. There was something magnetic and mysterious about him. I felt we were made for each other.

By comparison, Chris seemed younger and friendlier. I wanted to know more about them, but I could tell they were quite shy. The evening passed uneventfully. However, I became fascinated by the mystique of these two. They left without my knowing, and I was crushed.

The next evening on my shift, Chris Hillman came in again to see the same duo. This time, David Crosby was with him. David struck me as a charmer with a baby face. He also had the same mop-top hairstyle and scruffy, bohemian quality. This time, these two young men ordered "Hot tea," and that's all. During a break in that night's set, David left the table briefly. I decided this was my opportunity to approach Chris. I asked him, "Where is your other friend?"

"You mean Jim? Jimmy McGuinn? He didn't come out tonight. He's probably at his hotel."

"Hotel?" I asked.

"He lives at the Padre Hotel," Chris said casually.

"Are you two brothers?" I asked, because of the striking resemblance they shared.

"No, we're in a group," Chris said, as David approached the table, and the conversation ended. There was something about this information that sparked my curiosity.

I walked to the box office and found the LA yellow pages to look up the Padre Hotel, which was nearby on Cahuenga Boulevard near the Hollywood Bowl. I couldn't wait to get off work. It was after midnight. Bringing a bottle of red wine that I bought at discount from the Ash Grove kitchen, I drove to the Padre Hotel in the Renault. The Padre was a brick building about six stories high. I went to the front desk and asked for Jim McGuinn's room number. The older clerk didn't hesitate, and gave me the room number. Perhaps I seemed harmless. Up the elevator I went, a nervous wreck. I walked down the musty, carpeted hallway leading up to Jim's room. I quietly knocked on the door and he opened it slightly.

"Hi," I stammered. "Do you remember me? I work at the Ash Grove. You were there the other night."

"Oh yes," he said, and opened the door. "Come in."

I walked into the room. The scent of patchouli lingered in the air. It was intoxicating, a fragrance I had never encountered. There was a double bed, a dresser, a chair and a small desk. I placed the bottle of wine on his desk. We looked at each other and he asked cheerfully, "Want to see something?" Without any hesitation, he pulled a guitar case from under the bed. It was the blonde twelve-string Rickenbacker.

"Listen." He sat on a chair and started to play the guitar. It was Bobby Vinton's 'Blue on Blue.' He sang along. I was enchanted. I was instantly in love, mesmerized by Jim.

I looked at the surroundings. Jim's voice echoed nicely in that room with the high ceilings, and there was a faint white noise of traffic from the Hollywood freeway, right outside his window. His voice was stirring and seductive, pure.

After that song, he played 'Don't Worry Baby' by the Beach Boys.

We talked about music, traveling and his new group that he'd formed, the Byrds, spelled with a 'y'. He said they'd been recording new music at a studio near the Troubadour. It all seemed rather extraordinary, because what he was describing seemed artistic and full of possibility. There was a large care package filled with an assortment of chocolate bars, which his grandmother had mailed him from Chicago, sitting on his desk. We opened the bottle of wine and had a piece of candy. Jim took out a deck of cards and performed some sophisticated card tricks, which charmed me.

Companions through the night, we fell asleep on the bed with our clothes on.

The next morning, I awoke, surprised that I was still in this room with him. Time had passed in a different way, so quickly and yet I felt a gentle, everlasting connection had been made. It all felt like a dream. He awoke, a little disoriented, and self-conscious that I was still there. He gazed into my eyes and said, "Do you know that you don't have any pupils? Your eyes are so dark; you can't see your pupils." I'd never met anyone like Jim, because when I thought he was being humorous, he was actually dead serious. He looked intensely into my eyes, almost searching to determine who I was.

We walked out onto the street together, in the morning light, still wearing last night's clothes. Jim said he wanted to buy something at the health food store on Hollywood Boulevard. We walked there.

Reaching the health food store, we ordered Jim's favorite: banana-coconut shakes and cream cheese with black olive sandwiches on whole-wheat bread. The customers at the health food store were older women in their fifties. They smiled at us. We sat at the counter and ate. This became our frequent hangout. We returned to the Padre Hotel, and took up the entire afternoon lovemaking, exploring each other. Every touch was electric. Jim was a highly sensitive man, almost otherworldly. We lay together naked, and I quietly nestled under his chin for over an hour. "I can hear your heart beating," he said.

As the afternoon passed, Jim asked me if I knew how to play chess. "Yes!" I said. Jim took out a little magnetic chess set in a black case, and we played a game. He seemed impressed that I knew the game, and was a capable opponent. I won.

It came time for me to leave. Jim said he would come by the Ash Grove later that week. His group was meeting at Gene Clark's apartment, not far from the club, off Santa Monica Boulevard. They were rehearsing. I rushed home to shower and change.

When I came into work that night, I wondered if Jim would actually come by the Ash Grove ever again. I was eager to see him. I knew I was in love with him. The shift wore on. I told Nancy that Chris Hillman's friend Jim might come by during the week, and ask for me. Before I worked at the Ash Grove, Chris Hillman, a talented mandolin player before he joined the Byrds, had played the club as a teenager, and Nancy knew him from that time.

Later that week, while I was serving, I felt a presence behind me, and I turned and looked. Jim was standing at the door, shyly gazing at me. I brought him into the club and had him sit down at the pew that was at the right of the stage, with a small ridge for beverages. He wanted some hot tea, but noticing how thin he was, I ordered a plate of spaghetti and meatballs from the Trotsky chef. Jim was pleasantly surprised to see the meal in front of him, and eagerly ate it all with a smile. From that moment on, I knew the adage 'a way to a man's heart is through his stomach' couldn't be more true. Jim stayed for the whole show, and since it was a slow night, I was able to get off work early. He invited me to join him at Gene's apartment.

We drove in my car to a wood-slat apartment building off Santa Monica Boulevard.

"This is Dolores," Jim said to the other young men in the room – Gene Clark, Chris Hillman and Michael Clarke. I met Gene for the first time. He was well built, quiet, had a tense, manly face, with a warm, quick, nervous smile, and a deep, resonant voice. Michael was tall and blond. He hunched over a coffee table, leafing through a teen magazine, strongly resembling Brian Jones from the Rolling Stones. He nodded and mumbled, "Hi." Chris seemed pleasantly amused to see me again, and smiled, "Hi." In spite of his youth, he seemed very serious and had a brooding quality. I later learned that Chris' father had committed suicide when he was a teenager.

I took a seat on the sofa as Gene said to Jim, "Hey man, I want you to hear this new song I wrote." Taking out his acoustic guitar,

Gene strummed and sang a plaintive love song. I was struck by the melodic passion of the song, and the honest strength and timbre of Gene's voice. Jim played the unplugged twelve-string Rickenbacker as accompaniment, trying to find the right chords.

Michael and Chris smoked cigarettes and listened, watched Gene's guitar chord changes, and filled the small ashtray. This was one of many long, late nights I'd spend with Jim, as he jammed and coalesced songs with the other band members. It became so familiar to me that I'd sometimes rest on the sofa and fall asleep. Jim gently woke me when it was time to leave.

Back at the Ash Grove, a trend began where Byrds' members came to the club for shows, but hoped for, and usually got, a meal. One time, the Kentucky Colonels played. Jim and Chris attended the show. I was able to sneak them in free. Sometimes the other members joined them. When I could, I'd get them kitchen orders, like sandwiches, a cheese plate or, of course, spaghetti and meatballs. There was a hamburger joint on the corner of Melrose and La Cienega, and occasionally we'd go there, whether one or five Byrds, and spend my tips to get food. Of all the Byrds, Mike Clarke was the most voracious eater.

Taj Mahal came to town with a girlfriend in tow, Maude from Minnesota, and somehow it worked out that I could move in with her, and we'd have an apartment in Venice Beach. I was giving up on my studies. As my relationship with Jim progressed, I spent more and more time with him. Somehow, that was all that seemed to matter. Maude was blonde-haired, friendly and buxom. We got along well, and it was easy to live with her. We shared a big 1940s-era house, divided into two apartments. We lived on the second floor. The structure was just steps away from the beach – a California dream come true. Jim stayed with me on occasion; I had my own room. It was when I lived here that Jim told me that the band had an upcoming recording session for Columbia Records. This was due to the efforts of Jim Dickson and Eddie Tickner, two men in their thirties that I'd met briefly, who were managing the Byrds.

1965 - Forging New Adventures

The Byrds at a TV studio, 1965, snapped by Peter Fonda

One day I was outside painting a sign for the Ash Grove. Eddie Tickner pulled up in his Chevy station wagon that transported most of the Byrds' musical gear. Jim Dickson sat in the passenger side. Dickson said, "You look just like my wife, Harley." It appeared that I resembled everyone's wife. Eddie, in his early thirties, was a thin and elegantly dressed man from Philadelphia, who had a Borscht belt sense of sarcasm and humor. It took me time to get used to his style. When Eddie was around, there was a feeling of stability and that things were under control. Jim, on the other hand, was a volatile, husky native Los Angeleno, opinionated and intelligent, with piercing blue eyes. He felt his approach was always the best way. Despite this, he and Eddie rarely argued.

My Jim had recorded the backing track for the single 'Mr. Tambourine Man' with session musicians, supervised by Terry Melcher, one cold night in January. I heard that things had gone well; more sessions were scheduled and I was invited to a subsequent session. That's when Jim introduced me to Terry. I walked into a cavernous, well-lit room, large enough for an orchestra. Terry was a freckle-faced, easygoing young man who was very friendly, and clearly favored Jim. He welcomed me, which was reassuring, since I was the only female there. I also met Leon Russell, sitting at the keyboard, his hair slicked back, wearing a black leather jacket. He resembled a motorcycle gang member more than an established studio musician. He had bad boy good looks, and he knew it.

The session was at the Columbia studio in Hollywood near Sunset and Vine. Behind a huge, glass plate was an engineer's booth. Terry sat at the control panel with an engineer. Eddie, Michael and Chris sat on a sofa and Dickson was hovering over Terry. An engineer's assistant handled the large tape machine. Jim, Gene and David were in the studio, wearing headphones, laying down vocals to the backing track. It was magical to hear their harmonies blend, the studio's huge speakers and audio gear filled the engineer booth with overwhelming sounds. After several takes, Terry asked the boys to come in and listen.

When the session ended, Terry invited Jim and me to Villa Capri restaurant, which was near the studio. It was an old hangout for Frank Sinatra's Rat Pack, and Terry was certainly an insider, being Doris Day's son. The restaurant had a dark, 1950s well-appointed feel, with red leather booths and Italian murals on the wall. Terry ordered for us Steak Sinatra and a Caesar salad. I'd never been to a restaurant where they prepared the Caesar salad table-side. The food was exceptional, and the well-dressed waiters loved catering to Terry. It was to become one of our many visits to this restaurant. Terry and Jim discussed the session, the group dynamics and the ideas that Terry had for future recordings. There was hope that the single would lead to a full-length album.

A few weeks later, Jim and I picked David and Michael up in the Renault. Jim had gotten the acetate 45rpm single of 'Mr. Tambourine Man' from Jim Dickson. We were eager to hear the results. As we drove toward Gene's apartment, the car stalled at a stoplight. Michael, David and Jim jumped out and started pushing the car down Santa Monica Boulevard, laughing. The engine had died, but only temporarily. I was able to start the car again, once the engine cooled down a bit.

We continued to Gene's apartment. Jim and the rest of us gathered and listened to the acetate single, repeatedly. The first moment I heard Jim's twelve-string Rickenbacker play the opening notes, there was a palpable excitement in the room. The vocals and harmonies were beautiful, and I remember looking over at David and seeing a look of unbridled joy on his face.

Throughout the winter, I accompanied Jim to World Pacific Studios, where Dickson recorded demos of Gene's songs. It was during this time that Gene and David were competing to play the Gretsch rhythm guitar. The sessions would eventually become the *Preflyte* album, with a raw, playful, improvisational energy. Mike Clarke was learning to play drums. Many angry moments with David scolding Michael about the tempo flared up. Like Jim Dickson, David always thought his way was best. The clash of these two temperamental forces, Dickson and Crosby, would cause much drama in the future.

My Jim was clearly the person designated with leadership responsibilities in the band. Michael would shrug, "You're the leader. Lead." Jim's style was more about the natural flow of events, and he didn't like intervening in arguments. Things were usually somewhat tense, with Dickson the ultimate taskmaster, settling everything. 'She has a way about her / that makes her fuck around / now I wonder if she'll ever want to settle down,' was one of the lyric changes the boys playfully made to let off steam and crack up during the sessions for Gene's songs. Dickson said with a stern look, "That's funny guys, but let's get serious now."

I felt I'd been allowed to get to know Jim better when he invited me to wait for him while he attended a session at the spiritual organization, Subud. We drove downtown, to Subud's stately building on Hope Street. My first time there, I waited for him in an anteroom, curious about the mysterious practice, and the sounds that emerged. Men and women separated during the Latihan session. Jim's introduction to this Indonesian sect was through Richmond Shepherd, a New York actor from the Greenwich Village scene. Jim had said, "I'm high on pot." Richmond had said, "I have something else that will get you higher."

Subud was a popular meditation center for actors and artists, and had branches all over the world. I respected Jim's commitment to the ideals of Subud, which were restraint, respect and humility. It was the 1960s and people were exploring new ideas and concepts of faith and religion. Subud was founded by Bapak, an Indonesian spiritual leader. The basis of Subud is a spiritual exercise commonly referred to as the Latihan kejiwaan, said to represent guidance from the Power of God or the Great Life Force. Bapak claimed that Subud was not a new teaching or religion. He recommended that Subud members practice a religion, but left them to make their own choice as to which one.

After several visits and a few months waiting for Jim, I contemplated joining Subud. My time spent waiting there proved useful. Because I'd become a familiar face, I was invited by the ladies of Subud to sit in on their practice. I joined shortly thereafter, and Jim and I remained involved with Subud for the next several years of our relationship.

We became friendly with a young man at Subud who invited Jim and me to Sunday dinner with his family. He was in his early twenties, as we were. I don't remember his name.

Somehow, Michael Clarke tagged along, and we drove to Downey to have dinner with this man's family – mother, father, grandmother and siblings. It was an odd evening. Jim and I sat around the dining table and thought we were in a 1950s sitcom. All members of the family spoke in a kind of cliché TV-speak: "Pass the peas, please!" "Sure thing! Father knows best!" "Golly Gee, I can't imagine why, Granny!" in such authentic tones, as if to suggest we were being filmed for television.

The whole experience made Jim uneasy. Michael said to the grandmother sitting next to him, "Do you realize that we're made up of atoms, and we're not solid?" Jim added, "Yes, and do you realize that we're spinning in the universe at thousands of miles an hour, and only gravity is keeping us from floating off these chairs?"

The grandmother, flabbergasted, stared at Jim and scoffed, "That's not true!"

Our young friend from Subud said, "Oh Granny, they're just trying to scare you." The feeling of being in a *Twilight Zone* episode was uncanny. Jim made some excuse, after we finished our meal, about having to rush back to Hollywood. "Don't you want to stay for dessert?" Granny asked. We were halfway out the door. The young man at Subud never spoke to us after that experience. We realized Subud could be different things to different people.

At some point, the Byrds became friendly with a band of bohemian dancers and artists. Vito Paulekas taught sculpture to a group of teenagers who adored him. They all dressed up in colorful attire after class and danced on the beach together. It was either Chris or Michael, being the most handsome members, who drew the young teenagers' attention and interest, and somehow the Byrds were soon rehearsing in Vito's basement at his studio off Beverly Boulevard. I went to some of these rehearsals and met several of the teenage girls, who were sweet and naïve.

Vito was married to a woman named Szou. He had an intense, vortex-like energy, and I felt trepidation toward him and Karl Franzoni, one of Vito's associates. It was truly the beginning of the hippie movement, because Vito and Karl were like pied pipers, seducing the young women into a hedonistic lifestyle of abandon, communal living and casual sex. Their philosophy was amplified by drug use, primarily pot, but LSD and mescaline were not uncommon. I had not yet tried LSD, but other members of the Byrds had begun experimenting.

In the midst of this, the Byrds rehearsed using their newly acquired loud amplifiers, and rock music filled Vito's basement. In a haze of marijuana and cigarette smoke, everyone was dancing, including me. The Byrds were trying all of their collective material, which became the basis for their first album, *Mr. Tambourine Man*. These were mostly Gene's compositions.

It was during this time that the band became more cohesive musically, since they had an audience, and Michael developed a sense of what made a good beat dance-worthy.

To the troupe of teenage girls that followed Vito, I was known as 'Jim's Girl, Dolores.' Jim and I were always together, and I drove him and the Byrds everywhere in the Renault. Michelle, one of the girls, said once, "You two remind me of *David and Lisa*." She was referring to the eponymous film that had come out a few years before. I thought about it, and Jim and I did bear a physical resemblance to the couple depicted in the film – Jim with his golden hair and blue eyes, me with my long dark hair and bangs.

I'd become deeply involved in Jim's and the Byrds' lives and ambitions, but I still had to maintain an income, since we were all broke. Maude and I were still living together, although I spent less and less time in Venice Beach and more time with Jim at the Padre Hotel.

One night at the Ash Grove while I was working, Nick came into the lobby gallery, near the ticket booth, and he spoke to Nancy. "Nick's here. He wants to see you," she said to me. I nervously walked to the gallery where Nick was strumming an acoustic guitar – a Martin D28.

"So," Nick said, "I hear you're seeing this McGuinn guy."

"Yes," I said, with some embarrassment.

"Well, what are you going to do?" he asked, threateningly. "Are you going to see him, or me?"

I felt anguish that Nick had reached this point, where he had become aggressive and despondent. I wished I could tell him something he wanted to hear, but the words came out of my mouth, without any hesitation. "Well, I guess I'm going to see him," I said, swallowing.

A look of anger and hurt fell across Nick's face. He lifted the guitar by the neck, and with force smashed the body onto the tile floor. The back of the guitar splintered as wood shattered with a terrible, discordant sound, the bottom of the guitar dangling by the strings. People entering the club stopped to stare. I was shocked and disturbed, but relieved he hadn't struck me.

Nick looked at the guitar, realizing what his brute strength had done. He had a very pained look on his face, with a deep sense of loss. I felt terrible and sick to my stomach. Nick stood up and walked out the door, carrying the broken guitar in one hand and the guitar case in the other. No parting words were spoken. My nerves and my psyche were on edge, but I had to get back to work. 'Femme Fatale of the Ash Grove' resonated in my mind, as I pitied Nick's destruction of his beloved guitar. Everything that I did for the remainder of my shift seemed irrelevant compared to the hurt experienced through this encounter with Nick.

That night with Jim, I told him about Nick's visit and the smashed guitar. Jim said, "I would never break a guitar over a woman." I didn't know whether to laugh, or to just accept that the two men were vastly different: Nick, passionate, emotional and human; Jim, cold, aloof and detached. I prayed I had made the right choice. We went to sleep, and I held Jim, never thinking that we'd have an encounter as I'd had with poor Nick: Jim was a different kind of man.

Vicki Morris was Chris' girlfriend. She worked at Shelly's Manhole, a Jazz club on Vine. She was a waitress, like me, and we became good friends. Because she had long brown hair, people sometimes mistook us for sisters. A sad thing about Vicki is that once the Byrds started gigging regularly, Chris strayed and started seeing other women.

This was probably a long time coming, because Chris would get angry when we were all ready to go, and she'd still be taking curlers out of her hair and brushing up. Poor Vicki, she really loved Chris. I don't think she ever got over him. I always think of the Kinks' lyrics, 'So tired / Tired of waiting / Tired of waiting for you,' as Chris' anthem to Vicki. Jim, Chris and I often waited for her to get ready. Seeing how angry it made Chris to wait, and the impatience that Jim expressed, I became a speed-dresser, ready to leave in an instant.

Tickson Management, that is to say, Eddie and Dickson, began making efforts to get the Byrds into the public eye with live shows. One afternoon, Jim came into the Padre Hotel when I was in his room by myself. I was surprised to see him, and said, "Aren't you guys supposed to be playing a gig?" He said, "We hated it, so we left." I didn't ask any further questions. Jim wanted to go to the movies with Chris and me to see Gerry and the Pacemakers in *Ferry Cross the Mersey*. We drove in the Renault to meet Chris at the theater, near the Capitol Records building on Hollywood Boulevard.

We thoroughly enjoyed the film, which depicts the antics of the band Gerry and the Pacemakers, akin to the Beatles' *A Hard Day's Night*. When Jim and I returned to the Padre Hotel, Eddie Tickner was waiting in the lobby. He was furious, demanding to know why the band had left their engagement that day. He warned Jim that the Byrds would be blackballed if they did such a thing again. Jim nervously agreed not to ignore any future gigs, hanging his head low, like a scolded teenage boy. Eddie walked off in a huff, realizing the immaturity of this fledgling band of young men.

The next engagement that the Byrds had was opening for The Rolling Stones. The Stones were not well known in the US at this time, even though they had a couple of full-length albums under their belt. 'Satisfaction' had just been released. Tickson management set up a dinner with both bands and their entourages, so they could get acquainted, at Martoni's Italian restaurant in Hollywood. I sat in a booth with Jim, Chris and Michael. The restaurant had roped off the back section for us. The resemblance of Mike Clarke to Brian Jones was even more striking, seeing them interact in person.

Mick Jagger was polite and soft-spoken, laughing with David and whispering to Keith. Everyone was young, full of vitality and humor. It was a great gathering. The bands were set to play an outdoor concert down the coast in Long Beach the next day. Keith Richards and Charlie Watts were polite British gents. Each of the Rolling Stones had a striking female companion, mostly Americans. I remained at Jim's side, enjoying the atmosphere and the delicious Italian wine and pizza. Gene Clark was quiet and seemed a bit nervous. It was an occasion to feast, so deep down, everyone was happy.

The next morning Jim and I left early to meet the other band members at World Pacific Studios, where the equipment was to be driven down to Long Beach. Bryan MacLean, a teenage roadie, loaded the equipment into Eddie's station wagon. A limousine was to deliver the Byrds, and I tagged along, with Emmy, a teenage fan who'd befriended Chris. We rode down the freeway in the smooth limo, my first time ever in such a luxurious vehicle. Emmy said, "Look at those oil drills – they look like small enslaved children..." as we drove by the passing scenes.

At Long Beach, Bryan and the stage crew set up the Byrds' equipment for sound check. There was already a significant audience seated in the stadium. This was to be the Byrds' first show in front of such a large audience. I remember backstage, with the band, nerves were running high. Jim tuned his twelve-string, and checked it twice. When it was time for them to play, I went out to the dusty, crowded audience area and milled around. They put on a good show, although I could tell they were still nervous. The audience was receptive, but they were primarily Rolling Stones fans who were eager to see their band play.

Emmy had been flirting with Rolling Stones' drummer Charlie Watts backstage. She never went out front to see the Byrds play.

When the Byrds' set finished, I approached the backstage access area to join the band. They were exhausted by their performance and their pre-show nerves, but relieved that their show was well received, without any major technical issues. David seemed all the more egotistical as he fraternized with the Stones right before their show. We all stayed to see The Stones play, and that's when the Byrds saw how much work was in store for them to become a more crowd-pleasing band.

After the Rolling Stones' set, which left a roaring crowd wanting more, the Byrds shuffled off to the loading area where the limousine was parked. Each one of them piled in, and since Emmy had remained with the Stones, I was the only female. As I sat down next to Jim, David caustically barked, "No chicks in the limo." I was shocked at this, after all the times I'd spent with the group as the lone woman, without incident. "Dolores is with me," said Jim calmly, with an air of authority. The door slammed shut. We rode in silence for a while, David quietly sulking in his desire to be more like the Rolling Stones.

A month later, Jim and I were driving the band's station wagon to a venue that was to become the band's touchstone: Ciro's on the Sunset Strip. Eddie had made a booking for the band to play a solid week there. We were driving along Sunset, listening to KRLA radio station.

Suddenly the opening notes of 'Mr. Tambourine Man' played on the air. That second, I looked over at Jim and Chris in the back seat to see the expressions of surprise and elation on their faces.

The song had never sounded better than coming through the small radio speaker in the car. The twelve-string's clarity cut through the airwaves like a sword in the darkness, forging an altogether new sound, even sharper than when we listened to the acetate. We all shared the three minutes together in silent recognition of the achievement of the song. As the song faded out, Chris and Jim whooped and hollered with sheer adrenaline. I was so proud of Jim.

We arrived at Ciro's. There were stairs from the sidewalk that led to a huge entry. To the right was an elegant bar with mirrors. An iron railing led further down to a dance floor. Along the sides of the first tier were booths, and the second tier had tables and chairs. Over the dance floor hung an enormous mirrored ball. Eddie was there. Jim said, "We heard it on the radio, man! It was beautiful." For the first time in a while, Eddie seemed pleased. The equipment was set up, and when David, Michael and Gene arrived, Jim and Chris shared their joyous news. David was miffed that he hadn't heard it himself. Gene was in disbelief. Michael said, "Man, we've got to take the single to the other radio stations."

"I'm working on it," replied Eddie. "We've just hired a publicist for you guys. He just finished working for the Beatles. What do you think of that?"

Weeks before, Jim and I were listening to the radio when an obnoxious advertisement blared with an incredulous voice, "Who is Derek Taylor? Who is Derek Taylor?" This name stuck in our collective memory because of this ad. When Eddie said, "Derek Taylor is going to be working on your publicity," we all laughed.

Backstage there were waiters, well into their forties, who were talking to Michael. "Hey guys. Did you know there's a ghost in this club?"

Gene said, "Did someone die here?"

"Whose ghost is it?" Jim asked. The waiters were vague, but assured us that we should believe in and respect the ghost.

"I hope it's a good ghost..." Jim trailed off.

The Byrds did a sound check. It was loud. Ciro's, formerly an elegant supper club from Hollywood's Golden Era, now faded and showing its age, was not designed for rock 'n' roll volumes, but the acoustics were remarkable, as was the stage lighting. This was to be the Byrds' finest embarkation. They were to play three sets a night.

That night's first set was slow, but as the evening wore on, Vito and his dancers arrived, and everything changed. By the third set, the band and the dancers were literally creating a scene that was not only captivating to watch, but also, because of the loud amplification, emitted music that could be heard outside on Sunset Boulevard.

I'll never forget when Bob Dylan arrived one evening during the run of the engagement. A collective hush came over the crowd. Dylan was ushered to a booth where Dickson and Eddie sat. Thin, hunched over, dressed in black, his chiseled brooding face scanned the room. Those eyes, like a hawk, narrowed and peered into the soul of any lucky or unlucky person he wished to gaze upon. His commentary was brief and biting, and everyone held their breath. His voice was low and had a rapid, mocking, New Yorker-type accent. When he laughed everyone relaxed.

A brave autograph hunter tiptoed to the table, hands shaking, voice quavering, requesting the signature of the magical visitor. Dylan shook his hand at him. The fan backed away, tripping on the carpet.

Dylan's entourage consisted of Bobby Neuwirth and Victor Maymudes. They sat at the next booth, making sure to cut the hunters off, and turn away anyone who would bug 'His Mighty.' The booth slowly filled with beautiful women. As for me... I was just as fascinated as the next person, but I did my best not to show it. If anything, I became belligerent and questioned whatever he said. I think that did make an impression on him.

The Byrds walked onstage without fanfare and began playing 'Bells of Rhymney.' Carl and his crew had been hanging out on the dance floor. When the opening notes of the song chimed, they erupted into curvy-swirly dance moves that got the band and the rest of the crowd excited. There was definitely something new about this Scene. Dylan mentally recorded the Folk Rock sound, especially when his numbers were played. The way Jim sang and arranged 'All I Really Want to Do' and 'Chimes of Freedom' made a big impact on how Bob Dylan would render his future songs in the recording studio.

Dylan was kind enough to get on stage and play harmonica with the group. It was a glorious moment and frankly, quite historical. Dylan's approval was a blessing. After the show, we went to a club on Sunset Strip, Fred C. Dobb's. The owner had named it after the Humphrey Bogart character in the film *The Treasure of the Sierra Madre*. We all sat at three tables pushed together in a rectangle. Jim and I sat across from Dylan. He sat at an angle, legs crossed, one leg restlessly shaking back and forth, half uninterested. His pockets were full of bits of paper. He pulled them out of his shirt or jacket pockets, searching for one that had room to write. Finally, he'd grab a book of matches and scribble some thought or random phrase he heard someone say.

One memorable morning, while Dylan was still in town, we were invited to sail to Catalina Island with Dickson and his rich pal Lance Reventlow. The motley crew was made up of Eddie, Jim, Butchie (one of Dickson's girl buddies), Victor, Dylan and me. It was a grand yacht. Dickson had his own boat, *The Jubilou*, so he was able to help

Lance sail. However, the rest of us land lubbers were hung-over and ready to puke.

Dylan sat atop the roof of the cabin and Butchie sat next to him, whispering in his ear and generally falling all over him. The next thing I knew she was lying on the deck of the yacht, sucking Dylan's big toe. I was disgusted. Poor Bob, having to put up with this. He pretended it wasn't happening; he seemed unfazed. I guess he was disgusted too, because shortly after, he got up, and had to puke over the side of the boat with Victor holding his arm.

The Ciro's stint was only a week, but it seemed longer. So much was packed into that time. Celebrities great and small filled the old place. I remember Sal Mineo sitting alone at the grand bar. I had loved *Rebel Without A Cause* as a teenager. Seeing Sal in the club had an odd, familiar feeling, because he was alone and seemed at loose ends, just like the character in the movie he played.

Dickson had invited many of his Hollywood pals including Carole Eastman, Ann Marshall, Herbert Marshall's daughter, Peter Fonda and Dennis Hopper. After one show, we – the Byrds and their mates – were invited to a mansion in Griffith Park where John Phillip Law resided. It was an enormous castle. The fireplace was massive in the medieval sense, all it needed was a roasting pig on a spit and King Henry VIII with his hounds sitting at his feet. Our voices echoed as we ran up the turret to the crow's nest.

There was plenty of good pot that night that only David could acquire. The castle may have belonged to Boris Karloff in the old days. John Phillip Law was a handsome presence. I knew he was an actor, but I'd never seen him perform. He would later star in *Barbarella*.

As the week progressed, the strange-looking crowd that milled outside Ciro's, combined with word of mouth, brought in the curious. A *Los Angeles Times* article had appeared that gave a positive review of the Byrds' live show. PR man Derek Taylor had started showing results.

Thus began the first stirrings of the Sunset Strip Craze. The Strip had fallen out of fashion for movie people, but the restaurants, bars and clubs flourished. In the mid-1960s this burgeoning counterculture injected a new vibrancy into the area – eventually leading up to the Sunset Strip curfew riots a year later, involving police and crowds of teenagers.

Sonny and Cher arrived one night and Michael couldn't contain himself. "Cher is here. Man she is incredible, beautiful... those long legs." I spotted Cher sitting with Sonny at a table near the dance floor. I noticed a haunting, vacant look on her face. She had plenty of eye makeup on. I never wore makeup in those days, and I never really have since. Sonny seemed intense, with a very serious expression, scoping the crowd. Little did Michael realize they were enjoying the show and taking notes. A few months later, Sonny and Cher released 'All I Really Want to Do,' with Jim's arrangement. Dylan's songs were not Byrd property, and the music business was as cutthroat as the movie business. "They stole our song," Michael later bemoaned. Jim was equally dismayed.

Things moved quickly. Tickner and Dickson got an advance from Columbia and moved into new offices in the 9000 Sunset Boulevard Building. Billy James, a CBS A&R/Publicist from New York came on board along with Derek Taylor. There were local television dates booked on shows similar to *American Bandstand*. The Byrds' appearance was scruffy in the early days. Dickson had previously purchased uniform black suits that made Crosby look like Little Lord Fauntleroy. The band collectively objected to the cookie-cutter outfits, and went for the individual style; after all, the Stones did it. It also helped that the black suits were stolen one night. Maybe it was the Ciro's ghost.

Jim and I decided to live together. I gave up the place in Venice and Maude went on her way with Taj. Jim moved out of the Padre Hotel and found a small, furnished apartment that was owned by the magician Criswell. It was in a row of green stucco apartments, one block south of Sunset, just off Vine. They were located behind the old Moulin Rouge Theater, which was equipped as a television studio to broadcast the 1950s show, *Queen for a Day*. Oddly, this would be the venue for the *Big TNT Show* in which the Byrds appeared later in the year.

Jim and I walked up the narrow walkway to his new place to pay the first month's rent. A very distinguished silver-haired gent met us at the door. This was Criswell. There was the business exchange and talk about the band. Criswell gathered himself up and formally stated,

"I firmly believe you will be a success." Without much flair, he spun around on well heeled shoes and walked out, the screen door slamming behind him. We looked at each other wide eyed and I wanted to burst out laughing, but Jim appeared mesmerized. I didn't want to break his reverie, so I kept quiet. I looked into his eyes as I often did. They were deep blue glazed over with the image of being a star. Sometimes he dared me to look in his eyes and not blink. "Whoever blinks first is not telling the truth," he demanded. My eyes would burn, then water. Blink! "Hah, I knew it!" he laughed.

Many strange things happened between us in this apartment. Perhaps Criswell had left behind some strange vibes and restless spirits. The first incident occurred after one of the rehearsals at Vito's. An old friend of Jim's had arrived from San Francisco. She had access to all kinds of drugs, which was unusual at the time. Was she a dealer? I don't know and don't care to know. That evening she gave Jim some hallucinatory gem that truly freaked him out.

I had arrived from work and got ready for bed. I wasn't worried at first; I knew Jim might be in late. Then I heard his footsteps coming up the concrete walk. He had a distinctive way of walking. It was step, step, then the third step dragged and clicked a little. He knocked on the door.

"Dolores?" His voice trembled. I jumped out of bed and opened the door.

He rushed in. "I have to get out of these clothes," he said as he pulled at his shirt and flung his pants off. He ran in the bathroom and turned on the shower. I could sense he wasn't himself.

"What's the matter?" I asked. I was frightened. I stood in my nightgown outside the bathroom door.

"I took something Ginger gave me. I don't know what it was."

"Who's Ginger?" I asked.

"Forget that... she's an old friend."

"Some friend," I snickered, not realizing the gravity of the situation. He came out of the bathroom drying his hair, shaking all over.

"I'm so cold," he shivered. I grabbed some matches and lit the small wall heater. It had ceramic tiles that glowed red-hot with blue flame as the temperature increased. My hand shook nervously. "Get close to the heater," I instructed. I pulled the blanket off the bed and covered him as he bent down stretching his hands out to draw the heat toward him. We crouched together and then sat next to each other on the carpet looking into the flame.

"Are you feeling better?" I asked.

"Dolores... you're not a black widow? Are you?"

"Jim... of course not. How can you say such a thing? I'm a girl, a person."

"I was married to a black widow once." This was a revelation. "We had our marriage annulled. She was cruel. She read the Marquis de Sade in bed, and once she burned me with her cigarette. I found her in bed with Bobby Darin, when I worked for him. She just laughed and said, 'Come join us.'"

I put my arm around him and kissed the side of his forehead. Stunned at his confession, I only wanted to assure him of my love. "Look, look!" he exclaimed. "Did you see that? It was the devil jumping out of that flame! He's trying to draw me in..."

"I don't see that, Jimmy." I looked at the ceramic tiles, flames bouncing about. "It's just the gas flame. See? I'll lower it." I adjusted it and looked at him reassuringly.

"Let's pray," he said, looking earnestly into my eyes. "Repeat after me... 'I trust, with the help of God, everything will work out alright.'" I repeated the prayer and he nodded his head after I spoke each word. Together we prayed, "I trust, with the help of God, everything will work out alright." There was the blue glow of dawn outside. We had made it. No devils lurking in the daytime, as far as I knew, anyway.

"Let's go to sleep now," I said. "It will be better when we wake up." He held me tightly. Usually, it was me holding him.

Money began trickling into Jim's empty pockets. The recording of the full-length album began in earnest, and the guys were showing up at CBS studio eager to start, sans studio musicians. They were on their own, ready to prove they had talent. David was arm in arm with a go-go dancer he had met at one of the television shows. She was short and blonde and, best of all, she drove a Porsche. He now had a chauffeur.

Jim decided to rent a car instead of relying on my Renault. The rental was a cherry red car that he had for over a month. It ended up costing more than if he'd bought it. The worst thing was that someone ran a red light when I was driving to the studio and crashed into the passenger's side. I came into the studio sheepishly to break the bad news, and instead of being upset, they all laughed. David called me 'Crash' for several weeks after.

Eddie and Dickson didn't find it humorous. "McGuinn, you could have bought a little Carrera for that amount of money," Dickson chided.

My Jim looked at me and shook his head. "Women are expensive," he muttered. "They need the dress, the hat, the gloves, the shoes, and the other paraphernalia, not to mention jewelry. That's what I like about Dolores: a calico dress and sandals, Levi's, T-shirt and boots. She doesn't need all that other stuff."

In fact, I did need it. One day I was climbing up the stairs with Vito's wife behind me, when Szou said, "Really, Jim. You should buy Dolores some new underwear... something sexy." We were both embarrassed. I was wearing a pair of nylon bloomers I had bought in Boston to fend off the cold. My brother Marcus skillfully made my calico dresses with his sewing machine, and that kept me clothed. Up to this point, Jim had never bought me anything.

After one performance at Ciro's, we packed into a few booths at a restaurant on Sunset. The group included Dickson, Carole Eastman and a dark-haired woman who later appeared in *Five Easy Pieces*, as one of the hitchhikers. Also, there were other attractive women who I feared were after Jim. One of them said, "Jim, you sure have a fine-looking girlfriend in Dolores."

"Yeah," said another, "She's really beautiful." I was surprised at all the attention, and stammered a weak "Thank you."

When we got to the apartment, Jim was furious. I couldn't understand why he was so mad at me. "Oh. Don't you know? They were hitting on you. They were dykes hitting on you!" Frankly, I was shocked. I guess I was pretty naïve in those days. I didn't think 'dykes' could be such nice-looking women. That night in bed, Jim and I slept back to back, him still fuming and me wondering why I took the hit for his indignation.

The Byrds returned to Ciro's for two weeks in June. The place swelled with people of all sorts. By then 'Mr. Tambourine Man' was a huge hit and the Byrds were the latest 'in' thing. Michelle, one of the dancers in Vito's troupe, appeared one day wearing funny looking granny glasses. Jim liked them and purchased them at DeVoss, a men's store on the Sunset Strip. He bought several colors and found them ideal to hide behind when he was on stage. He wore contacts and had terrible vision.

I had been neglecting my friend Karen. She had been accepted into Julliard and had plans to go to New York City in the fall. Emmy had a grandmother living in Harlem. Nancy Kubo had moved to Boston and was living with Jackie Washington, a young black folk balladeer.

The Byrds were getting ready to go on a bus tour in the Midwest, then traveling on to New York and to London for yet another tour. The girls were after me to help them drive across in Karen's yellow VW Bug. I thought about it and discussed it with Jim. He thought it was a good idea that I go. We could meet in Youngstown, Ohio and I could join the crew on the bus.

The weekend before we left, Jim suggested that Karen and I should try acid. We were dumb enough to do this. Jim had a rehearsal and they were to tape a TV appearance the next day. That evening, Karen and I split the tab of Owsley and waited.

Suddenly the room seemed too small to contain us. We decided to drive to the beach in my car. As we went out the door, the plants along the concrete walk were quite alive and talking to us. We marveled at their ability to communicate. I could see the pollen on the flowers... everything had a space between it, as if I could see on the molecular level.

Off we went in the Renault. We managed to get to Santa Monica Boulevard, driving west to the Pacific Ocean. We stopped at a gas station and the attendant – there were gas attendants in those days – was dressed in a khaki uniform. His face melted before my eyes, and Karen had to pay the bill as I cringed in horror.

We parked and walked on the beach all night long. The blue-green waves as iridescent giants roared to the sand lapping at our feet. We walked and walked for hours not needing to speak. Soon, dawn was breaking and a tide pool held a crab in it. We looked down at the creature and it smiled, all knowing. Karen stared at me and the three of us shared the mystery of life. I knew that there was a fragility to everything. Our LSD trip was ending, and our trip across the US was about to begin.

We arrived at Jim's apartment, raw and generally wrecked. What had just happened? For one, we were starving. Jim was getting ready to leave for his TV show taping. He looked all showered and dressed to the max. I began to look in the fridge.

"Why don't you order something?" Jim suggested.

"That's a good idea," my voice said, coming out of someone I did not recognize.

"How about chicken?" said Karen.

"That's right," said Jim, "Super-Ego uptight, try Chicken Delight." Chicken Delight was the local equivalent of Kentucky Fried Chicken, which did home delivery. "Very funny, Mr. McGuinn," I muttered. I couldn't find the humor until later. Karen and I laughed and laughed. Jim did have a wry sense of humor. He walked out the door with his step, step, click.

After recovering a few days later, we left Los Angeles from Jim's apartment. Karen's yellow VW was packed with suitcases, snack food, a road atlas and, under the passenger seat, a black air gun that Jim had given us for protection. It was a metal dart gun that looked like a real pistol. We wrapped it in a red bandana and hoped that we would not have to use it. We departed in the afternoon. The Byrds were performing at Henry Fonda's birthday party that evening. I was sorry to miss this, but I had an adventure of my own to embark upon.

The trip went forward as we drove on the interstate freeway without any event, until we reached Texas. We had a flat tire on the highway and pulled over to change the tire. Emmy had fallen asleep curled like a kitten in the back seat and it was impossible to wake her up. Karen and I decided to change it without her help. It was the front tire on the driver's side. We pulled out the spare and the jack, and went to work. Not one passing car stopped to help us. There were a lot of gawkers and some hecklers, all male. It was the Sixties in Texas, which was still the 1950s. A black woman and a Mexican gal, who would ever think to help them? We managed to get through the ordeal with Emmy waking after we had finished.

A few times we got lost after taking wrong turns. This happened at night and it was very scary, driving with no light, on deserted, windy, tree-lined back roads. We decided to stop at a motel and spend the night outside of Dayton, Ohio. Karen showered first. Emmy and I were chatting away, glad to have a place to rest for the night. We heard a thud in the bathroom, but didn't think anything of it. After a long while, Karen emerged from the bathroom.

"I just fainted in the shower," she said.

She looked dazed and disoriented. We jumped up and helped her sit on the bed. "I'm sure you're just hungry," I said.

"No bumps or bruises?" Emmy asked, looking at Karen's head and back. This was to be the first indication of Karen's health. We later discovered she had sickle cell anemia. Her mother was white and it had never occurred to her that Karen would inherit her father's gene for a syndrome that was in people of African descent.

In Dayton, we stopped for gasoline. A group of white high school teenage boys pulled up next to us. They instantly became verbally abusive. They were cursing and spitting out racial slurs I had never heard young men say. I pulled the gun, still wrapped, from under the seat and placed it on my lap. I thought seeing the gun might scare them. Karen paid the attendant, who also looked frightened. Emmy crouched in the back seat. We took off, praying the mean boys wouldn't follow. We were shocked and shaken: this wasn't Texas and it wasn't the South. How could this be happening in Ohio? The Byrds were supposed to play that evening... what kind of reception would they have?

We drove a few miles and looked at the Byrds' itinerary, trying to find Youngstown, Ohio, where the gig was located. It was at a venue called the Idora Park Ballroom. The bus was parked near a side entrance and we went in. We were stopped by a security cop, until Bryan MacLean intervened. He took us to the dressing room, which was someone's office.

Jim was sitting at a large desk. A big smile came over his face and he got up and gave me a big hug. "Boy, is it good to see you!" he whispered in my ear.

"Me too, you." I laid my head against his chest. "It has been a scary trip. This morning we ran into a few teenagers that were saying terrible things."

"Is that so?" Jim pulled us apart. He looked into my face. "I can't tell you what we've been through. The audiences have been heckling us. When Carl's people get on the dance floor, it's a nightmare. It was probably not a good idea to bring Carl and the girls, they are too extreme for this part of the country."

The concert began with the audience standing menacingly around the dance floor. Jim's twelve-string rang out the familiar opening notes of 'Mr. Tambourine Man' and the dancers twirled onto the dance floor... me included. The audience stood in stoic silence, watching us as if we had dropped off some strange planet. We didn't care. The music elevated us to that very planet, and we were oblivious to everything around us. The sheer joy of this music, so pure and magical, filled the hall with its glorious sound. I was so happy to be back with the artists who created it.

Karen and Emmy left for New York the next morning. I had planned to meet the girls there after the bus tour. The group had a few more dates to complete, including Chicago and Louisville, before leaving from New York City to England. This was to be the Byrds' launch to international exposure. First, the bus tour had to wind down.

This was my taste of life on the road in a tour bus. It was miserable. The bus had a narrow aisle, hard, upholstered seats, a faint mildew smell and a restroom in the middle. How the musicians and entourage had endured this trip thus far, the drudgery of the grinding, shifting gears and the constant hum of the engine, was hard to imagine. There was also a faint waft of marijuana in the back. The bus driver was John Barrick, a friend of Jim Dickson's. He was a good-natured man with brown hair and glasses, always fresh in his white, collared shirt and khaki pants.

I sat in the back, reunited with Jim, who seemed very accustomed to this form of travel. He was playing an acoustic guitar with Chris and David nearby. Gene and Michael were sitting with young women, chatting to pass the time. Jim was playing a folk song, and I asked him to play the Pete Seeger song 'Turn! Turn! Turn!' He of course admired the song, because he was a big Pete Seeger fan. He had also helped Judy Collins in the studio with a version of it. Jim knew the chords well and promptly strummed and hummed the tune as he emulated Seeger's voice.

The other Byrds smiled at the mimicry and David chimed in readily with his beautiful harmony. It was magical, a true sing-along, as other bus passengers nearby enjoyed what they heard. Chris said, "We should record this song." Jim smiled and said, "We should." David concurred. It didn't matter what the next song that day was, because Pete Seeger's song had made an impression. Jim had set about arranging it for the band, as he did with most other numbers.

The Chicago performance was eventful because it was Jim's hometown and his parents, Dorothy and James, and kid brother Brian, were attending. I was nervous to meet them.

Byrd fans in Chicago, 1965

Both his parents were very sweet and gracious. Dorothy was so proud of Jimmy, and his handsome father beamed with an Irish grin. "He left home after high school to join the Limeliters," she exclaimed, "and he never came back. Now he's famous on his own!" Dorothy was a petite blonde with a bubbly personality. James was a handsome, distinguished-looking man. He stood very tall and had a stern yet warm aura. They were familiar with fame and success, having written a best-selling book about bringing up Jimmy, their son, titled *Parents Can't Win*. They were to become a big part of my life.

Derek Taylor flew in from LA to rendezvous on the last few dates of the US tour. After the Byrds' Chicago performance, Jim's parents came backstage. Jim was soaking from the summer heat, wearing his usual coat and tie. I brought him a towel, and Dorothy remembered that nurturing gesture for many years to come. Later we went back to the motel and Jim cleaned up – he was eager to take Derek and me on the town, to show us his old haunts.

First we drove past the Biograph Theater, where Jim told us Dillinger was gunned down in the 1930s. We made our way to Old Towne, where Jim had studied folk music, and where the Gate of Horn stood. We went to an old, famous jazz club, the Black Hawk, where Jim had seen a lot of music as a teenager. We had beer at every stop. By the time the bars shut down at four in the morning, we were very merry, and wanted to keep the party going. We were energized.

Jim thought nothing of calling on his parents at four-thirty in the morning, to sit in his family kitchen on Division Street to have another beer. We rang the doorbell, and Dorothy came out in her robe, surprised to see us. She joyfully let us in, and we all convened in the kitchen. She brought out some bottles of beer and we sat around the table, Derek, Jim, Dorothy and I, and described to Dorothy the events of the night. Just some hours before, Jim had been on stage. It was a heady night, jammed full of impressions and happy feelings. I always loved that Dorothy could enjoy a spontaneous beer for breakfast; that was how youthful she was.

In the car on the ride to the motel, Derek told Jim, "You and Dolores should get married." I was pleasantly surprised to hear this. Jim had no idea why Derek would say that at that hour. Then he added, "You seem to be meant for each other." The rest of the ride was quiet.

The remaining time on the bus tour was grueling. The last stop was Louisville, Kentucky with a small dingy motel room, greasy food, and plenty of complaints from the group. "Just wait till I get hold of Eddie Tickner," Michael muttered. "This is *da pits.*" Everyone agreed. Jim didn't complain; he was the most experienced traveler. From Las Vegas with Bobby Darin to South America with the Limeliters, he had seen the best and the worst. He shared an interesting observation: "Some hotel walls in Latin America never meet, there was always a space between them where the wind would whistle in the room." I tried to imagine how that sounded. The rooms were so stuffy in the July heat it might have been a welcome breeze.

We made it to New York City and the dance troupe, along with Bryan and Carl, were sent back to LA, much to their disappointment. The Byrds stayed at the Gramercy Park Hotel. It was quite a difference from the Midwest motels we'd stayed in on the road. It was to become a future favorite place to hole up when Jim and I visited New York. While we were there, the Byrds did a lot of publicity – Murray the K, a local DJ, had Jim and David on the show. A few photo shoots took place, near the Columbia Records building in Midtown. Guests came to visit Jim at our hotel room including Bobby Neuwirth, a friend of Bob Dylan's who really hit it off with Jim.

Bobby became Jim's New York buddy. They played guitars together all the time, exploring old folk songs. It was wonderful to see their budding friendship, and Bobby was always very warm and inclusive toward me. One night, Bobby said to Jim, "You are the Stephen Foster of our generation, man! You should play, 'Oh Susannah' in tribute to him!" Jim took this advice to heart, and the Byrds worked the song into their repertoire. Michael Clarke despised the song (just listen to his performance on the *Turn! Turn! Turn!* album). "This is a dumb song!" Michael exclaimed. He always wanted to play the blues, like the Rolling Stones.

Derek Taylor was to shepherd the boys to London, first stop on their British tour. I was not invited. Jim was eager to travel to England, and Michael couldn't wait to visit Carnaby Street to peruse the latest fashions. I knew they were going to have a lot of fun, just the boys – no chicks allowed, as David had said. It had been predetermined that they would meet the Beatles, since Derek was their former publicist. There was a sense of wonder about the outcome of this tour, and excitement about meeting their heroes, who had become their peers in a very short time. Jim and I said our goodbyes, hugging haplessly as I gradually got into a cab that delivered me to the steps of a Harlem brownstone, where Emmy's family lived. Jim was off to the newly named John F. Kennedy airport for his international flight. I was going to miss him.

Emmy's brownstone home was very large. The entry was an anteroom where you left your raincoats and galoshes. Going into the house, you turned right to the dining area and kitchen, left to the parlor, and straight upstairs to the bedrooms. We only spent one night there, planning our escape to Boston in the morning. Emmy's grandmother made fried chicken and sweet potato turnovers for the trip. It was delightful.

We got up early the next day, and drove up the Massachusetts Turnpike. When we arrived in Boston, Karen parked her car at a gas station and we called Nancy Kubo. We were worried because Nancy sounded very hesitant about our visit. She gave us Jackie's address and the house, it turned out, was in Roxbury, the black neighborhood in Boston.

Jackie was out of town, and Nancy was afraid he would not want three extra women in his house. We could stay, but it was not certain what would happen after Jackie returned. Emmy was not happy with the reception. She returned to New York on the bus straight away, and had decided to make it back to LA as soon as she could. Karen and I stayed with Nancy, and went out job hunting the next day. Karen got a job at Club 47 waitressing, and I got a job at a club in downtown Boston as a go-go dancer. This was funny: Karen and I, it appeared, had switched roles.

The outfit I wore was a striped T-shirt and bellbottom pants, nothing too outrageous for conservative Boston. The Beatles single 'Help!' had been released, and it reflected my pitiful state as I danced mechanically on the small wooden platform. 'Satisfaction' by the Rolling Stones was another popular number.

This was a painful time... I missed Jim, but he was thousands of miles away. Karen and I were struggling financially and crashing at Jackie's was not what we had anticipated. Jackie was underwhelmed by the idea of us staying there, and made it clear that we should move out as soon as we could. The dancing job turned into a fiasco. This young Italian hoodlum kept coming to the club. After two weeks of hanging out in front where I danced, he decided he wanted to take me to meet his mother, because he intended to marry me! His cruelty and oppressiveness became evident when I took a break and sat at the bar. He approached, uninvited, and sat next to me, and as the conversation escalated, he said with a flat delivery, "You're going to marry me, or *I'm gonna break your knees*. Then, you'll never dance *again*." I was petrified. My only recourse was to get out of Dodge.

I had only intended to travel east with my friends and meet Jim on the road. Unfortunately, I'd become mired in Boston, struggling to get by. I thought I'd have made enough money to get back to LA easily, but this was not case.

The Byrds were back from their British tour, and had returned to LA. I missed Jim terribly. We had not been in touch during the tour. We did have one brief conversation when he had returned to California. I said, "I really want to come back to LA. Boston is not working out." There was a long pause on the other end of the phone line. "Uh, okay," Jim hesitantly muttered. "I'll talk to Eddie about getting you back here." Karen did not want me to leave her, but I was so glad to get on the Greyhound bus to New York.

I called Eddie Tickner and told him I was in New York, and asked if Jim and he had spoken. Eddie said yes, he knew I wanted to return to LA. He gave me Barry Feinstein's number, and said he'd have him pick me up at the Port Authority Bus Station – a very scary place in those days. Barry was a photographer and had been on the Midwest tour taking photographs of the Byrds. He took the fish-eye photo on the first Byrds album. That photo was taken at a little park west of the Troubadour. I called Barry and he gave me the address of his Midtown apartment and told me to get a cab.

He met me at the front entrance and he gave me a big bear hug before he paid the cabbie. Barry said Eddie had arranged to fly me back to LA and all we had to do was kill time until the plane left LaGuardia airport that evening. We went to a local Jewish deli; there is nothing like matzo ball soup and half a pastrami sandwich to make one feel human again. I was relieved to be returning to the West Coast and very thankful to Barry and Eddie for making it happen.

Once in Los Angeles, Bryan MacLean picked me up at LAX, and he dropped me off at Jim's apartment in Hollywood. I knocked on the door and Jim answered. He hugged me briefly. The Temptations were performing on the Strip that night, and Jim was preparing to leave. I showered quickly and off we went. He seemed a little timid, as if he had a guilty conscience, but I just assumed it was the month's separation. Later I learned that he had been with a girl Derek had pulled from the audience at one of the concerts in London, and had taken her to the hotel that night. "She was blonde and blue-eyed and very young," he confessed.

I was hurt. He had stated on more than one occasion that he'd always dreamed of being with a blonde, blue-eyed woman. Much later, he and David wrote a song about the girl, 'I See You.' Jim was very sensitive, and could see how much I missed and loved him. I think he felt protective and wanted to help me recover from the time apart. I realized I had many guardian angels. I thought at the time that Jim was one of them.

Perhaps Subud's influence made him want to be honest and upfront, with a devotion that was unusual, considering the amount of women attempting to seduce every member of the group. In addition, Jim's aloof, intellectual presence may have been intimidating to the teen fan base of the Byrds. Subud's teachings encouraged monogamy, because promiscuity depleted and eroded one's essence. I attribute Jim's fidelity over the course of our relationship to this Subud ideal. The other Byrds fell into the seduction of the hedonistic lifestyle, early on.

The most exciting event took place shortly after the Byrds returned from Europe. The Beatles were booked at the Hollywood Bowl. Everyone in town was talking about their arrival. On talk shows, the A-list actors described the glimpse of the quartet they caught at a restaurant or airport, and their attempts to get tickets for their kids to the performance. We had a direct link: Derek Taylor. The Byrds had met the Beatles in England and were looking forward to seeing them on our own turf in the USA.

They were staying at a home of one of the Gabor sisters, tucked up in Beverly Glen. Jim went to see the Beatles early in the day. This might have been when he and David took LSD with John and George. When Jim returned home, we got ready to drive to the Bowl. The crowds were impossible: teenagers spotted Jim and shouted, "There's McGuinn!" They didn't chase him, however, because they were there for the Beatles. The concert was loud and raucous. The roar of thousands of screaming fans filled the Hollywood Hills and did not cease for the entire show. The audience loved them and except for the fact that the band could not hear themselves, the energy was reciprocal.

The Beatles planned to have a few people over after the concert. The time designated for us to leave the show was when the band began playing 'A Hard Day's Night.' That was not their last number, but it gave us ample time so that we could avoid the exit traffic and make it to their house. We hurried to a rental car, and just as we heard the final notes of the song, we were pulling out of the Hollywood

Bowl. The roar of the audience could be heard from Highland Avenue below.

When we arrived at the Gabors' home, the house was swarming with cars, teenagers on foot, and police patrol cars with their lights on at the front gate. There was one of the band's road crew with a list, checking the names of those allowed to enter. Derek happened to drive up at the same time and we had no trouble getting in. The house was sprawling and spacious, modern late-1950s style. It wrapped itself in a horseshoe around a large swimming pool that jutted against a brick wall set next to a hill on the other side. Jim and I sat on a couch in the well-appointed living room facing the pool. Crosby, Gene and Michael all hung out, milling around nervously. There was an air of anticipation.

Without fanfare, the Beatles walked in, having changed and looking excited, yet slightly exhausted. Each of them exuded confidence and the familiar qualities that made them so special. They asked about the sound and complained about the monitors. Each one went his own way with another Byrd or someone else. Jim and I were invited to George's room.

Yes, there I was with Jim McGuinn and George Harrison. Jim and I sat across from George at a small table in his room. Jim started rolling a joint, a skill at which he was very adept. They began talking about religion. Jim explained Subud's philosophy and George, in that soft, gentle, mellow voice, spoke of the metaphysical and our transient nature in the universe. George also expressed his enthusiasm about David sharing a tape of Ravi Shankar's music.

They talked late into the night and brought out acoustic guitars, and began playing riffs back and forth. I left the room in search of a restroom. Ambling around, I ran into sweet-looking Paul, hand in hand with a petite blonde in a red velvet dress, coming out of a bedroom, her teased hair slightly lopsided. I later learned there were high-paid call girls invited to the house. The bathroom had 360-degree mirrors, white wall-to-wall carpeting and a large recessed bathtub.

At about two in the morning, I went outside to the patio with the well-lit swimming pool. John and Ringo were sitting on chaise lounges chatting. I couldn't believe it, but there was Emmy, a piece of paper in hand, interrupting them, asking for their autographs. "It's for these poor teenage kids behind the fence. They are begging me for your autographs."

They snickered. "Well we're 'begging' you to leave us alone," John mimicked.

"Here give me that!" Ringo grabbed the pencil and paper from Emmy's hand and signed it.

"Thank you. Thank you." Emmy bowed and bumped into me as she turned around.

I held her by the elbow and whispered, "Emmy how did you get here?"

"Oh, I came with Christopher." We walked a little way. "You shouldn't be asking these guys for their autograph," I scolded.

"I know, but I just had to... you ought to see these kids, just dying to see their heroes."

"Emmy, they are trying to get away from all that attention and just be normal."

"No big deal." She shrugged me off and went to find the 'poor teenage kids.'

I went back to the bedroom where David had joined Jim and George. This is one night I didn't fall asleep. I stayed up knowing this was something I wanted imprinted forever. At around three-thirty in the morning, the visitors were thinning out, so Jim and I said goodbye and drove home.

We were invited for a swim the following afternoon. When we arrived, the same traffic jam existed. We got through the gate and went toward the kitchen. John was at the door wearing white trunks, white espadrilles and a blue-striped shirt with the cuffs rolled up. He held a mug of hot water and dipped in a tea bag he gripped by the paper tab, up and down, and in and out of the mug.

"Would you look at this? This is what they call a cup of tea in America. Come in Jim. Come sit by the pool."

We followed him outside. Ringo seemed to be in the same spot I had left him, except he was gathering up the sun. Paul sat next to him, relaxed, dressed in a T-shirt and trunks. "Jim McGuinn and partner." Paul declared. "McGuinn... that's Irish, correct?"

"How Irish can you get?" John remarked. Jim mumbled something and we sat down uncomfortably.

"Nothing wrong with Irish," said Ringo in his Liverpudlian accent, and everyone laughed.

The afternoon passed with them playing music by the pool in the bright California sun. Derek came out and interrupted the session. He reminded the Beatles they had to get ready. Elvis Presley was sending his limo to pick them up to meet them. The Byrds were not invited to meet Elvis, and I don't think they ever were. We left saying goodbye to George. He was very gracious and wanted Jim to visit him next time he was in London.

We went to visit David at his apartment the following day. He came to the door shirtless wearing a pair of Levi cutoffs. "Come on in," he said as he swallowed a mouthful of cooked lima beans. He placed the white bowl half-filled with buttered lima beans on the nearest table and dropped the tablespoon into the bowl. "Have I got something to tell you!" he exclaimed. "This cat and I took one of the chicks at the Beatles' place home yesterday. She lives in Holmby Hills and she invited us in. It was a huge pad. She took us to her bedroom and over her round bed was a mirror, man. A great big mirror on the ceiling, so you can see what you're doing. She invited me back. I didn't ask her if she was going to charge me, or her price."

We all laughed. "Wow!" Jim exclaimed. "I knew some of those chicks were call-girls, probably sent by some wise guy in the record company. By the way, David... do you have any pot?" Marijuana was hard to come by in those days and Jim usually relied on the joints that friends gave him. Jim never bought more than a lid.

The Byrds were set to play the Hollywood Palladium, a welcome home event. Unlike Ciro's, the stage was elevated and the dance area was a beautifully polished hardwood floor. There were tables and chairs set up on carpeted levels. The Byrds' show was scheduled for just after the Beatles left, and just before Dylan played the Hollywood Bowl, around the end of August 1965. The Byrds event sold out. The group wore new outfits they'd purchased in London's Carnaby Street. They were now making a fashion statement. The Byrds put on a good show, and the audience enthusiastically welcomed them back.

When Dylan arrived in Los Angeles for his engagement at the Bowl, he stayed at a hotel on the Sunset Strip. We were invited to visit and when we came in he said, "Well look who's here, Mr. and Mrs. McGuinn." We laughed and felt welcomed by the King. He sat in a chair and commanded everyone's attention. It's not that he wanted it, he just had that magnetic quality that drew all eyes toward him. He smoked non-stop and always with the crossed leg that shook constantly. Benny Shapiro was Dylan's agent who worked at William Morris and he had a home in the hills just above Ciro's. He gave a huge party for Dylan a few nights later. Vito's gang was there of course. It seemed every room had a different thing going on: guys with guitars playing music with avid listeners singing along; couples making out; people going in and out of a 'special' getting-high room; lots of talking and eating in the kitchen; and a gathering of elders in the living room, going over business.

Jim was playing acoustic guitar and I wandered around. Michelle, from Vito's troupe, came up to me and shouted, "Dolores, Marlon Brando is here! Come and see! I'm going to grab him." She took off and I tried to follow. I went around the corner and there he was, sort of weaving. Marlon Brando and I met face to face. I was taken aback by his beauty. He wore a white shirt with a loosened necktie and a tan suit. The jacket hung over his arm. His hair was short; he resembled a youthful Julius Caesar. He looked fit and not overweight. He had been drinking. Michelle appeared, grabbed his hand and started pulling him into the living room.

"Wait," he said, pointing at me, "*That's* the girl of my dreams!" With that, he was gone. I was startled by his remark. There I was and Marlon Brando, one of my heroes, had just said that I was the girl of his dreams! I quickly chased after them. Next thing I knew, they were sitting on the sofa. Michelle was jabbering away hanging onto his arm and he, looking quite trapped, bored and overwhelmed, drink in hand, was drunk as a skunk. I went back to find Jim—he was still playing with a small audience gathered around him. I sat as close as I could get to him and promptly fell asleep, dreaming of being Marlon Brando's girl, no doubt. Jim woke me up to go home.

During this time, recording continued at Columbia. Jim and I settled into the Vine Street apartment and the rest of the Byrds were on the Strip hanging out and meeting all sorts of people. David had a motorcycle he bought from Peter Fonda and he talked about meeting Steve McQueen and Wally Cox. He also met folks with high quality pot. Chris was still having Vito's teenyboppers straighten his hair, and Michael had a different girl every night. Gene, the most serious of the group, had women falling for him.

There were more local television appearances and club dates. Peter Fonda sometimes accompanied the band and me at the studios. He was attractive like his father, slightly older than Jim was. They had mutual friends from the East Coast. Peter and Jim became buddies, appearing in each other's home movies.

The Trip was a venue that Elmer Valentine had recently opened near the Playboy club on Sunset Strip. He also owned the Whisky a Go Go further west on the Strip. He had booked the Byrds to play at the start of October. Jim and I walked toward the Trip after parking a new red Porsche he had bought from Alan Pariser, one of Dickson's friends. We saw David running toward us. Jim and I looked at each other and knew something was up.

"Dolores. Dolores, you know we all really love you. You are a special person, and you mean a lot to all of us," David gushed. "Gosh David," I said not believing my ears. "Thank you." What did I do to deserve all this flattery? I was thinking David was doing a major turnaround.

We walked into the club and Chris rushed up and gave me a big hug. This was too much. It wasn't my birthday and all this attention overwhelmed me. We walked into the dressing room and there it was, painted on the wall in big black letters: "The Byrds are cool, but Dolores is a Mexican Bitch!" I was stunned. Who could have written such a mean, cruel slur? I felt the tears burning my eyes and my knees weaken. Jim held me by my waist and whispered, "I love you. Do you want to go outside?"

Everyone in the room - the Byrds, Jim Dickson and Eddie Tickner - gathered around us, and for that moment, they all came together as one. They separated as quickly as they had united. Jim and I left the room and Elmer Valentine stopped us and said, "I'll take care of that as soon as possible. I don't know how that happened."

The show went on. The audience packed the club. I sat next to Eddie and his wife Rita. I scrutinized the faces in the young crowd. Who hated me enough to splatter it on the wall for everyone to see? I felt like I had been kicked in the gut. Something strengthened and renewed me... it was the first time that Jim had said he loved me. The hurt lingered; I had never seen myself as different. Jim had never referred to my ethnic origin. He always treated me with respect and listened to my opinions. He took me everywhere, and did not exclude me. He laughed when I once tangled with Dylan at Ollie Hammond's and said I was a suffragette. The women's lib movement had not yet evolved, and the civil rights era was just beginning to make its mark.

We began looking for another place to rent. The onslaught of female teenyboppers had discovered the residences of the entire group. Jim loved Laurel Canyon. The charming cottages were tucked away in the winding hills. There was a village grocery and a restaurant underneath. It served Hungarian goulash with noodles that melted in your mouth. The area had a European flavor different from the city of Los Angeles. The houses rented at a premium and were hard to find.

We were able to rent a small wood frame ranch-style home off Woodrow Wilson Drive. The place was very tiny and cozy. You walked into the living room, to the right was the bedroom and to the left was the kitchen and bathroom. There was a tan carpet in the living room and bedroom. The slatted windows had a lever to open or close them. The house belonged to a character actor who had turned realtor and owned other properties in the Canyon.

One night as we lay in bed together, we heard a couple arguing, neighbors who lived above us on the hill. The sound carried far from their cantilever house. Jim and I lay in the dark quietly as this unhappy couple discussed purchases and money matters in raised, angry voices. I realized then that Jim and I had never once had an argument, or raised our voices to each other. This remained the case throughout all of the good years of our relationship.

We also enjoyed concentrated chess games when we lived at this house. Sometimes they continued very late into the night, and I'd get so sleepy that I wanted the game to end. When this happened, I intentionally made a move that would enable Jim to complete the game and win. He thought he was pretty clever, but I just wanted to get to bed.

The *Big TNT Show* was set for November 1965, produced by Phil Spector, a much-admired boy-wonder in the recording field. Gathered together were the musical hit-makers of the time: Ray Charles, Ike and Tina Turner, Donovan, Joan Baez, Petula Clark, Bo Diddley, the Ronettes and the Byrds. It was to take place at the

Moulin Rouge Theater, near our old apartment on Sunset and Vine. The event was filmed and took most of the day. The audience was enthusiastic and there were as many boys as girls in attendance. They were a youthful, clean-cut crowd, whose lives would be changed by the Vietnam War, the pill, and 'hippie doom.'

After the taping, Phil Spector invited us to his house in the hills, a lavish, 1920s, white stucco Spanish-style home with a tile roof. I remember it being dark and not well lit. We sat at a long table, almost the length of the entire dining room. There was a red tablecloth and many candles. Everyone had been drinking. Spector sat at the head of the table. The food was forgettable. There was a lot of conversation and Derek Taylor began arguing with Spector about the state of the current music scene, and the balance of British and American acts. Another topic was Jim's leadership of the Byrds, over Gene's. Both Jim and Gene quietly listened to the loud argument and Derek's hypothesis.

The Byrds were appearing on TV shows and recording their second album, again produced by Terry Melcher. Things had taken a serious turn with the band. The British tour had been a bolt of awareness of what they should be. At this point, because of their sudden widespread success, the Byrds were offered money to appear in many commercials, including Coca-Cola. David refused to 'sell out,' as he called it, and another opportunity slipped for a broader appeal.

Shortly after, the Byrds embarked upon another tour of the Midwest, Dick Clark's Caravan of Stars. The final stop on the tour was an appearance on the beloved *Ed Sullivan Show* in New York City. Jim said his goodbyes to me. I always felt sad when he was leaving town for a prolonged period, knowing I would not see him for a month. We'd grown very close, and since I wasn't working, I wouldn't come into contact with many people outside of the swirl of the Byrds' network. It had become a part of my life.

I called my mother to let her know that Jim and the Byrds were performing on *The Ed Sullivan Show*, and to tune in. She had not met him, and had only heard what I had told her. She didn't even know what he looked like. I realized that I'd been in a bubble, with the rest of America going about its business, but my new companions, the Byrds, were on a blazing path of success. The year 1965 was winding down. They had skyrocketed to fame, and I had come along for the ride.

Jim bought me a paint set for my birthday in November, and I started to paint during his absence. The smell of linseed oil filled the small cottage, and I painted still-lifes, experimenting with this new medium of oil paint. I was pretty isolated, and realized that my choices were dominated by Jim's career – I would probably have never tried to spend time on the East Coast again, had the Byrds not been on their Midwest tour. Jim also bought a small color TV, a rare thing in those days. It was remarkable to see color on television. I'd grown up mostly without television, and then later, as a teenager, with only a black and white TV set.

On the appointed night, I tuned into *The Ed Sullivan Show*. The show had recently started broadcasting in color, which was a treat, since there were often many colorful acts performing. It was thrilling to hear the familiar voice of Ed Sullivan announce, "Ladies and Gentleman, The Byrds." I watched their lip-synced and live performance with happiness, knowing they'd reached a new level, going into millions of homes that night. The color was gorgeous as well, and they each had a unique persona. David was always wearing a green suede cape, which hid his chubbiness. The other Byrds appeared tall, lean and graceful by comparison. David was cherubic. However, he was also a little devil at heart.

When Jim returned from New York, he told me that David had created such conflict with the show's producer, Ed Sullivan's son-in-law, that the Byrds were forbidden from ever appearing on the show again. I was shocked that David could sabotage the group's professional standing, especially since he was smiling throughout the entire lip-synced performance of 'Mr. Tambourine Man.' Eddie Tickner never forgave David for such a lapse in judgment. David always wanted the last word. Jim was also dismayed by the developing egomania of David, as was Chris. The *Turn! Turn! Turn!* album was released in time for Christmas. Jim had just gotten a box of the LPs from Columbia. He took one out, removing the shrink-wrap so we could listen to the record. While the opening notes of the song played on the stereo, Jim took a ballpoint pen and mischievously scribbled doodles over the band on the album cover: a Van Dyke beard on himself, and a Hitler mustache on David. We both burst into laughter. The record sounded great, and 'Turn! Turn! Turn!' was already a number one single.

Gene's songwriting was becoming more evident and lucrative for him. In fact, his royalties from songwriting created a tension in the band, because he drove up in a Ferrari one afternoon, as the other Byrds looked on in envy at the new toy. I was fascinated that there was that much money in the Byrds' pot, and that he was getting most of it. Jim and I were still struggling.

Other people wrote both Byrds' number one hits, but Gene's songs were always the B-side of their popular singles. Therefore, his earnings were astronomical in comparison to Jim's and David's, let alone Chris or Michael's. Jim and David muttered to themselves at some point, "We'd better get cooking on the songwriting." No doubt this rivalry was the seed that later caused a rift with Gene.

One quiet evening before Christmas, I was baking banana bread when there was a knock on the door at the Woodrow Wilson cottage. I answered. It was Bob Dylan and a heavily bearded Allen Ginsberg. They came in with a flurry, much to our surprise. Ginsberg lit up a joint and began looking around the room, looking at our meager furnishings. Dylan and Jim started talking, and Dylan quipped to Jim, "I thought you'd be living in a mansion by now." Jim seemed embarrassed. "I want to help you make more money, man," Dylan said, "You taught me how to sing my songs."

Ginsberg asked me, "Have you heard Hare Krishna chant?" as he offered me a toke. "No," I said, bewildered, as I inhaled indiscriminately. Instantly he took out two sets of little finger cymbals, and he began clinking them and chanting, "Hare Krishna, Hare Krishna, Krishna, Krishna, Hare-Hare, Hare Dharma, Hare Dharma, Hare Dharma, Dharma, Dharma, Hare, Hare, Hare, Krishna, Krishna, Krishna, Hare, Hare-Hare – Sing Along! You'll feel better!" I was surprised to see such uninhibited joy from this jovial man, as if we'd been friends a long time. I joined the joyful chant, as Jim and Dylan continued to commiserate in hushed tones.

"That was an exciting evening!" I said after Dylan and Ginsberg had left about an hour later. The room still contained the electric energy of two strong forces. Later that evening, I pulled out one of my books of poetry, and searched for Ginsberg's poem, 'Howl'. I read it to Jim, and we laughed excitedly, intrigued by Ginsberg's vision and organic brilliance.

Jim did not always take to surprise visits so well. One night, my brother Marcus, his wife, Barbara, and my friend Karen brought along a visiting Frenchman to our home. I opened the door and happily greeted them, and they stepped inside. They were all dressed up, having been out to dinner. Jim was working on his electric light-box experiments: an aluminum box with Christmas lights that blinked off and on with various toggle switches. He seemed very irritated at the guests, and did not get up to leave his worktable. Turning his head slightly, he managed to mutter "Oh, hi," when they walked into the living room.

Barbara and Marcus were surprised at Jim's coolness. Karen and her date seemed uncomfortable. Even though I offered drinks and asked them all to sit, no one felt like they wanted to stay, because Jim's attitude was unwelcoming. They quickly left.

After Christmas, The Byrds were rehearsing their loud music in our small cottage. Gene, David, Chris and Jim were amplified and rehearsing vocals on 'Eight Miles High,' a new song about their trip to London. I was serving beers, but everyone was preoccupied with smoking marijuana. Gene had brought a lid. David smoked a lot. Suddenly there was a knock at the door. I looked out the kitchen window, and saw a police patrol car at the top of the driveway. My heart raced as I called out, "Oh, Jim...! The police are here."

With that, Gene grabbed the baggie and ran to the bathroom, immediately flushing the pot down the toilet. Jim calmly got up and opened the front door. The young officer said, "We have a noise complaint, sir."

Jim said, "Well, we were just rehearsing for our next record, officer." The officer then realized the celebrity status of the musicians who were present and said, "Well if you could please lower the volume, I'm sure the neighbors will appreciate it." Jim nodded and said, "Thank you, officer."

The door closed and everyone breathed a sigh of relief. Gene came out of the bathroom with a look of irritation that he'd lost all that good pot, and we all started laughing. David looked into the bathroom and saw the remains of the marijuana leaves still floating in the toilet bowl. "Oh man, too late." If the police had come inside the house and seen that pot, I'm sure we would have all been arrested. That had happened to an acquaintance of Jim's, who spent time in jail for marijuana possession.

I always felt closer to Chris than any of the other Byrds, maybe because I'd met him first. We three would get together and sing folk songs like 'When First unto This Country' and 'Man of Constant Sorrow.' I accompanied their guitars on autoharp. Chris encouraged my singing, whereas David never let me sing along with the band. David said I disrupted his harmony; he constantly shushed me. Chris snapped a photo of me one afternoon, when he came to show us his new 35mm camera, outside the Woodrow Wilson house.

The year ended, and the success of the Byrds and their new record, *Turn! Turn! Turn!* saw Terry Melcher out of a job. I will never understand why someone who produced two successful albums would be treated like this. David and Jim Dickson had convinced my Jim to aim higher, and change the formula, since Melcher's work was creating a redundant sound. Jim Dickson produced the recording sessions for the new collaborative song, 'Eight Miles High,' and Jim and David's song, 'Why'.

The session was recorded in an RCA-owned studio. I was sitting in the listening booth with Jim Dickson and the engineer. 'Eight Miles High' had a haunting quality, unlike the melodic hits the Byrds had previously made. Jim often listened to John Coltrane and Ravi Shankar, and integrated their sounds into his style of guitar playing. Gene had come up with the title of the song, after Jim told him they were "about six miles high" when they were traveling in the air. Jim truly felt that the song was about their jet flight and arrival in London, and the impressions taken in during their visit.

David, of course, thought that the double meaning of 'high' was important, because they were high during most of the journey. Getting high was as common for David as eating a meal is for most people. David had once said, "I joined this group for the drugs and the chicks." I think that attitude always irritated Jim. The recording was unlike any of the Byrds' previous work. Their rapid evolution intrigued me. Columbia executives listened to copies of the demo. They informed Jim Dickson that the song had to be re-recorded.

Since Columbia could not legally use the recording from an RCA-owned studio, for reasons that are now considered archaic, the Byrds later returned to the Columbia studio, this time with a newly mandated producer, Allen Stanton. Jim Dickson, disgruntled, sat in during the re-do session for 'Eight Miles High.' It seemed to me the studios were identical, but Jim Dickson said the RCA studio was more intimate and the band seemed more comfortable there. He had wanted to take over the producing of the new record in Terry's absence, but Columbia saw different. Allen Stanton was a corporate, necktie-wearing, ad-man type. He was quite formal, wore glasses and was very straight looking... very different from the young, handsome and hip Terry Melcher. Not only did I miss Terry, but I also wondered if the Byrds were in good hands.

After the flip side to the new single, 'Why,' was recorded, the Byrds went off to New York, yet again for a publicity trip. It was during this scheduled flight that I later learned that Gene Clark had refused to get on the jet, having a premonition of the plane crashing. Jim had given an ultimatum on the spot, "You can't be a Byrd if you don't fly." My thoughts are that Gene had had a very bad series of LSD trips, and he'd broken up with his most recent girlfriend. Gene was highly sensitive, emotional and moody. He was the type who internalized all of these feelings from recent traumatic events. His rapid rise to celebrity status built a pressure that caught up with him. It was something he just could not cope with.

When Jim told me, I was saddened and worried about the future of the group. Even though Gene was not the only one involved in the creation of the music, he was the mainstay of the vocals and the songwriting. He was the 'silent leader.' Gene had a strong stage presence. I was worried that the creative part of Gene's contribution was irreplaceable. Jim also felt concerned; the responsibility for the group's future lay in his hands.

Gene went into hiding; no doubt stunned himself about his decision. A line in the sand was drawn. There was nothing that anyone could do or say; it was a done deed. When Gene left, David and Jim realized they had to become better collaborators. They jammed more frequently together, sharing song ideas, and they experimented musically with new influences.

During one San Francisco trip, David drove his Porsche, and Jim and I followed in our Porsche to meet Owsley Stanley, the chemist who cooked all the doses of LSD that were in use at the time. David probably wanted to pick up his monthly supply of LSD and the newly minted STP.

We drove to Berkeley, to a long wooden building in a pasture in the middle of nowhere. Perhaps it was an old railway warehouse. We walked into the quiet building and came across a most bizarre scene. A long dining table for a party stood in the center of the building. The table was set as if there had been a large banquet, but everything had been left to decay, like Dickens' Miss Havisham from *Great Expectations*. Little Chinese bowls and teacups were set up with dried tealeaves in them, empty beverages sat next to food shriveled on the plates: everything had been left, abandoned, as if everyone had got up to leave the party, and never returned. Perhaps it had been a celebration for Chinese New Year. It was a ghostly, foreboding place. We never found Owsley. David said, "I guess they split, man." We drove back to San Francisco.

Around this time, David also invited us to a party at Wally Cox's house in LA. Wally was a character actor who played nerdy, milquetoast types. He had appeared in several television shows in the 1950s. Contrary to this persona, he was a motorcycle rider and very intellectual. I'd heard that David met Wally on Sunset Boulevard, when the two were stopped at a traffic light on their motorcycles. They became instant friends. Wally's house was in the Hollywood Hills. Jim and I arrived after dark, when the party was in full swing. It turned out to be a casual affair. John Derek was playing billiards with Christian Marquand. There was jazzy music on the stereo, cocktails in hands, and everyone dressed casually in shirts and slacks. David was already there and passed a joint to anyone who wanted a toke.

I was sitting on a love seat, and Jim was standing across from me, arms folded, a bit uncomfortable in the Hollywood social scene. Who should enter the party from an adjoining room but Marlon Brando? The other guests pretended not to notice. Brando and Wally were good friends from the New York Actor's Studio days. Marlon spotted me and sat right next to me on the love seat. I was thrilled. I looked over to see Jim's reaction. He acknowledged the presence of Marlon by coldly turning away from direct view.

Marlon said, "Hello again."

I'd had a drink, so I was relaxed enough to flirt. "Hello again."

"What's your name?"

"Dolores DeLeon," I said, my voice quivering a little.

He asked, "How do you know Wally?"

I smiled. "I don't, really. We were invited by David," I said, as David approached, joint in hand, offering Marlon, "Hey man, want some?" Marlon politely refused and David walked away.

"I don't smoke that stuff. I like being in control. So tell me about yourself, where were you born, Dolores?"

"In a little mining town out West." He smiled and seemed charmed.

"West of what?" he asked.

"A little town named Ray, Arizona. My dad was a miner there."

"What brought you to Los Angeles?"

"I came to seek my fortune," I said, sipping my glass of wine. He laughed, and about that time, Wally's big Saint Bernard dog walked up to Brando, and slobbered all over my dress. I started wiping my dress, and Brando said, "Not to worry," and with his bare hand, wiped the dog's saliva directly off the dog's jowls, and onto his pant leg. It seemed very earthy and manly. He laughed as Wally Cox's wife came and fetched the dog away. "Come on, you!" she said.

"You're not squeamish, are you?" Brando asked, and I said, "Not really."

"Who are you here with, besides David?"

I smiled and nodded my head over toward Jim, who still stood there, with his arms wrapped protectively around his waist. Marlon snickered and said, "You can tell he's unbalanced and fearful, the way he's cradling himself." I was surprised at this brash assessment, but then again, I was in the presence of one of Hollywood's most confident men, whose acting ability made him an expert at reading character.

Marlon continued chatting with me, about personality types, and I noticed that David and some other guests were drawn to Marlon, as if he were holding court. David sat at Marlon's feet, as did Christian Marquand. David, Christian and Brando chatted back and forth for some time. A young brunette woman sidled up next to Brando, and slid her arm around his shoulder. He said to me, "This is Pat Quinn." She smiled provocatively. "Look at Christian. He's French. And the

French are thought to be very seductive, and yet he's a big teddy bear." Christian laughed at this comment. Time seemed to stand still as we all felt a connection with each other, sitting there.

"Well, I guess we'd better get going." Brando said, standing up, which dispersed the group of admirers, except Pat. He looked at me directly and said, "Are you coming with me, or are you staying with him?" as he tilted his head in Jim's direction. It was the second time I'd been asked that question... I thought of Nick back in the Ash Grove. In that split second I knew my whole life would change if I went off with Marlon. I glanced over at Jim, and my heart felt for him: shy, aloof and somewhat socially inept.

"I'm staying," I said hesitantly. It might have been different if Marlon had been alone, but I could sense that with Pat, Marlon's intention was a ménage à trois. He linked arms with Pat and said, "Adieu," and as they walked away, she smiled at me haughtily.

I walked from the love seat toward Jim, and he asked, "Having fun?"

I said, "What do you think of that?"

"So, Brando likes you, so what? Ready to go?"

We drove home in silence, the Porsche engine revving through the dark, winding Hollywood Hills down to our little abode on Woodrow Wilson Drive. At home, I climbed into bed and Jim stayed up for a while, tinkering with one of his light-boxes. I could tell he was hurt. I felt him get into bed several hours later.

The next morning, I made coffee and sipped it quietly in the kitchen. I had made my choice, once again, knowing I loved Jim, and nothing, not even Marlon Brando, could come between us. I guess that night I discovered that my love for Jimmy could endure many temptations, and I just felt that I wanted to be with him for the rest of my life, and grow old together.

Jim woke up sheepishly, and, as if he'd been thinking the same thing, he put his arm around me and asked, "Will you be my Bonnie?" We hugged.

"Always," I said, as we held each other closer. Marlon had brought us closer together, and I think Jim appreciated me more.

1966 - Prejudice vs. Fifth Dimension, Baby

Jim with Lear Jet model, 1966

Remarkably, the recordings for *Fifth Dimension* went well, and the album took shape. Jim and David rose to the occasion and filled the void with newly arranged folk songs and some originals. 'Mr. Spaceman' was one song that Jim wrote. I remember him rehearsing it in our home as he pulled the words out of his brain. He asked me what I thought, and I said, "It's fun."

Later that year we were watching *Star Trek* on television, and there was a feeling of wanting to explore new worlds. Jim's other main song, '5D: Fifth Dimension,' was another exploration based on a book we'd read, a sort of picture book about possibilities in other dimensions. We continued to practice at Subud as well, and Jim's consciousness was truly expanding.

David seemed jubilant about the vacancy that Gene's departure allowed. There was more songwriting space on the record, and more space onstage for his growing ego. The recording sessions for *Fifth*

Dimension continued, without Gene. David finally had the opportunity to write a few songs and sing his beloved 'Hey Joe,' which everyone groaned about. "Everyone's recorded 'Hey Joe' except me, and I'm the one who brought it to everyone's attention, man. I should have recorded it two albums ago." Along these lines, 'Captain Soul' was a concession for Michael Clarke's desire to play more blues. Jim was feeling out of his element as these forces came into play.

The Byrds were always one step ahead of the musical genre of the time, truly innovators. This made for an audience that was never prepared for their next move. However, their experimentation opened the gate that allowed other musicians to take that musical genre and have more success. Jim seemed to enjoy the amount of creative space he was allotted by Gene's absence.

The '2-4-2 Foxtrot' song was an expression of Jim's fascination for technology and the sci-fi obsession that he'd had since he was a boy. We went to an airfield where the Lear Jet was docked, and Jim brought the state-of-the-art cassette recorder he'd purchased in London to capture the sounds of the jet engine starting. John Lear, Jr., a handsome heir to the Lear dynasty, took us around the hangar and showed us other aircraft, much to Jim's elation. John Jr. had been in a terrible airplane crash and told us he had a metal plate in his head. He had sandy blond hair that was neatly combed. I never would have guessed he had a metal plate. We later went to dinner with Lear Jr. and his beautiful wife at a resplendent French restaurant. John Jr. was a Byrds fan.

The following day, Lear Jr. flew Jim, David and Peter Fonda for a short flight to Las Vegas. That is when the pilot's communications were recorded for '2-4-2 Foxtrot'. When I saw David and Jim later that day, they were as excited as schoolboys, happy to know someone who could 'take them for a trip.'

Allen Stanton used his ability in the studio, incorporating Jim's audio tapes into the Lear Jet song. What they were all attempting was very unconventional for the time, and Allen seemed successful in combining studio professionalism with experimentation, keeping the group intact in the process, when they may have dissolved under other producers. I have always wondered what Terry Melcher could have accomplished as a producer on *Fifth Dimension*. Sadly, Jim had lost touch with Terry in the process of moving forward with the record, and I'm sure Terry was hurt.

One morning, as I was preparing coffee, I felt nauseated. I had missed a period. Now my thoughts were certain that I was pregnant. I had morning sickness, but I decided to wait to tell Jim. Another month went by. We were sitting down to dinner. "I'm pregnant."

He paused, reflected on what I had said, and asked, "What are you going to do?"

"I plan to keep it." Jim sat quietly, and he seemed to lose his appetite.

Jim broke the silence by asking, "How are you going to manage?"

I knew the conversation would go in this direction, since Jim had seemed tentative about any future marriage or family plans, because of his negative past experience. But that didn't stop the pain of his detached, cold attitude. I felt emboldened, defiant.

"I'm going to have this baby, whether you support me or not."

"I thought you told me you couldn't get pregnant," he muttered.

"Well, I guess I was wrong," I said.

With Nick, I'd never used any birth control. Because we had a serious relationship, I took the leap of faith, thinking birth control didn't matter. I never became pregnant with Nick, and throughout those years, I questioned whether I could become pregnant. At the Ash Grove, a co-worker there began taking the pill, and I noticed she became quite bloated, and later developed a blood clot in her leg. This horrified me, and I vowed never to take the pill. Somehow, I'd managed, despite my different encounters, to avoid pregnancy. I'd told Jim about this early into our sexual relationship. Furthermore, despite the year of monogamy with Jim, I had not become pregnant.

"I've managed without you in the past, and I can manage without you if you're not supportive," I said bravely. He took this in, and we quietly finished dinner. I didn't know what Jim's feelings were, since he remained quiet the rest of the evening.

The next day, Jim suggested I go to see 'Dr. Feelgood,' literally, the man who prescribed Jim and David the various pharmaceuticals, Valium, caffeine pills and an occasional Ritalin, for their professional needs. Jim used Ritalin for stretches of late night driving, and later, for music inspiration. I went to see the doctor down on Vine, an office close to the Hollywood Presbyterian Hospital.

I entered the doctor's office and took a seat. I was called in, and the doctor examined me. He confirmed that I was pregnant. He said that he wanted me to come in for prenatal visits every six weeks, and advised me not to smoke or drink. That wouldn't be hard, since cigarette smoke was making me deathly ill, on top of the morning sickness. He also said that his partner would actually deliver the baby, which was due in October. In those days, the suspense of whether you had a boy or a girl was kept until the final push of birth. Ultrasound and amniocentesis were not in common use. I knew I was going to have Jim's baby. I knew that until Jim left me, we would go through this together.

Bob Hippard was a friend of Jim's from Chicago who'd finally come out to Los Angeles with his pretty wife, Cheryl. I'd met them at one of the Byrds' LA concerts. Bob was a gregarious, thoughtful man with short-cropped hair and a warm sense of humor under his conventional exterior. Cheryl was a flight attendant with Continental Airlines, and along with her charm, she epitomized the elegant poise and beauty that the job required. They were both wonderful people, and Jim and I became very social with them during this time. Bob, I later learned, was instrumental in getting Jim motivated to go out and seek musician auditions during his downtime after the Limeliters. Bob was a true friend to Jim. Bob came to Hollywood to make it as a screenwriter. For now, he was a cabbie. He and Jim smoked pot together, while Jim bounced song ideas. Cheryl and I told stories about what had been going on with each of us. She became very dear to me. Both she and Bob were very enthusiastic about my pregnancy.

'Eight Miles High' had hit the airwaves, and its futuristic sound was unlike anything else on the radio. It was great to hear the collaborative work of all the Byrds, including Gene Clark, reaching a receptive public. Jim, David and Chris had a press conference with a sitar, and the journalists called the future of their music 'raga-rock,' and Crosby spoke proudly of his "introducing John Coltrane to McGuinn and Ravi Shankar to the Beatles."

It was disturbing to learn, as the song climbed the charts that a Midwest censor was labeling the song as drug-influenced, and therefore needing to be withdrawn from the airwaves. Jim was upset that the song was misunderstood. About this time, San Francisco was emerging as a cultural destination for recreational drug use, and the secret life of rock musicians getting high was now becoming public knowledge. San Francisco radio embraced 'Eight Miles High' as the anthem of psychedelic culture. This was a small consolation. 'Eight Miles High' deserved to be a much bigger hit because of its innovation.

Fifth Dimension was completed and the next step was to set up publicity and take the album cover photos, scheduled to happen during a few different trips to New York City. Eddie Tickner had booked me onto the flight with the Byrds going east. This was to be a very romantic trip for Jim and me. We landed at JFK airport and Eddie had arranged for us to have a Lincoln Town Car, which Jim would drive. The other Byrds stayed at hotels in Manhattan.

Chip Monck, a New York-based stage lighting designer, had a girlfriend who lived in Long Island. Chip was full of all kinds of stories. He would later be responsible for all of the lighting at the Woodstock concert. Chip had invited us to stay at a cottage in Long Island, which was part of his girlfriend's divorce settlement. It was a little, one-room guesthouse with a bathroom. There was a path leading to the large main house.

Later, Chip sent Eddie Tickner a bill for Jim and me staying there, the decorating fees apparently. We only stayed a few days because Jim did not like having to rely on Chip and his girlfriend for our meals, and we had to drive quite far to get into Manhattan. One time when we were driving, we saw sand bars and the ocean lapping, and Chip said to Jim, "Can you imagine an old pirate vessel out there in these waters, and the little skiff coming to the shoreline, with all these pirates to bury their treasure around here?" Jim said, "Yeah man... that's a picture. I always had the feeling I was on a whaling vessel at one time. I must have been a sailor in another life."

During this time, 'Strangers in the Night' was a big hit on the radio for Frank Sinatra. Jim and I listened to that song multiple times during our drives to and from Manhattan. Jim sang along with Frank on the radio, and we'd laugh. The song grew on me. To this day, if I hear that song, I think of those misty drives through Long Island into New York City with Jim at the wheel of a black Lincoln Town Car.

The Byrds did a photo shoot for publicity and the Fifth Dimension record cover in Norman Griner's Midtown studio. I was waiting, and watched during the session. These photo shoots were typically boring, especially when it came to David demanding certain angles being taken, Michael getting restless and impatient, and Chris wanting to smoke. However, it didn't matter, because the camera loved the Byrds. No matter what sulking expression they made, or from what angle the photo was taken, they were extremely photogenic. They were drinking some cups of red wine, bored, when they sat on the large colorful Turkish rug and photos were snapped. One of these photos became the record cover.

Afterward, Jim and I enjoyed lunch at the then-fabulous Brasserie restaurant not far from CBS. It was a well-appointed, European-style restaurant with a Manhattan immediacy, very bustling, and fantastic food. It had been one of Jim's favorite restaurants for some time. His other favorite restaurant was the Minetta Tavern in the Village, veal piccata being his favorite dish. The Minetta was a dimly lit, atmospheric Italian restaurant with Old World charm. "Possibly a gangster hangout," Jim said quietly. It was always great to be in New York City, on the wind of a success. Jim had taken a leap from living as a struggling musician staying at the Albert Hotel, and now he'd returned, with a sense that *this was his city*. He'd made it. Some of our New York friends who we'd see in the street – because you always run into people you know on the street in New York – were Richmond Shepherd, Bobby Neuwirth and Antonia Lamb.

Antonia was a friend who'd known Jim before he went to California, who'd helped him survive during his early New York City days. She had long brown hair and a thin build with an endearing, crooked smile. He recalled having tea with her, and that she'd read his horoscope. I sensed that she had wanted to be involved with Jim, but she was already married to a man named Lee Lamb, a lanky man with a chiseled face who was the father of their two children. Eddie Tickner hired Lee that year to fill the position of road manager for the Byrds tours. A musician himself, Lee did not like the job's challenges, and was stoned most of the time. He was soon fired. Despite this, Antonia and I remained lifelong friends. She moved up the California coast to Mendocino and pursued folk music, astrology and writing.

One memorable gig got us lost in the heart of New Jersey. The Byrds and I were piled in the Town Car. Jim was driving. We stopped at a mini-mart grocery store on the side of the road in the New Jersey suburbs. Michael Clarke got out of the car to stretch his long legs. Chris lit up a cigarette, and as they walked toward the store, three husky blue-collar type men in their bowling shirts brusquely walked out. These men looked at Chris and Michael like they were beings from another planet. "Hey what's this? Why do you guys have such long hair?"

Michael replied, "We're the Byrds."

One of the men looked incredulous. "Hey *Chawlie*. He says, he's the *Boyds*. Who are the *Boyds*? I've never *hoid* of the *Boyds*." By that time, David and Jim approached behind Michael and Chris.

David said, "Yeah man, we're the Byrds. A group." Charlie said, "Yeah, I *hoid* of the *Boyds*. My *dawta* has the record. What's the name of that song?"

Michael said, "Mr. Tambourine Man." The three New Jersey men burst into laughter. "If you're a *Boyd*, let's hear you sing it!" they challenged. This was a disturbing moment, and I feared for the Byrds' safety as these men were mocking them. Michael responded, "Hey man, we don't have our guitars. We can't just sing at the drop of a hat."

Charlie said, "Okay then. Give me your autograph for my *dawta*." He pulled out the receipt from his recent purchase. Jim and the others signed the receipt quickly on the hood of the men's car, and we hurried into the store. Inside, Michael started laughing nervously, "Hey man... that was close. What a trip. Let's get out of here!"

From inside the store, I watched one man slap his buddy on the back playfully, as they got into their car and left. There was a collective sigh of relief. I realized that despite the Byrds' success in Los Angeles, the rest of the country hadn't caught up with the fast-changing progressive lifestyle. This brush with the other side of America reminded me again that we were in a unique sphere.

Back in Los Angeles, my pregnancy was becoming apparent. A few people, like Bob Hippard and Cheryl, had known I was pregnant all this time, but now it was physically obvious to most. My brother Marcus asked, "Are you getting married?"

"Not yet," I replied, sheepishly. The other members of the Byrds may have known sooner, but my traveling with the group had subsided for now. There was no formal acknowledgment about my expanding girth by anyone. No one seemed to want to dwell on it.

Karen and I went to Olvera Street in downtown LA and bought some loose-fitting Mexican wedding dresses that were maternity-size for me. She was excited. I was mostly solitary during this time, when Jim was on the road. One afternoon at the Woodrow Wilson house, I heard a sporadic knocking at the front door. I opened the door and no one was there. When I looked down, there was a large tortoise wanting to get into the house. I let him in, and soon he became a pet. He didn't have a name, but his presence was reassuring.

Karen had invited me to attend the cinema while she was working at a movie theater on Melrose and Western. One afternoon, I decided to take her up on it, and she let me in to see a film by little-known-at-the-time Roman Polanski. It was *Repulsion*. Catherine Deneuve plays a young woman living in London with her older sister in a narrow flat. When she's left alone on a weekend, she slowly loses her mind and has psychotic visions of assault, while in possession of a skinned, decaying rabbit. In my pregnancy and loneliness, this film was profoundly disturbing. That night I had a nightmare that I had given birth, and that my child looked like a turtle. The next morning, I decided to put Mr. Turtle outside and let him fend for himself. My nerves were still rattled from the movie.

When Jim was back in town, we went to Subud. I waited for him, because they wouldn't let me practice Latihan at my stage of pregnancy – about five months at this point. We arrived home and heard some strange news. David told Jim that Dylan had been in a terrible motorcycle accident, but that he had survived. We were in shock and wondered what effect this would have on Dylan's future music career. Jim Dickson tried to find out more information, but there was an air of secrecy – no one knew how serious the accident had been. My Jim was reflective during this time. Life appeared vulnerable, even for pop stars.

I later found out that one of Jim's good friends from New York, Judy Moll, who had relocated to Laurel Canyon in the mid-Sixties, was summoned to help the Dylan family with Bob's recovery. Judy was to become a live-in assistant, and help with whatever was needed. At a later time, she revealed to me and Jim that Dylan's accident had been so severe that he could hardly hold his guitar to play it, that he had to re-learn how to play the guitar. This was a sad revelation. Dylan, at the height of his career, to be in such condition, would show the measure of his ability and strength, able to re-emerge from such a compromised state. Judy spent several months with the family in New York.

Years in formulation, a hit single emerged from a selectively handpicked group of musician/actors who'd auditioned for the part of being in a television show about a pop group. They were called The Monkees. There had been stirrings in town about the audition process. Stephen Stills purportedly auditioned for a part and was rejected. The sheer commercialism of the venture was evident, and Jim found the packaging of Beatles' style pop culture degrading.

What was even worse, however, was seeing Monkees' songs climb the charts effortlessly because of TV exposure, while the Byrds' brilliant single 'Eight Miles High' stalled. This reminded me of the Sonny and Cher rip-off of 'All I Really Want to Do.' The Byrds were cutting edge, with David the sole aggressor in regard to staying competitive in the LA scene. The Byrds didn't appreciate the inorganic feel of the Monkees' chart success but felt an obligation to watch the television show, to see what the phenomenon was all about. It was painful to witness the inane antics on *The Monkees*, knowing what the actors must have been paid for mugging at the camera, the charm of *A Hard Day's Night* reduced and co-opted into a formula for mass American consumption. The times they were a changin'. Jim and Chris eventually wrote a song about this disillusionment and commercialism, 'So You Want to Be a Rock 'N' Roll Star.'

The annual Renaissance Pleasure Faire took place in the San Fernando Valley that spring, and David was eager to check it out. He encouraged the other Byrds to join him. It was a very colorful setting; people were dressed in medieval costumes, the women wearing long velvet dresses. There were court jesters, jugglers, knights in armor and vendors selling pottery and incense.

Jim did not have a good time, but he gleaned the positive aspects of the event. He couldn't stand the dust, or the cluster of people, or the traffic. Our Porsche got very dusty that day. Jim was eager to get home, while David drew inspiration from this gathering of theatrical artisans, later penning a song with Jim about the essence of the experience, 'Renaissance Fair.' Jim was fascinated by Bach and Baroque music, and I believe he infused the spirit of Baroque into the melody of this song.

The Vietnam War was escalating, and through evening news coverage was made all the more immediate with footage of the carnage. I'd cringe when seeing some of the horrible images of explosions, mayhem and injured soldiers. Jim had failed his draft entry when he passed out after his blood was drawn for testing. He woke up and asked the big sergeant, "Am I alright?" "Yeah buddy, you're alright. You can get up and go." The sergeant dismissed him. Chris, on the other hand, stayed up two nights in a row before his draft exam. He slicked his hair back and wore a leather jacket and tight jeans. Apparently, he didn't look the all-American type, because he was also dismissed from being enlisted. Michael Clarke had a trick up his sleeve: on the information form, the question asked, 'Have you ever engaged in homosexual behavior?' Michael slyly checked off, 'Yes,' but then erased it with the new entry, 'No.' That was enough to get him dismissed. Gene had escaped due to a knee injury.

Roger in photo booth, late 1966

I was grateful that there was no possibility that Jim could be drafted. He could not have possibly handled military service. I had two brothers in the service but the environment we grew up in had toughened them. Jim had had a more privileged childhood. In some ways, the success that came with the Byrds extended that childhood, as he became excited about the newest technologies in electronics, radio and television, consistently purchasing new toys. Gadgets, and supplies for soldering and creating electronic connections, were his form of experimentation when he wasn't playing music. He continued making elaborate metal boxes with an open back, toggle switches on the front, and lights that blinked on and off.

One day he arrived from a film supply store with a large 16mm projector and Bolex film camera. Jim had long admired Stanley Kubrick, and aspired to pursue film experiments. We'd watch some of the commercial 16mm film prints he'd purchased, projected on the wall at night: a documentary on Craig Breedlove, the fastest race car driver in the world, and the sci-fi films, *Forbidden Planet* and *War of the Worlds*. We watched *Forbidden Planet* countless times. After the fourth or fifth time, I'd memorized the dialogue. By the tenth time, I could hear the movie's bizarre theme 'song' of electronic blips and special effects sounds in my ears during the daylight when the movie wasn't playing. We lived in Jim's world, and that was becoming increasingly eccentric, helped by his ability to indulge in his fantasies.

He began filming his special effects lighting boxes on 16mm, and playing back Beatles songs while projecting his work. He looped the film so that the visual experience was uninterrupted. Marijuana was not necessary... I was pregnant and I couldn't tolerate any nearby smoke. During my pregnancy, Jim refrained from smoking as well, at least in the house.

We had a special visitor one night. David Crosby brought George Harrison over. George looked handsome as ever, but very tired. David was taking George around town in his blue Porsche. They smoked pot and we watched some of Jim's films. The soundtrack was the Beatles' 'Tomorrow Never Knows' in addition to a cassette tape with sounds of screaming females during the Byrds' British tour. Everyone seemed amused and supportive of Jim's new hobby. Almost as soon as they'd arrived, David and George were off again, speeding away in David's Porsche. These recorded sounds of screaming young fans surfaced again in the song 'So You Want to Be a Rock 'N' Roll Star.'

The Mamas and Papas had moved to California from the East Coast, and Jim had known all of them previously from his New York days. We'd visit Cass Elliott at little get-togethers during my pregnancy. She lived off Barham Boulevard, in a ranch-style house. There was a trailer next to the house. She served food and everyone spoke about the New York days and the current state of the music business. She was a sweet, jolly woman, who called Jim "Jimmy." Men at the party were drawn to Michelle Phillips because she was so beautiful – the perfect blonde. She embodied the southern California spirit. All of the Byrds said she was 'groovy.' I was not friendly with her; we were opposite types. Certainly, she presented a threat, as she was Jim's image of an ideal mate.

Because of Subud, I had complete faith in Jim's fidelity. Jim never seemed to eye women in the same way that most men did. No staring at bosoms or lewd comments the way Michael Clarke did. No lustful side glances. This seemed reassuring to me, especially since we weren't married, and I was very pregnant at the time.

I had made dinner for us one night, a spaghetti Bolognese in my college friend Nancy's cast-iron skillet. Before I could wash the dishes, we were supposed to head out for Jim's performance at the Whisky A Go Go after dinner. I left the skillet in the sink, soaking in dish soap and water. The show was part of a weeklong engagement, and I was glad it was close to home. When we returned after the show, I finished cleaning the kitchen and the skillet.

The following day, I was going to make a beef stew. I made the stew and it cooked for a long time in the same skillet. When the stew was ready, we ate dinner together. Jim was silent during the meal. I wasn't sure what was wrong. I had noticed a faint soapy flavor, but I didn't want to mention it. I asked after dinner, "So, what do you think?" Without skipping a beat, Jim replied, "It was a Thrilling dinner." The liquid dish soap was named 'Thrill' and the soap fragrance had permeated the meal. We both laughed.

The Byrds were set to play a ten-day residence gig at the Village Gate in New York City during October. Our baby was due some time in mid-October. I wondered if Jim would be in town when I was going to give birth. By this time, I'd grown used to Jim's frequent touring. He loved the road. We always got reacquainted on his return.

The Hippards had been watching over me and keeping tabs, along with my brother, Marcus, while Jim was away. Marcus was worried that I was to be alone before my due date. He called our mother, who planned to come out and stay with him once the baby was born. My mother had never met Jim, she'd only heard about him. She had seen him on *The Ed Sullivan Show*, where my younger brother Larry pointed out, "He's the one with the funny glasses." She was concerned about me, to say the least. An unmarried daughter having a baby with a longhaired musician was not acceptable, but I didn't care. Jim and I spoke daily, and I updated him: no baby yet.

I was grateful that he was returning to LA and I hadn't given birth. It was almost as if the baby was waiting for Jim to come back home. Karen and I had bought some baby clothes, and Marcus bought a wooden crib that rocked. Karen took me to visit a young friend of hers, Lisa Lamelle, who was also pregnant, and set to deliver twins. We were due around the same time. Lisa had been to birthing classes, and she told me what to expect. My baby was going to be delivered at Hollywood Presbyterian Hospital. Lisa introduced me to Paul Fliess, a pediatrician in Los Feliz. Jim and I discussed possible names for our child. I asked, "If it's a boy, how are you with James McGuinn?" "Yeah, that's fine," he said. We didn't select any girl's names, because when I suggested 'Miranda' after my favorite uncle's last name, Jim nixed it. "No, I hate that name." There was a woman on the Byrds' British tour, Miranda Ward, a very pushy promoter's assistant.

On October 18, I began getting contractions late in the afternoon. Jim drove me to the hospital in the red Porsche. We checked in and Jim left me there, because the nurse told him, "It's going to be a while." It sure was... I shouldn't have gone into the hospital so early. They put me on a gurney and I lay there for several hours. My elbows were painfully brushing against the starched sheet and my back and buttocks were sore as the contractions progressed.

When I started going into the final stages of labor, the nurse said that she'd call my husband. I was taken to the delivery room early the next morning.

Jim had come in around five in the morning, after the nurse had called him. He arrived at the hospital and was ushered into the waiting room, where he promptly fell asleep. After remembering nothing of the physical birth of our son, I awoke in a hospital bed. I had been given general anesthesia, which was common at the time, and had a 'twilight birth.' I asked the nurse if my husband had arrived. She said, "He isn't here, honey. He must have left." Almost an hour later, Jim came straggling in the door to see me and said, "I've been waiting for you to have the baby. I fell asleep on the chair."

"They said you weren't there."

"No, I fell asleep in one of the chairs. What do we have?"

"It's a boy."

"Can I see him?"

The nurse came into the room. "Visiting hours are three to five. You'll have to come back."

"Well, I think I'm going to go home now," Jim said. He kissed my forehead and said bye. I fell into a deep sleep.

When I woke up, there was a young Mexican woman in the next bed, a new mother herself. She and I exchanged pleasantries in Spanish. She'd had a boy as well and asked about my husband. I shared that he was one of the Byrds. She did not look Hispanic; her hazel eyes sparkled cheerfully. When her husband walked in the room later that day, a well-built dark, fine featured man, she burst out, "*Mira, honey, el nino de ella es un pajarito.*" (Look, honey, her son is a little bird.)

Around three in the afternoon, Jim returned with Bob Hippard to see the baby. They went to the nursery and saw the nurse holding up our infant.

"Boy, McGuinn, that's your son! Look at that nose," Bob laughed.

The following morning the registration people came in and wanted to know what name we had chosen. I said, "James Joseph McGuinn IV." They took note, then asked, "And what is the father's occupation?" I responded, "Musician." Later, Jim became indignant when he saw the birth certificate. "I'm not a musician. I'm an entertainer."

The doctor came in and said, "Everything went okay. But I've given you an injection to dry up your milk, so you can start the baby on formula." My right leg was hurting, and I alerted the doctor. "Oh that must be where the anesthesiologist placed the IV." "Why didn't he put it in my arm?" I asked. He ignored the question. Jim took me and our new baby home, and I was glad to get out of there. We drove home in the Porsche, me cradling baby James in the passenger seat, not even a seatbelt around me, with all of the bottles and formula they had given me in the back seat. When I came into the house, it was clear that Jim had thrown a big party the night before. There were ash trays filled with cigarette butts, and bottles half full of beer. I put the baby in the crib, rocked it gently and he soon fell asleep.

Patrick and me, 1967

Jim and I started talking in the living room as we cleaned up the party mess. We sat down and started a conversation about his recent New York travels. All of a sudden, baby Jimmy started crying. I was in the middle of a sentence, speaking, when the cries of the baby became louder and louder. "Well, I think someone's calling you," Jim quipped. This was to be a big adjustment. I gave the baby the bottle, and he took it, and drank. He promptly started barfing. I was uncertain what to do. No one could prepare me for this new experience. My life was no longer my own.

Very early the next morning, Jim left for another gig up the coast. I heard the baby crying and started to get out of bed. Suddenly an excruciating pain shot up my right leg, where the IV had been. I could not walk to the crib. I had to crawl. I was profoundly disturbed by my sudden disability.

I called my brother immediately to ask if our mom, Hope, could come over. She came as soon as she could, shocked at how tiny the house was, and started to clean. The baby began crying, trying to nurse as I held him.

"Dolores, this child wants to nurse, you should not give him a bottle, you should just let him nurse." I decided to let baby Jimmy nurse, and he was much happier. Not long after, the baby went flush, probably a reaction to the medication they gave me to dry up my milk.

We ordered a diaper service. Once I started nursing, the baby was well behaved. I realized that in the medical field, my opinion was not respected. The doctors had their own agenda. For example, getting a woman to use formula instead of breastfeeding, and not encouraging natural delivery but using anesthesia instead, were all forms of money-making that were part of the 1950s medical establishment. I was glad to meet Paul Fliess, who had updated views on common practices.

When Jim returned from his San Francisco gig, he called his parents, and told them the good news: they were grandparents. Dorothy was very excited. Marcus invited us for dinner that night. Karen, Jim, baby Jimmy and I came over for a wonderful home-cooked meal of roast beef, mashed potatoes and string beans – my favorite.

Marcus had a little handmade bench in the living room. Jim sat on the edge of the bench, and it tipped over and Jim fell to the floor. Both Jim and Marcus were embarrassed. "Sorry, I hadn't put the dowels in," Marcus apologized.

Before the meal, I placed baby James on a blanket in Marcus' bedroom. Karen came into the room, and she and I gazed down at the sweet baby on the bed. When we turned to leave the room, a huge black butterfly swooped past us and fluttered over him. Karen whispered, "Oh, that's a good sign." Where the butterfly came from, I have no idea.

All of the Byrds came to Woodrow Wilson to visit, and were amazed at the little being. Mike Clarke said, "I want one of those!" They all had a sense of wonder and took turns holding our child. Gene and Michael seemed to be the most experienced in holding a baby. "Wow McGuinn! Wow!" David exclaimed.

At Subud, Jim shared the news of his new son with the other members. I wasn't with him, but members encouraged him to write to Bapak for a name for our new son, feeling that the name "James Joseph McGuinn IV" would carry a lot of baggage and that there was something that could resonate better with the Universe. Jim put the request in writing, and the letter was hand-carried to Indonesia by another member who was traveling there.

Having a baby changed our lives. There were certain shows that I just couldn't attend with an infant, but initially we tried bringing baby James with us on the road for small stints. I remember bathing him in a motel sink on more than one occasion. This baby loved the water. The house on Woodrow Wilson Drive was becoming very small – too small for the three of us.

We decided to move to Yucca Trail, a two-story, two-bedroom home that the former actor/real estate agent suggested. This house in Laurel Canyon was across the hill from where Chris Hillman lived. The day we moved in, my brother Marcus helped us. Jim had come down with the flu and kept saying, "Do we have to do this now?" in a feverish delirium. I said, "All you have to do is get yourself in your Porsche, and drive to the new house. I'll make the bed there for you."

Once Jim got better, the Hippards came over to see our new place and admire the baby. Bob and Jim co-wrote a song, 'C.T.A.-102' about human radio waves being heard by alien beings. Jim also enjoyed taking Polaroid photos of UFOs flying by our new house. The effect was achieved by double exposing the Polaroid film, once with a backdrop and then a second time using colored floodlights, angled from below.

Following the release of this song, Jim received a letter and an attached article from *The Astro-Physical Journal*. It was written by a radio telescope astronomer named Eugene Epstein, who was reaching out to Jim after hearing 'C.T.A.-102' on his car radio, driving home from work one night. Jim was delighted to visit Eugene at his office at the Jet Propulsion Laboratory in Long Beach.

On a terrestrial note, Jim took a trip to Stuttgart, Germany, to buy a new, mustard colored Porsche 911-S. He sold the red Porsche at a discount to my brother Marcus, who loved it. By this time, all of the Byrds had Porsches. Jim described his joy driving the newly purchased car full speed on the autobahn from the Stuttgart factory to the port in Hamburg. Jim flew back to LA, but the car took the slow-boat to Long Beach, California, where we eventually picked it up and drove it home.

That was about the time that Cyril Maitland, an Australian photographer, snapped photos of our baby son, Jim and me one quiet afternoon together. The photos appeared in a teen magazine. The Byrds always had great coverage in these magazines, thanks to Derek Taylor. Derek and his wife lived in Nichols Canyon, and were gracious enough occasionally to babysit for us, when Jim and I attended Subud. Marcus and his wife Barbara also took care of baby James on Subud days, Tuesdays and Thursdays. Jim and the band were in the studio again, and I was taking care of the baby in the night hours when they recorded. Jim brought back rough-mix tapes on reel-to-reel that we'd listen to together the next morning. I was surprised at how Chris had blossomed as a songwriter. The bass playing on the entire album was a tremendous example of his growth as a musician. I was happy he had come out of his shell.

I was intrigued by the infusion of a country music tinge in these new songs, abetted by session work from guitarist Clarence White. I had known Clarence from the Ash Grove, when he performed with his family, The Kentucky Colonels. Susie, his wife, had also recently had a child, Michelle. The addition of Clarence's guitar playing to Chris' songs added depth and character.

This album gave me faith that the band could survive without Gene. David's harmonies stood out. The songwriting was fresh and had vitality to it, and pointed to new directions, although I thought 'Mind Gardens,' with its borrowed Shakespearean line, was a bit pretentious. 'Everybody's Been Burned' was superior. Jim and the lads seemed to have found their groove.

Gary Usher, their new producer, worked quickly and imaginatively. Younger than Allen Stanton, he was a great match for Jim's creative experimentation in the studio. Hugh Masekela played trumpet on 'So You Want To Be A Rock 'N' Roll Star' and he was managed by a man named Larry Spector, whom David had befriended. Jim had high expectations for this song. He hoped it would bring the group back to the charts with a number one hit.

Larry Spector was courting David and the Byrds. One of Larry's overtures was an expensive meal at Ernie's in San Francisco with me, Jim, Chris and his new girlfriend Anya. The restaurant had been featured in Alfred Hitchcock's *Vertigo*. Jim did enjoy fine dining experiences and gourmet meals. I'll always think of Chris shifting uncomfortably in his seat, amidst the red plush walls and smug waiters, as I gently cut my steak, listening to Larry's forecasts of fame and money.

I remember a visit to Spector's Rodeo Drive office, where I noticed that he had a huge cement planter encircled with sculpted angels. I admired it, and told him so. A year or so later, he delivered it to us, when we moved into our new home on Alomar Drive in Sherman Oaks. He was a stocky, short, bald-headed man, overly friendly, who later turned out to be rather deceptive and devious.

Jim's kid brother, Brian, came to visit us from Chicago during his Christmas break from high school. He was mystified and intrigued by the world his older brother inhabited.

One of Larry Spector's early suggestions was that Jim and I should get married. He told Jim it would improve his tax deductions: mother and child, dependents. Jim reiterated Spector's suggestion, and I happily accepted. It came as a complete surprise. I was somewhat relieved that our son would legally have Jim's name. Not only this, but also I loved him dearly. I thought we would grow old together.

Chris Hillman, hearing of our plans, offered us a ring that he intended to give to a friend. It was a beautiful gold band with delicate flowers engraved around it. Jim presented it. Chris would later say with a smile to me, "You married the wrong Byrd."

On one afternoon in late December, before the year was up, the Hippards, Jim, Brian, baby James and I boarded a flight to Las Vegas. On the ground, we rented a car, and after driving around in search of a chapel that was open, we got married. Cheryl waited in the car with the baby, while Bob and Brian were witnesses. It was a quick, unconventional wedding, and we didn't even enter a casino. Although Jim was good at playing cards and doing card tricks, he didn't believe in gambling. "The house always wins," he said. Afterwards, we had lunch at a nearby diner, and then promptly flew back to Los Angeles. I called my mother to tell her the good news. Brian flew back to snowy Chicago but he didn't want to leave LA.

1967 - Change Is Now

Chris and Gene jamming, 1967

I used to trim Jim's hair. Chris wanted me to cut his hair as well. On the appointed day, he was late. Jim kept phoning him, and there was no answer. We figured he was on his way via his motorcycle, and had made a pit stop. Suddenly, across the hill, we saw a huge plume of black smoke and flames erupting from the forest below. With his newly acquired video camera, Jim began filming the fire.

We heard fire trucks, which had difficulty getting into those narrow canyon roads. Chris showed up at our house with the front of his hair and eyebrows singed, bewildered. He said he had been working on his motorbike in the garage, when the pilot flame from the water heater combusted with the fumes of the gasoline, and everything erupted into flame.

His house was built entirely of glass and wood and it burned quickly. Chris had managed to rescue Anya and his cat. The house burned down to the ground. There was nothing left but a bowie knife and a Mexican stone mataté, used for grinding corn. It was tragic and highly disturbing, and I felt terrible for Chris.

Chris and Anya stayed at Michael's house, while Michael stayed with a girlfriend. Michael had moved into our former house on Woodrow Wilson Drive. One day Chris and Anya came over to our Yucca Trail home, commenting, "We're going to have to find a motel... we're headed to the drug store to buy lice medication. Mike's bed is full of crabs!" We all laughed.

Chris tried to claim his insurance money for the home fire coverage, but the company resisted at first, since Jim had sold the videotape of the burning house to the local TV news station, and the insurance company thought the fire had been premeditated. Chris eventually straightened it out, and moved to a new house in Topanga Canyon with Anya.

A few weeks later, a telegram arrived from Indonesia. It read: *Name baby son Patrick [stop].* I was fascinated by this process. Patrick seemed like a good name that suited our son. Jim liked the name so well that he decided to ask Bapak for a name change for himself: this is the well-known moment when Jim became Roger, and I became Ianthe, based on the letters that vibrated well in the universe for each of us. Jim had written some names that had sci-fi or two-way radio references that began with the letter R: Ralph, Raymond, Raul, Ram-Jet and Roger. He was quick to decide on Roger. It was used in every sci-fi or military movie: "Roger, over and out," Roger being affirmative.

Someone in Subud recommended Ianthe for me... a Greek name meaning wild, violet flower. It was far better than the other choices of Irma, Inez, or Irene. Irene was Jim's grandmother's name. He loved her dearly, but felt Ianthe suited me. Ianthe was a difficult name to carry. It was always misspelled or mispronounced. I was still Dolores to Jim Dickson and Eddie Tickner and of course to my mother.

Roger and I received our new names confirmed on paper a few weeks later. Jim legally changed his name to Roger, and our son's name to Patrick, appearing with our son at City Hall to complete the process.

The new single, 'So You Want to Be A Rock 'N' Roll Star' emerged on the airwaves. It was exciting to hear the Latin beat and

Hugh's trumpet playing infused with the Byrds' harmonies. It climbed the charts and seemed on its way to becoming a hit.

Roger continued a busy schedule of performances with the Byrds. With an irregular rehearsal schedule, the band became very inconsistent onstage. They performed in San Francisco, at the Fillmore, playing on the same bill as very strong groups like Cream, Big Brother & the Holding Company and Jefferson Airplane. Sadly, the Byrds' music was not as powerful live as it sounded on this new record, and the vocals sometimes suffered from Gene's absence. I never said anything to Roger about this, because I was trying to remain positive.

On one occasion backstage at the Fillmore, Mike Bloomfield came into the dressing room, happily greeting us. "Hey Jimmy!" he said, having known Roger from Chicago Old Towne days. Roger calmly said, "My name is Roger now. I'd like for you to call me Roger."

Mike looked incredulous. "Your name's not Roger. It's Jimmy. Jimmy McGuinn. It'll always be Jimmy McGuinn!" Roger was taken aback and looked pale. Everyone got quiet. Mike stormed out of the room and nothing more was said.

We didn't stay long at the Yucca Trail house. Maybe it was the fire in the Canyon. Roger felt spooked. It could have also been the draftiness and the steep stairs leading to the living room. I had slipped once holding Patrick, and now he was beginning to crawl. We went searching in the Porsche to find a new place, and we located a new home on Sycamore Trail, in the Hollywood Hills south of Burbank. There was a 'For Rent' sign out front. We knocked on the door of the adjacent home as instructed, and a distinguished older man answered. He was welcoming and invited us in.

The home was partly furnished, since the man who lived there was moving in with his neighbor who, it turned out, was his boyfriend. Roger liked the way the house was decorated. There was a high ceiling with large Impressionist prints hanging on the wall, and an open living room with lots of windows. Roger decided it was the perfect spot to place a new billiard table he wanted to purchase, which he later did. We moved in that summer.

Tickson management had been pursuing movie soundtrack work for the Byrds, and an early result of this endeavor was the lighthearted song 'Don't Make Waves.' Jim and Chris procrastinated over the songwriting, but managed to whip up the song in one afternoon. It was recorded soon after. Crosby had disdain for any 'selling out' and he was very unenthusiastic during the project.

That June, the Byrds geared up to play the Monterey International Pop Festival. This was to be a major event in the music scene, organized by John Phillips of the Mamas and Papas and producer Lou Adler. All of the best groups were to perform. Tickson music had booked the Byrds on the bill. Derek Taylor attended with his wife, and served as the festival's publicist.

David Crosby had given Roger a sample of some brownies laced with marijuana. "For the trip to the gig," he advised Roger. We packed the mustard 9-11S with our clothes and a wicker laundry basket that held eight month old Patrick. There were no seat belts or car seats in those days. We decided to make the trip in the evening.

We broke into the bag containing the brownies, and listened to the latest Beatles tape, as we sped along the winding Pacific Coast Highway. Patrick was sound asleep in the basket on the jump seat in back.

It must have been forty-five minutes into the drive when Roger started rubbing his chest and taking deep breaths. "I'm feeling weird... I can't feel my hands."

"Are you OK? What's the matter?"

"Oh my God! Did you see that?"

"See what?"

"It was something running alongside the car."

"Roger, I didn't see anything, you're seeing things. I think it's the pot."

"Yeah, you're probably right. It must be the brownies. I wonder what's really in them." He released his foot off the gas pedal and the car slowed down.

"I don't think I can keep driving, things keep coming at me."

In the meantime, I didn't feel any effects. I hadn't eaten a whole bar.

"Roger, Roger!" I shouted. "You better pull over. I'll drive."

He was so hyper by then, he hugged the car at the nearest spot alongside the road. We exchanged seats. I got into the driver's side, put the car into gear and took off. The car was fast with five speeds and a speedometer that went to 160 mph. I loved it. With all the turns, one had to keep changing gears when the car slowed down or else you would lug the engine. I wasn't thirty minutes into the drive when suddenly the cars coming at us appeared to have their lights on bright, almost blinding me. I felt I was in a tunnel. The car was taking over, it wasn't me driving.

"Roger, I don't think I can do this. You'd better drive... are you able to drive now?"

"Yeah, Ianthe. Just pull over as best you can. I told you this pot was strong... you wouldn't believe me."

We arrived in Monterey weary and eager to tell Chris and Anya about our wild ride with David's potent brownies. It turned out the brownies were made with hash, and not pot. We laughed about this episode, although the drive itself had been a bit terrifying.

I was not prepared for the cold weather up north. I didn't bring any cold weather garments for me or the baby. On one windy, cold afternoon, Michael was wearing a knit cap, and I was holding Patrick. I asked him if I could borrow the cap for Patrick. "No!" he said. "I love this hat." I was shocked and angry that he had no consideration for the baby, and I was angry at myself for not bringing something that would cover Patrick's little bald head. Roger went out to the vendors' area, to see if we could find some kind of cap for the baby, which thankfully we did. There were other items available for sale: posters, incense and, remarkably, an inventor named Moog had an information booth about his new synthesizer keyboard for sale. Of course, Roger was fascinated. He promptly negotiated a purchase for one of the prototypes with Moog himself, right at the booth.

There were hospitality tents available for the musicians and press to co-mingle. It was here where I met Grace Slick and Janis Joplin. Janis was very warm and kind. Maybe there's something about a mother with a child that is endearing to other women. She had a crooked but genuine smile. I couldn't understand why people from her hometown supposedly didn't like her. She was gregarious and sweet.

Grace Slick, the alluring, intelligent singer for Jefferson Airplane, was originally from back east. Roger and I went to lunch at a fancy health food restaurant, typical of northern California, with her, band-mate Paul Kantner, and Patrick. Patrick started fussing, so I nursed him, there at the table. Paul and Grace were surprised at this open display of breastfeeding. She had a little bit of hardcore 'one of the guys' attitude to be a musician. Like Janis, she wasn't afraid to express her opinion or put someone down. She was not reserved or cautious in anything she said. Nevertheless, the sight of my bare breast was enough to startle her.

There were long tables in the hospitality tents. I began to notice the extravagance of the new, hip showbiz fashion – The Who had long velvet coats, and Jimi Hendrix looked equally exotic. The Byrds appeared tame by comparison.

Cass Elliott was very friendly and welcoming as usual, admiring Patrick, holding and bouncing him for a while. The Byrds would perform in the early evening. I sat out in front with Anya and Patrick to see the show.

When I saw how nervous they all seemed, among these larger, more polished acts about to take the same stage, I sighed with concern and hoped for the best. They opened with 'Renaissance Fair.' There were some potentially bright moments, marred by their nerves, which increased the tempo of many songs, as when they played 'So You Want To Be A Rock 'N' Roll Star' with Hugh Masekela on stage. I was happy to hear that they were going to play an old favorite, 'He Was A Friend of Mine,' until I heard David launch into his anti-government spiel. I could see the impassive expression on Roger's face, and the look of irritation on Chris' face. Michael sat in the back, behind the drums, chewing gum.

It was embarrassing how frequently David spoke to the audience, as if he was the master of ceremonies, and his introduction to 'Hey Joe' seemed petty and pointless. I felt that the impression they made at this show was upstaged by newer, bolder, musically tighter acts. I overheard a male audience member behind me make a comment that I know would've hurt Roger: "The Byrds are passé."

After their set, I went to the hospitality tent to find Roger looking miserable and tired. Sometimes Roger would ask, "How did that sound?" He didn't tonight. Chris was stomping around, smoking a cigarette. Crosby was off socializing with the Buffalo Springfield. He was going to rehearse with them, volunteering to perform as well, since one of their members hadn't shown up. At that point, Chris and Roger felt that David had sabotaged the Byrds' performance. It hadn't been the first time, *The Ed Sullivan Show* being the prime example. I think David must've thought somehow he was doing the right thing, but clearly, he was making decisions that put the band in an unflattering light.

Roger was so stressed out after the Byrds' performance that I couldn't enjoy the rest of the night. I don't remember seeing any of the following acts that evening. It was getting late, and Patrick was tired. We sped off to the motel and went to sleep.

On the drive back home to LA, Roger was quiet. I knew he was angry and uncertain what to do. We got home and tried to forget this northern California weekend. "The coldest winter I spent was a summer in San Francisco," Mark Twain is purported to have said.

I cut my hair short, because having a child and wearing long hair was becoming too much to manage on a daily basis. Roger was upset when he came home and saw my new haircut. He thought it looked boyish, and wanted me to let it grow.

The unrest was spreading: by the end of the month Eddie Tickner and Jim Dickson were fired by Roger and the Byrds. This was initiated by Crosby and Larry Spector. Roger had somehow been convinced that Spector, who also managed the Monkees, might bring the same success to the Byrds. "He even picked up my laundry, man!" David said of Spector, as if Tickner/Dickson had ignored the band's basic needs. David had written 'Lady Friend,' a beautiful song that created egotistical conflict in its wake, and it became their next single after the Monterey Pop Festival.

The Byrds' Greatest Hits album would soon be released to positive reviews and enthusiastic record sales. This hit would fill the coffers and bide time for production of the next album.

Eddie and Rita Tickner had been very honest in their dealings with the Byrds, and even though Jim Dickson had distanced himself from the band, he still had a deep emotional connection to David, Roger, Chris, Gene and Michael. The sudden firing of Tickson Management created turmoil, as complex as a divorce.

Roger loved experimenting with cameras, 1967

Around this time, the band performed 'Lady Friend' on *The Tonight Show*, and I watched it at home. I was disappointed that Johnny Carson was not hosting that night, substituted by the deadpan comedian Bob Newhart. This performance was shortly after the Monterey Pop Festival, and the tension between the band members onstage was palpable.

A few days later, Roger and the Byrds had some New York gigs and Roger took me along. My younger brother, Larry, seventeen years old, was enlisted to be our summer baby sitter while he visited Los Angeles along with my mother. They would care for Patrick at the Sycamore Trail house while we went to New York.

We were back in New York, like old times, staying at the Gramercy Park Hotel. This trip was eventful, and packed with excitement. Jacques Levy and his very sexy female companion introduced themselves to Roger after one of the Byrds' shows, and invited us to an off-Broadway performance of *Oh! Calcutta!*, a play Jacques was directing. The curious thing about the show was that the actors were totally nude onstage. This was a new precedent, and it was slightly uncomfortable to watch bouncing boobs and organs. We turned to look at each other when one of the well-endowed actresses danced freely across, as we sat in the first few rows, our eyes wide open.

After the show, we had dinner with Jacques, who had graduated college as a clinical psychologist. This seemed to give him more credibility when he asked Roger if he was interested in writing a musical with him. The story involved a young man named Gene Tryp, who he'd based on Ibsen's tale, *Peer Gynt*. Roger seemed enthusiastic, and invited Jacques to Los Angeles to collaborate on writing songs. This would happen when they both had time available.

Back in LA, Roger and I were invited to dinner at Michael Nesmith's home. Larry Spector also managed Nesmith, a member of the Monkees. Roger and I drove up to the Hollywood Hills home where Michael lived with his wife. There was a high iron gate with a security intercom and camera. I could tell Roger was mildly envious as we passed through. We were greeted by a large German Shepherd, and then met Michael's wife, Phyliss, who was friendly and sweet. She prepared Cornish game hens with vegetables for dinner.

During dinner they commented about their dog biting Larry Spector on the hand when he had come to deliver their laundry. We all laughed at this curious character. After dinner, Michael showed off his new in-home recording studio, lavishly appointed with the latest audio equipment. By this time, Roger was green with envy, and I think Michael knew it. However, it was interesting to share notes with people who knew Larry, because he seemed too good to be true.

Inspired by Michael's domestic life and accumulation of toys, Roger and I decided to buy a house. Rita Tickner had been setting aside money in Roger's account for this purpose. My brother Marcus had been scouting a new home for himself, and had located a charming ranch house, too small for his family, on Alomar Drive, atop the hills of the San Fernando Valley suburb Sherman Oaks. The house overlooked the valley below and had two avocado trees in the backyard, which seemed to ascend boundlessly into the hills. Roger liked the large living room, which had space for his billiard table. There was a hill above the driveway, leading down to the property, where Roger wanted to place a security camera.

Larry Spector, now in charge of Roger's financial affairs, set about purchasing the house for us. What I didn't know was that during this process, Larry had me sign a quick claim deed on the house. This meant that the house was solely Roger's property. It was a well-guarded secret between him and Larry that I had no legal right as co-owner of the house. Years later, this would be devastating news to me.

We didn't have much furniture, coming from the furnished rental on Sycamore Trail. The only thing we owned, that had to be moved, was the billiard table. I loved this new house: it had high open-beam ceilings, a dual stone fireplace, two bedrooms, two bathrooms, all-wood floors and windows facing west that offered tremendous views of open sky and hills. There were sycamore trees in the front yard where we put up a hammock and a tree swing. We would entertain an array of characters in this wonderful house.

Late one night, shortly after we'd moved in, I awoke and found the bed empty. Where was Roger? I quietly walked about the house. Everything was still, and the bright moonlight came flooding through the windows. I walked the length of the house and peered out the kitchen window, facing the driveway. I strained to see: I thought I saw a white horse coming down the hill! As the figure approached, it appeared to be a centaur, but it was actually Roger, quite naked, gracefully walking in the moonlight, his body thin and beautiful.

I called out to him, "Roger, what are you doing?"

He calmly replied, "It's such a beautiful night. I just had to come outside and feel the air on my body."

He came inside and held me, and we went back to bed. The idea of Roger as an apparition gave me a new perspective on his sensual nature.

Soon after, Roger, Chris, David and Michael took a trip to Hawaii, for a gig and a songwriting retreat for their upcoming record. I was happy to stay in LA and get our new home in order. Spector and I went furniture shopping in Beverly Hills to accessorize the billiard room with elevated director's chairs. Marcus and I went to a less-expensive furniture store, White Front, to buy a hound's-tooth patterned sofa and a black leather reclining chair for Roger. I found some wonderful pieces of wood furniture at former-prop-house shops on Ventura Boulevard in the Valley.

I went to have lunch with Karen one afternoon. She seemed in good spirits, and I realized how long it had been since we'd spent time together. She now worked at the Ash Grove as a waitress. We shared war stories. Then she told me she'd started seeing a young songwriter, Tim Buckley. The affair didn't last long, since Tim was married.

Back from Hawaii, with stories to tell about his time off with the boys, Roger used the mantle on the fireplace to position his growing collection of TV sets, one of which was for the security camera. The Moog Synthesizer was soon delivered and installed. Roger was delighted by the complexity of this instrument, which brought many strange sounds into the house. News spread that Roger owned one of these expensive instruments, and curious visitors, including Jane Fonda and Roger Vadim, stopped by for a demonstration.

The Moog was put to use during the recording sessions for *The Notorious Byrd Brothers*. Roger was very fond of Carole King's songwriting; she was a Brill Building alumnus and had written songs for many recording artists, including the Monkees. I remember hearing her demo tape for 'Goin' Back,' when Roger brought it home to listen one day. The song itself didn't strike me as having any power or edge, but I'd learned my lesson not to say anything about music to Roger. He was pretty intent on recording the song with the Byrds, along with 'Wasn't Born to Follow.'

I had heard that the recording sessions were not going well with David in the studio. The main issue was a song called 'Triad,' which depicted a ménage à trois, with David as the center love interest. Roger thought the song was in poor taste, as well as being in conflict with our Subud beliefs, and that it would further cultivate David's radical counter-culture image that was on full display at the Monterey Pop Festival. Conversely, David hated 'Goin' Back' and thought that the lyrics were inane.

We paid a visit to David in Benedict Canyon one afternoon. Things were still cordial among us. David passed a joint around and went on diatribes about songs-in-progress on the album, in full opposition of 'Goin' Back.' He was surreptitiously exerting his desire to be a leader in the band, wanting to have the final word. Patrick was a toddler now, and saw a blue enamel tea kettle that David had in his kitchen for boiling water. Patrick pointed to the teapot, having recently become fascinated by them, and said, "Mine?" David poured the water out and said, "Here, you can play with it," handing it to Patrick. Roger and David continued discussing the production of the record.

As our visit came to an end, Patrick held the teapot and started walking out the door. David said, "I don't think so, little man." He stooped over and took the teapot from Patrick's grasp. Patrick immediately started wailing, "Mine!" "No," David said, "It's *mine*," in no uncertain terms. David was not willing to relinquish the tea kettle. It was another reflection of David's personality: not willing to give in, even to a toddler. I scooped up Patrick as he began crying, "Mine!" His hand was in his mouth and his finger was pointing at the blue teapot that David was placing on the stove. "No Patrick, we're going home. You've got other teapots at the house," I reassured.

Some days later, Roger returned in his Porsche one afternoon, after hanging out with Chris. He came in and sat down in the dining room.

"We just fired David," he said.

I couldn't believe my ears. "What? Why?" I asked.

"Chris and I have had just about enough of his egomania. He doesn't want to be in the group anyway." I felt Roger had decided to take control of the group, and I could see that he was joyous. He even laughed, "I don't think he expected it. He thought we were coming to jam with him. I felt sort of guilty, but we had decided to do it, and we went through with it."

David was a thorn in everyone's side, including young Patrick. It seemed an inevitable decision for them to make. David had steadily grown into a tyrant, since the early days when Roger had playfully scribbled the Hitler mustache on the *Turn! Turn! Turn!* record sleeve. Now Roger had liberated the musical future of the Byrds. It would be up to him and Chris to complete the album. The single 'Goin' Back' was released, and tour dates loomed. How would the gap in the band's lineup be filled?

Remarkably, Gene Clark was briefly enlisted. I found out when he came by the house to rehearse vocals with Roger one afternoon. Gene sat in one of our rattan chairs in the living room, as I was working in the kitchen. I heard constant squeaking of the rattan in the next room. I looked over to see Gene squirming in the chair, laughing nervously, chain smoking, lighting one cigarette after the next.

Gene seemed uncomfortable in his own skin as he worked on songs with Roger. Their reunion didn't last more than a few weeks, but they did play some shows in the Midwest together, and appeared on the *Smothers Brothers* TV show, lip-synching 'Goin' Back.'

When I heard that Michael Clarke had dropped out of the band, I thought the entire venture was unraveling before our eyes. "Now what?" I thought. How could Roger keep the band afloat after such major blows?

Larry Spector and his lawyer came through with a renegotiated contract with Columbia and the two remaining Byrds, producing a windfall of cash. When Tickson discovered this, they filed a lawsuit. Roger was now in the middle of a tricky legal affair, yet he had to maintain touring and album production, while being a father and a husband.

Chris had taken his share of the renegotiated advance and purchased land in New Mexico. It would now fall upon Roger to be the sole compensator to the former band members. He couldn't quit the Byrds even if he had wanted to. I felt terrible that all of the responsibility fell on his shoulders. Roger's ultimate words were, as always, "I trust it will work out alright," which became his mantra through these trying times. He decided to buy a black 1968 Cadillac El Dorado to help ease the pain.

Unbeknownst to Roger, Larry Spector and his lawyer generously compensated themselves with the cream of the cash from the renegotiated contract before distribution. This siphoning went undiscovered for months. Larry put on a good front, and remained the Byrds manager for some time to come.

The Notorious Byrd Brothers was completed by the end of the year, amidst a busy tour schedule of live performances. Chris had enlisted his shy and quiet cousin, Kevin Kelley, to play drums on these dates. They continued through the end of the year as a trio. It was ironic that with the lushness of *Notorious*, the Byrds had to set forth as a minimalist rock trio.

Roger let my younger brother Larry tag along with him when the Byrds had a weeklong engagement at the Whisky A Go Go. Larry couldn't have been happier to see this side of the music business, having aspirations himself. Larry was also a tremendous help taking care of baby Patrick. I was relieved Christmas was ahead and we could take a break. We decorated a large Christmas tree for our son. My mother came to stay, cooking up a batch of pork and beef tamales, which became one of Roger's favorite dishes. Roger seemed to find comfort in our domestic life as the year ended.

1968 –Tromping Muddy Pastures with Rolling Stones

Roger and Chris backstage at the Fillmore in San Francisco, 1968

Roger's family moved to California. They'd been increasingly curious about the life Roger was leading and wanted to get away from the bitter winters of Chicago. They eventually settled in the same neighborhood we had previously lived in, off Barham Boulevard, south of Burbank on Primera Avenue. I was happy that Patrick would get to know his grandparents, and they were very loving and welcoming. Dorothy and Jim Sr. set about furnishing and painting their new house. I will always associate the smell of fresh oil-based paint with them, because Roger's father was also an amateur portrait artist.

Their younger son, Brian, was living with them too. Dorothy did not recognize Roger in his Cadillac as we drove by one afternoon. Roger said, "Cadillacs make their owners invisible to the outside world." The McGuinns' home had a sweeping view of Burbank below. They had converted their garage into a dining room, and the first time that Roger and I came over for dinner, Roger asked, "Well, what do you think of your new dining room, Brian?" Brian replied, "VAAROOM." The paint couldn't hide the years of car smell that permeated the room. The family had a unique sense of humor.

1968 was the year Roger and I grew closer to Chris and Anya. We spent time visiting them in their Topanga Canyon home. Roger and Chris depended on each other now, as the sole original members of the group. Anya and I spent many hours together when traveling to shows. Once she told me about several angry outbursts that Chris had had on the ranch, which frightened her, since she was alone in the canyon wilderness. I saw an emerging dark side of Chris, but I tried not to dwell on it. The four of us saw many excellent movies that reflected the zeitgeist of the late 60s, such as Kubrick's *2001: A Space Odyssey*, Antonioni's *Blow Up*, and Zeffirelli's *Romeo and Juliet*.

Larry Spector invited Chris, Roger, Anya and me to dinner at his thirty-first floor apartment off the Sunset Strip. We all drove in Roger's Cadillac. It was a smooth, quiet ride. When we arrived at the apartment, we waited at the door for some time after Roger rang the bell. He rang it again. Finally, a young man unlocked the door. He was the assistant who helped Larry in his office. He was about twenty years old, thin build, an all-American kid, whose hair was mussed up on one side, as if he'd been asleep.

He greeted us cordially, if somewhat nervously. Larry Spector came out, a little flustered, wearing his usual white shirt and khakis.

We sat down to drinks as a black maid announced that dinner would soon be ready. Dinner was uneventful. On the elevator down the thirty-one floors, Chris and Roger burst into laughter, having held it back for some time apparently. Anya and I looked at each other, wondering what the joke was all about.

It wasn't until we were driving in the car that Roger and Chris made it clear to us that the delay was because Larry had just been having sex with his young charge, the lad who answered the door. I couldn't believe my ears – Larry a homosexual? It made sense, but I was surprised that the whole incident went over my head completely.

The Notorious Byrd Brothers was released, and I remember listening and dancing to this record with much enjoyment, holding Patrick in my arms. The Byrds had reached a new level of achievement through experimentation amid the turmoil that had ensued. Roger and Chris had become a great songwriting team. Some of my favorite songs are 'Draft Morning,' 'Change is Now,' and 'Wasn't Born to Follow.' A couple of songs on this album had country-flavored nuances in certain sections, buoyed by Clarence White's energy again.

One day, Roger and Chris came over to our Alomar home with a brown haired, lean and handsome young man in tow. "This is Gram," Roger said, "My wife, Ianthe." Gram lazily extended his hand. "Why, this is a pleasure, Miss Ianthe," he said with a southern drawl. Gram was so utterly charming and sincere, it was arresting. I'd come across many characters since the Ash Grove, and there had not been anyone as smooth and gracious as Gram. I brought them cold beers as Roger threaded up a tape to play Gram, saying, "This is what we've been working on."

Gram charmed Roger, too, at least at first. One evening, we were all driving in the Cadillac with Gram, Chris and Anya, on our way to the Palomino Club in North Hollywood. It was an old-school honky tonk, where authentic country music could still be heard. Excited about our destination, Gram belted out, a cappella, Hank Williams' 'Your Cheatin' Heart,' Porter Wagner's 'Green, Green Grass of Home' and Willie Nelson's 'Crazy' as we drove. The rest of us joined in on the chorus. He spoke about the Grand Ole Opry, and how he'd always dreamed of performing there.

I looked over at Roger. He listened quietly as he drove the Cadillac. Gram's pure country background didn't seem to be the type of direction Roger wanted. *Notorious*, with its Moog experimentation and jazzy time signatures, was diametrically opposed to the hillbilly country sound that Gram embraced. Chris was seduced by Gram's fresh enthusiasm, and eventually convinced Roger to venture in that direction. Gram's kind and generous spirit, encouraging me to sing along, was a far cry from David Crosby's continual shushing. Chris called me 'Miss Mousy,' because of my high, harmonizing voice.

125

I was happy that they'd found someone so charismatic to add to their lineup. He was going to play piano on their upcoming tour dates, but later switched to guitar. Roger subsequently brought home a rehearsal tape of songs they were working on for the upcoming album. I was surprised when I heard Gram singing most of them, and that they were all country songs. Earlier Roger had talked about a different kind of project that encapsulated many forms of American music. Now, with Gram, the project focused on country music alone. Roger took a back seat, and seemed resigned. Gary Usher also encouraged the new direction that the album was taking.

The Columbia contract stipulated that the band had to produce two records per year. In hindsight, I'm amazed at the group's productivity and the high volume of creative output during the Sixties, each album with its own texture and identity, introducing new musical genres. The Byrds were always so far ahead of the current trend. But audiences were not prepared for the changes ahead. That's why I feel the record sales suffered.

They ventured to Nashville to record the new album. I was excited, because the songs were good. To a degree, I'd grown up listening to Hank Williams and Patsy Cline in Tucson, so I had nothing against country music. The band timed the recording to take place along with a performance at the Grand Ole Opry on the Ides of March. The venue was incongruous with the Byrds' prior repertoire, but Gram got his wish.

When Roger returned from Nashville, he was upset. Just as David Crosby had sabotaged *The Ed Sullivan Show*, Gram angered the audience and the venue management when he deviated from the Opry set. The recording for the album went well, but Roger seemed road weary after the experience of working with Gram. "The audience didn't like us," Roger said. "We were booed. They weren't ready for us. On top of it, one of the radio interviews went terribly bad. The DJ was downright rude."

Shortly after the band had been in Tennessee, Martin Luther King, Jr. was assassinated in Memphis. Roger and I heard about it on the evening news, on three TVs at once. Realizing that the rest of the US was troubled, we feared that the Civil Rights movement would take a violent turn. What followed were riots all over American cities, and it marked the end of the Sixties peace movement. Robert F. Kennedy pleaded on television to honor King's death with non-violent response.

The Dylan song 'You Ain't Goin' Nowhere' was already on the airwaves in America. This was the song that Roger had tried to get played on the radio in Nashville. I loved Roger's interpretation of this song, and was upset to think of some DJ in Nashville not "getting it." Once again, the Byrds were ahead of their time, and the audience didn't exist for their new music.

Despite the Opry fiasco, the local LA gigs with Gram went well, and the music had a new energy and vitality. Chris Hillman seemed in his element, and was beguiled by Gram's spirit. The music was ready, and a European tour was quickly organized.

During this time, Chris and Roger had become like brothers, sticking together through some very tough times, playfully nicknaming themselves 'Wally and Beave' after the Fifties TV show, *Leave it to Beaver*. One such adventure was a weekend camping trip we took: Roger, Patrick and I drove in the Cadillac, following Anya, Chris and their bloodhound into the mountains of Big Bear. It was a long, bumpy ride on dirt roads once we got off the main highway.

Roger, having formerly been a Boy Scout, put up tents with Chris. Roger had bought a huge turquoise tent for the occasion. I tied little bells onto Patrick's shoelaces, so he could be heard wherever he went. The terrain was dusty, full of pine trees. Chris ignited a campfire. Roger had brought along a portable, battery-powered black and white television, which he pulled out and placed by the campfire. "We're supposed to be camping in the middle of nowhere, Roger," Chris dryly said. We all laughed and had a good time, into the night. We peacefully slept in our tents.

The next morning, we awoke to discover Chris' hound had chased a porcupine and its mouth and snout were full of quills. Poor animal! Chris wanted to get the dog to the nearest veterinarian he could find. They rapidly broke their camp and left, leaving Roger, Patrick and me. Roger didn't seem comfortable without Chris there. "We should probably leave and get breakfast in the nearest town." We broke camp, and returned to civilization. That was the only time we ever went camping.

Anya and I were going on the European tour with the band; I packed some cool weather clothes. My mom would take care of

Patrick in Tucson while we were gone for two weeks. We boarded the jet for the East Coast and stayed there a few days. Gram had a friend in Boston he wanted us all to meet, Jet Thomas.

As we were driving up to see Jet, who was a Harvard professor of theology, Gram said to me, "I want to be like Hank Williams." I didn't know if he meant he wanted to die young, or he wanted to follow in Hank's musical footsteps.

Jet, a southern Baptist minister, invited us into a small apartment on the Harvard campus. Chris, Anya, Gram, Roger and I came in and sat down. Jet had some fresh strawberries, the first of the season, and he set a bowl on a coffee table, and offered us the best marijuana to go along with them. It was an afternoon full of music. Gram, Chris and Roger took turns playing the acoustic guitar and we all sang old hymns and folk songs together. Jet's southern hospitality carried us through the rest of our trip.

We flew from New York to London. Doug Dillard joined the Byrds on this tour, playing banjo. This was my first time in London. I loved it. Anya, being a British native, shepherded us about. I was enchanted by the city's atmosphere: narrow streets, glistening after the rainfall, cool air, black taxis and of course, the mod dress shops and boutiques. Anya took us to a restaurant for lunch. The King of Jordan was eating there with his bodyguard. I wouldn't have known it was the King of Jordan if Anya hadn't pointed him out. I remember ordering some delicious fish and chips in a pub, wrapped in newsprint.

We stayed at the Mayfair Hotel, a resplendent place with stern but polite doormen and cheery bellhops. Gram was clearly feeling heady about his entry into the life of successful, touring musicians. While at the hotel, Roger and Gram composed a song, 'Drug Store Truck Drivin' Man,' in our room one evening. It was about the Nashville DJ who'd mistreated them just a couple of months before. I enjoyed the harmonies and Gram and Roger worked well together.

The Byrds performed two shows at the Roundhouse that were packed. I recall Paul McCartney being in attendance. The audience was taken aback by the new country music material. Of course, they really wanted to hear the older songs from 1965. But Gram's presence captivated the audience, even if the music didn't.

We flew to Rome the next day. Mine was the only bag that the customs officials inspected. Luckily, I never carried anything incriminating. The drivers and traffic in Rome were terrible – people didn't stop for red lights. The city, however, was gorgeous. Chris, Anya, Roger and I went sightseeing to the Trevi Fountain and the Coliseum. Anya knew her way around Rome quite well. She was a perfect tour guide, and refreshed our memories of ancient cultural history. We attempted to enter the Sistine Chapel, but Anya and I both wore stylish miniskirts. The Church forbade the short skirts and we couldn't enter. We were all disappointed.

The Italian food was delicious. Any little restaurant along the street provided an array of simple and beautiful cuisine. We all had a memorable lunch: I had linguine Alfredo and Roger ordered his veal piccata. The pizzas were personal size, smaller than the American style.

We spent several days in Rome. Some evenings we played poker. Doug Dillard and Gram Parsons were poker aficionados. Of course, I remembered the rules from my poker-playing days with Nick Gerlach in Venice Beach. Dillard wore a fringe cowboy jacket that I don't think anyone in Italy had ever seen before. He got many stares.

The Byrds performed at the Piper Club in Rome. This show was also jam-packed, and the audience was greatly appreciative, especially of the new country music. Gram had a ball, seeing the enthusiastic response. Roger seemed confident that this edition of the Byrds could succeed, if he could keep Gram reined in.

Back in London, we were invited to Mick Jagger's apartment after the Byrds' performance at Middle Earth. Keith Richards and Mick came to the show, and were very supportive of the country-infused music. Mick had a huge, spherical violet iridescent globe in the center of the room, giving it a wizard's den vibe. We all stayed up well past four in the morning, having fun in Mick's apartment, talking, drinking and smoking. Mick was the consummate host.

Mick thought it would be an adventure to visit Stonehenge at dawn. Two Princess limousines pulled up to the apartment and the nine or ten of us piled in. It seemed like we drove for hours. I was in the car with Keith and his girlfriend, Chris, Anya and Roger.

The limos dropped us off far away from the monument, and Mick decided that we'd walk through a pasture to witness the sun rise. It turned out to be a wet, cloudy morning. We began the trek, Mick leading the group with his robe-like attire flowing in the breeze, as we tromped through a sopping, muddy pasture.

I saw the monument from far away, the circle of stones, and I reflected on the mystical strength of this location. Mick said that the Druids had placed the stones together. When we reached the monoliths, we all hugged them to brace ourselves, as the wind was quite cold. Keith passed around a bottle of whiskey. Chris and Anya pointed out the nearby road that led directly to the monument. We could have driven there and saved our cold, wet feet and shoes from the mud! We all laughed, sobered up by now.

Mick decided to remedy our chilled state. We were driven to Stratford on Avon, where Shakespeare had lived, to a teahouse, which was very quiet at that hour. The staff was pleasantly surprised to recognize Mick Jagger and his entourage. There was a big fireplace. We ordered hot tea and scones.

Mick sent someone to a nearby clothing store to pick up several pairs of dry white socks, each of us getting a pair. We all changed into the socks immediately and warmed ourselves by the fire with our hot tea. Mick once again displayed his generosity and hospitality: he was a true gentleman.

Keith and Gram had bonded during this visit. Gram had a puppy-like adoration for Keith, and seemed star struck. He'd only been a Byrd for a few months, and now here he was hanging out with the Rolling Stones. Roger quietly observed the proceedings. There had been some discussion and warnings about the Byrds' upcoming South African tour from Mick and Keith. Roger was not fazed by this.

We returned to Los Angeles, happy to see Patrick. We brought back some European presents for him. After a few days of jet lag recovery, Roger received the news that Gram could not record under the Columbia label, as he was still contracted to Lee Hazelwood, and it would take time to resolve his participation in the Byrds' new record. Roger promptly set about re-recording vocals that Gram had sung lead on in Nashville. It pushed Roger's vocal approach into a new style, and he seemed comfortable with that direction. There wasn't much anyone could do, and I think Roger was relieved that the project was back under his control.

By this time, my only interaction with the recording sessions was hearing the rough mix-down tapes that Roger came home with each night to evaluate. Having a young child at home was very demanding. The European trip had been a romantic return to our pre-child days. Our separate responsibilities of parenthood and career had returned.

The Byrds were booked at the LA Memorial Sports Arena for Robert Kennedy's presidential fund-raising campaign, a high profile event that took place on May 24. I remember hanging out backstage and seeing other, eclectic, entertainers. The British actor Peter Lawford, Robert Kennedy's brother-in-law, was rushing about as if he were the stage manager. The Byrds performed a few songs, among them 'He Was A Friend of Mine.'

After the show, the performers lined up backstage, and Bobby Kennedy passed through and cordially shook everyone's hand, thanking them as he left. I was standing next to Roger, and Bobby shook my hand. He was shorter than I had imagined, but his eyes were a deep blue, with a penetrating quality that I will never forget. He had an otherworldly goodness. Roger and I had faith in his skill to get America out of the Vietnam War and restore sanity to the discrimination and poverty that were tearing the United States apart.

Jacques Levy came to LA in June to begin the process of putting a project together with Roger. He stayed at the Sportsman's Lodge on Ventura Boulevard in Studio City. Every afternoon he would show up at our house. Sometimes he'd have dinner with us, and then he and Roger would set to work on writing songs for the musical they had in mind, *Gene Tryp*. They took inspiration from the bank of TV sets Roger had placed on the mantle, getting random ideas from the various programs, volume always turned off. It was an innovative approach to writing songs.

One particular evening, I went to sleep early, but awoke to a commotion from the dining room, and went in to see what was happening. "Ianthe," Roger exclaimed nervously, "Bobby Kennedy's just been shot." I couldn't believe my ears, and the three of us stared numbly at the TV images. The Ambassador Hotel was the site of Kennedy's California acceptance speech. Someone had shot him after he left the podium. It was awful to think that Bobby might die from the gunshot wound. Roger and Jacques stayed glued to the television sets.

Saddened and still in disbelief, I returned to bed, praying that Bobby would survive. I kept envisioning the kindness and humanity in his eyes when I had met him in May. I cried as I fell asleep. The hopes we had placed in the Kennedy brothers were destroyed again. My heart went out to the Kennedy family; how would they survive yet another assault?

The next morning, my fears were confirmed when I awoke early and saw Roger and Jacques, still working by the TV sets. I looked into Roger's eyes. He looked saddened and said, "Bobby's gone."

It was with the loss of Robert Kennedy weighing heavily in their hearts that Jacques and Roger pursued their project. Some beautiful songs came out of their collective sorrow: 'Chestnut Mare,' 'Just a Season' and the ironic 'I Want to Grow Up (To Be a Politician).'

South Africa called. The Byrds were off to England shortly after the Kennedy tragedy before flying to Johannesburg. At the stopover in London, Gram saddled up to Keith Richards and the word was that South Africa was off limits to English performers. It would be career suicide. Roger had promised Mariam Makeba that he would see for himself the living conditions apartheid had created. He'd been told that the Byrds would play for integrated audiences, but, as it turned out, the promoter was unscrupulous, and had just told Roger and the Byrds' management what they wanted to hear.

Nonetheless, Gram abandoned the group the night before departure, and chose to stay in London with his new pals, Keith Richards and Mick Jagger. The Byrds' roadie, Carlos Bernal, was recruited to fill in on rhythm guitar, much to everyone's dismay. Roger called me from England to tell me of these events right before they flew to South Africa. I'll never forget how, in the face of adversity, Roger remained calm and said, "I trust it will work out alright." He was faithful to his professional commitments.

Larry Spector accompanied the Byrds in what turned out to be a disastrous tour. I did not hear from Roger during the ten-day period. I was expectantly waiting for word from him, considering how plagued the tour had become.

Roger walked into the house the morning of his return and said, "I think I'm having a nervous breakdown." He looked worn and thin, sleepless, his usually handsome face sallow and drawn. My heart sank when I saw how decimated he'd become in just a few short weeks. He collapsed into the chair and told me of the terrible conditions, deceptions, and death threats to the group. How African blacks had to walk on one side of the street and whites on the other. The service people were not allowed to speak to white people at all. Roger said that a simple radio interview where they expressed their beliefs may have caused the death threats the band received just prior to departing South Africa.

I was appalled at what he'd been through. After he had slept and had a meal, he played a tape he'd recorded during an interview with the fatigued band members, where Chris imitated a German accent, "Johannesburg reminds me so much of Germany," sounding like a Nazi SS officer. I could see how South African white culture would not understand Chris' dark sense of humor. I was relieved that they were home safely.

Roger had to find a new member to fill the vacancy that Gram's absence left. Chris felt that Clarence White would be the easiest to integrate into the band, since they all knew him. Roger agreed that having a skilled guitarist in the band was the best option. Clarence was recruited. His wife, Susie, and I became close friends. His daughter, Michelle, was very close in age to Patrick. Susie and I offered each other valuable support and understanding over the coming years.

One afternoon, Chris arrived at our house furious, enraged. Roger and I were just finishing lunch. Chris stormed in and said, "I just found out that Anya has been sleeping with Carlos." We were both shocked and taken aback.

Carlos, a well-built, handsome Mexican-American roadie with curly black hair, had been a part of the Byrds' road crew for about a year. I don't know how he and Anya got together; she'd never confided this clandestine affair with me. I knew she really liked Gram, who seemed the more likely seducer than Carlos did.

Roger and I sat quietly as Chris blew off steam, saying he was going to punch out Carlos. "If I get my hands on him...." he said, leaving the rest to the imagination. I'd never seen Chris so angry, his face red with fury. South Africa had frayed everyone's nerves, and Anya's betrayal was devastating to Chris.

Carlos and Anya, as it turned out, had run off to New Mexico together, to hide out. I never heard from her again, other than hearing that she later moved back to England. Once, in the past, she'd asked Roger, at the height of his business troubles with Larry Spector, if happiness might be measured in letting go of all of success' trappings, to just drop everything and be poor again.

"No!" Roger said, emphatically. This was telling, because I think Anya just decided to remove herself from the chaotic ride she'd been on as the wife of a Byrds member. I was sad that she ended on such bad terms with Chris. I heard about her death from cancer years later, and only thought of the good times we had shared together in London and Rome.

Clarence was a perfectionist, and soon convinced Roger and Chris to replace Kevin Kelley with a drummer he'd formerly worked with, Gene Parsons. Gene and Clarence came to the house once, to play billiards with Roger. This would become a familiar sight. Gene seemed innocuous, a burly mechanic, without the charm or good looks that Michael Clarke had, but his technical ability was an improvement. At a time when they needed it most, he helped the band's sound coalesce with his rhythmic consistency.

Shortly after Gene was added, the Byrds were scheduled to play at the Rose Bowl in Pasadena. It was an afternoon performance at a music festival, and Susie and I sat out front with the audience. The Byrds did a quick set. Clarence and Gene were smart additions to the band. The guitar playing wowed the audience, and the drums brought a full sound to the music. Finally, I thought, the group can regain some stability.

However, this was to be Chris' last show as a Byrd. On the ride home, Roger had been keeping a secret.

"Chris left the group today," he said, with a sense of exhaustion. "He just smashed his bass and walked out, after threatening Spector."

My heart sank. "What does this mean?" I asked Roger.

Roger answered calmly, "Do you know what this means? Chris has left the group. He took his advance money and bought that property in New Mexico. He's left me holding the bag. I have to reimburse all of the other members of the group, and all the affiliates of the group, and now I have to find a new bass player."

Things couldn't get any worse, I thought. I had a heavy heart, feeling that Chris had abandoned us. This breach of loyalty wounded Roger, and if he had been cool or distant before toward fellow band members, this experience cemented an emotional armor that made Roger even more detached.

I feared that every month would bring some new, tremendous challenge. Larry Spector found an able replacement on bass, John York, who'd played with Clarence before in The Gene Clark Group. Handsome, confident and intelligent, John seemed like a good replacement, yet I later discovered that he was unsure about the music and joining the Byrds.

A taping of a unique television show, *Playboy After Dark*, took place at the end of September. The new edition of the Byrds did blazing renditions of two Bob Dylan songs, 'You Ain't Goin' Nowhere' and 'This Wheel's on Fire.' I was struck by Hugh Hefner's harem of glamorous, sparsely dressed young women.

The apartment where taping took place was a penthouse in a high rise, next to The Trip, on Sunset Boulevard. I thought it was interesting that the guests were able to drink actual alcohol, which seemed non-standard for the time. Of course, cigarette smoking was acceptable, and people smoked quite a bit. I stood in the back, as the color TV cameras took up most of the floor space. I was glad the Byrds did a spot-on performance. Roger seemed satisfied that the new group could hold their own.

Around this time, Christian Marquand had asked Roger to write a song for his new movie, *Candy*. Roger was to collaborate with an established film composer, Dave Grusin. Dave was a friendly, well-dressed man who came to the house a few times to work with Roger. On one occasion we all went to dinner at a restaurant near the house, The Ruddy Duck.

While we ate dinner, Dave joked that if he couldn't continue a successful career as a film composer, his worst nightmare would be playing piano at a Holiday Inn lounge. Roger and I laughed. Dave was a very modest, kind fellow. The song 'Child of the Universe' was completed, recorded and placed onto the film's soundtrack. Roger enjoyed the experience.

Another collaborator that Roger worked with was a fellow Subud member, Joey Richards. He was an overweight young kid with a beautiful singing voice who was in awe of Roger, seeking advice about his own musical aspirations. He eventually became part of the chorus for the LA production of *Hair*. He and Roger composed a song, 'Bad Night at the Whiskey,' which would wind up on the *Dr. Byrds & Mr. Hyde* record. The song was a statement about the teenagers on the Sunset strip, and their growing, excessive use of LSD and other drugs.

Roger continued recording sessions with John York, Clarence, and Gene Parsons during the fall for this album, and sang on every track. It was a quick production with Bob Johnston. He was a full-blown Nashville producer who'd just worked on Dylan's last album, *Nashville Skyline*. Bob had produced several of Dylan's records and seemed to have an agenda with the Byrds. He thought he could return them to the charts, but the recordings I heard seemed derivative of past work. My feeling is that he thought Clarence, Gene and John were simply hired hands, and that there was no soul left in the band. It had gotten around in LA that David Crosby was saying, "McGuinn is beating a dead horse," behind Roger's back.

UCLA had an exhibit called the Kinetic Art Show. It was a science fair/innovation-driven arts expedition that radio telescope astronomer Eugene Epstein invited Roger and me to attend. We were to have dinner with him and meet his friend Carl Sagan and Sagan's wife, Linda. We met at a little bistro in Santa Monica.

Carl, Roger and Eugene enjoyed each other's company. They were like old friends who hadn't seen each other for years, even though they'd just met. Linda was very sweet and talkative, and tried to explain to me what neutrinos are. The Sagans were young and vital, full of ideas that were beyond the scope of average people. It was an enlightening and uncommon experience to spend time with them.

Carl was intrigued by Roger's use of space science and sci-fi in his songwriting, and requested copies of Byrds' records, in exchange for a copy of his recently published book, *Intelligent Life in the Universe*. Sadly, Roger assigned the task of sending the records to someone at Larry Spector's office. The records were never delivered, though Carl Sagan's book arrived promptly. It was only later that we learned Carl Sagan hadn't received the Byrds' albums and was mildly offended by Roger's neglect.

My mother came to town just before Christmas. As a holiday tradition, she would make a large batch of tamales. Roger and I decided to have a big holiday party, and let bygones be bygones. Tamales and Mexican cuisine on the menu, we invited everyone, including my family and the McGuinns, the current and former Byrd members, Chris, Gram and Peter Fonda. We thought of it as a time to reestablish communication after the challenging experiences of the past year. It was healing for Roger to be amiable with Chris and Gram, now that the Byrds were stabilized with new musicians. Everyone loved the tamales, which were an exotic delicacy for that time. My mother, Hope, cooked the best Mexican food. It made quite an impression at this party. In fact, she always contended that Chris and Gram enjoyed her burritos so much, they chose it as the name for the new band they'd started, The Flying Burrito Brothers. It's a likely possibility.

Dorothy McGuinn was in her element, enjoying the food and festivity. She'd had a few beers, and feeling jolly, revealed her age, a top secret that she normally wouldn't share, to those in proximity to her. The acoustics in the house were such that her voice carried into the next room. Roger came around and said, "Mom, we heard you in the pool room, and now we know how old you are." We all laughed. "Oh dear!" she cried. We were running low on booze, and Gram offered to drive down to Ventura Boulevard to pick up some more. I decided to join him, when he said, "C'mon, Ianthe, let's go and take a ride in my new Mercedes!"

I borrowed Dorothy's mink coat, which her husband Jim had bought her with their royalties from *Parents Can't Win*. The mink fit perfectly - Dorothy and I were the same size - and I hopped into Gram's red convertible. We sped down the hill.

Gram spoke excitedly about his new band with Chris, and invited us to see them play at some club in Topanga Canyon. We looked rather exotic in the grocery store: Gram wore a burgundy velvet suit and I had the mink coat, so we made a flashy impression on the cashier and customers as we picked up the necessary liquor. We dashed back up the hill.

My sister Bernice had recently moved to Los Angeles with her family. She wore a tight white crochet mini-dress. She looked like a Latina Elizabeth Taylor. Gram met her and began flirting. As the evening wore on, he was getting ready to leave the party, and he asked Bernice if she would join him for the night. Bernice came into the kitchen and told mother and me about his proposition. Mother erupted, "Don't you *dare* go with him, Bernice! *No!*" For once in her life, Bernice obeyed mother, and did not join Gram that night. Bernice still regrets not escaping with Gram to this day. She reflected, "Those tight velvet pants left nothing to the imagination."

The party was a big success, and we enjoyed the twilight of a tumultuous, eventful year with dear friends and family.

We embarked on a trip to Chicago right before New Year's Eve. We took Patrick with us, his first trip to visit his great-grandparents, Louis and Irene Heyn. They were in their late seventies at the time, and graciously hosted Roger, Patrick and me in their family home that had survived the Great Chicago Fire, near Lincoln Park. The house was very warm inside with the radiator heat, which contrasted with the freezing air and slushy ice on the streets of Chicago. Patrick loved the sights and sounds of a new city, and the exotic snow.

Irene, smitten with Roger, still called him Jimmy, and looked at him lovingly, her elbows on the table, as we sat there for supper. "Jimmy, oh Jimmy," she sighed. She'd prepared a big family dinner, roast chicken and mashed potatoes. We had a continuation of the warm holiday spirit. They still had their Christmas tree up, waiting for Jimmy and Patrick.

Louis, who was called Bompa, had a sweet ritual of leaving a 'Blue Jay Gift' at the bottom of the stairs. He had started this treat-giving tradition with Jimmy and Brian when they were small boys. Patrick was now the 'Blue Jay' recipient. Every day we stayed there, Bompa would say, "What did the Blue Jay leave you? Go and see." Patrick would be delighted to see a single-serving paper cup of ice cream with a wooden spoon. The Heyns loved children.

The Byrds had a show at the Kinetic Playground in Chicago, performing with Muddy Waters. I remember the enormous size of this once-grand venue. Muddy Waters put on a great, loud show with his band. The Byrds, with Clarence now an important part of the live sound, also impressed the large audience. A little-known act called Fleetwood Mac performed after the Byrds. I don't think I stayed to see their set, but there were multiple sets that night by all performers, to ring in the New Year at midnight, 1969. We all celebrated with champagne backstage after the show.

I was happy we were able to bring Patrick to Chicago. Roger and I drove back to his grandparents. Patrick was asleep in our bed. He and I flew back to Los Angeles shortly after, and the Byrds continued on a Midwestern tour for a few dates.

1969 - Juggling Chaos and Second Child

Patrick with newborn Henry, 1969. Patrick asked, "Who gave to me?"

The constant traveling was dizzying, but I would soon re-join the Byrds on a leg of their East Coast tour in February as they promoted the release of *Dr. Byrds & Mr. Hyde*. Patrick would once again spend time with his grandmother Hope in Tucson, while we traveled. Roger believed that he now had to take on many live bookings in order to pay off the debts owed to the other Columbia Byrd contract holders, since the radio hits weren't coming. It's a good thing that Clarence was on board, because their shows were better than ever, wowing the Byrds' audiences with his electric string-bender guitar.

On one travel day, John York and I sat with Roger at a diner. Roger left for a few minutes. John asked me, "Do you listen to anyone else besides the Byrds?" I thought about it a minute, and realized the answer was "No." In fact, thinking about it, I'd been living my life completely in support of our son Patrick, and vicariously through Roger's career, listening only to Byrds music. John looked at me with a bit of a smirk, and said, "You really should broaden your musical spectrum. The Beatles just came out with an amazing record." John was referring to *The White Album*. His cocky attitude was strange, given that he was a Byrd, and on payroll at that. I never told Roger about this comment.

Roger ended up firing Larry Spector, and took on management duties for the Byrds, when it surfaced that Larry had taken a substantial sum off the top of the Byrds' Columbia contract. This of course infuriated Roger.

The Flying Burrito Brothers were simultaneously on tour during the winter of 1969, and were on the same bill as the Byrds at the Boston Tea Party. It was fun to see Chris and Gram, and their music was exciting. An air of competitiveness could be felt between the Byrds and the Burritos, which thrilled the audience, as each act put on such energetic shows. Yet the friendship between Roger, Chris and Gram prevailed.

One night back in LA, Roger and I, accompanied by Jet Thomas, who was visiting the West Coast, went to see the Flying Burrito Brothers at some club on the top of Topanga Canyon. It was a cozy joint with beer and bar food. Clint Eastwood sat at the bar, very enthusiastic about the Flying Burrito Brothers' music.

Chris and Gram were quite the showmen, and their blend of country and rock sizzled that night. Roger was feeling romantic, and he asked me to dance for the very first time ever, to the song 'Do Right Woman.' It was joyous to be held in his arms, listening to great music, as he was usually the one performing the music on stage. I felt all was right with the world in his arms as he held me tenderly.

I soon realized I was pregnant. Roger and I had wanted to have another child, a companion for Patrick. It was a blessing. I visited a new obstetrician, Dr. Frankel, an associate of Dr. Fliess', and he confirmed that I was expecting – another October baby. Roger was happy with the good news.

Peter Fonda made a new film and invited us to a rough-cut screening. When Roger and I went to see the movie, then untitled, bringing young Patrick with us, Patrick ran back and forth before the movie in his loose, baggy T-shirt. Dennis Hopper commented,

"Whose kid is that?" "Oh, that's McGuinn's kid," Peter responded. The film was an exciting story about two motorcyclists making their way across a conservative American landscape. I liked all the characters, and was disturbed and saddened by the ending.

After the lights came up in the screening room, I was happy to see all three characters alive and well, because the death scenes were so realistic. Dennis Hopper, Bob Rafelson and Jack Nicholson were quiet and laid back. The music in the film had been a highlight, driving the action forward with an eclectic rock soundtrack. Peter was concerned he would not be able to get all the necessary clearances.

The movie would become *Easy Rider*. Roger was involved in the soundtrack's completion, because it turned out Bob Dylan had no interest in including his recordings in the movie. Bob asked Roger to record 'It's Alright Ma, I'm Only Bleeding.' Fonda had wanted an original Dylan composition as well, to sum up the film. As the story goes, Dylan, after watching the same rough cut, had written lyrics on a napkin, which he gave Peter Fonda, containing the opening verse, "The river flows/ It flows to the sea/ Wherever that river goes/ That's where I want to be." Dylan told Peter, "Give this to McGuinn. He'll know what to do with it."

Roger set about completing the song that Dylan began, playing the guitar in our living room. We were good friends with Peter. He and his wife, Susan, had a son, Justin, who was Patrick's age. We'd go swimming in their pool in the Hollywood Hills. Roger and Peter had become closer over time. It was said that Peter imitated Roger's demeanor in his role of Wyatt, the motorcyclist, and that Dennis Hopper emulated David Crosby's persona. I would say that Dennis didn't know David that well, but just meeting David a few times was enough to observe his idiosyncrasies.

Peter said to us, on more than one occasion, that the graveside scene in New Orleans was a cathartic moment about his mother, who had committed suicide. We had no idea that the film was to become a cultural landmark of American cinema. It was a tremendous success, and it was a huge benefit to the Byrds' career to have songs in a hit movie soundtrack, since Roger accepted a modest fee for the songs used.

Inspired by the film, no doubt, Roger bought a Triumph motorcycle, another new toy. He would zip around the neighborhood, during the daylight hours, to visit Clarence and others. He would occasionally take Patrick, sitting on the gas tank, along Mulholland Drive. I am shocked now to think that neither of them wore helmets and, for that matter, had any harness support whatsoever for Patrick. After one long ride, I remember coming out to greet them, and saw that Patrick had dozed during the trip, leaning his head, asleep, against his father's arms. I thought that was the last time Patrick should ride: it seemed very unsafe. Roger hadn't even noticed his sleeping son.

Another toy Roger acquired were two Citizen's Band Radios, one in the house, and one outfitted in Sidney, the Cadillac. Roger would stay up all night, talking to truckers and other CB enthusiasts. His handle was 'Big Byrd.' He would also communicate with me at the house, when he was running errands. It was the closest thing to a mobile phone at the time. My handle was 'Velvet,' and the truckers loved that.

One afternoon when my mother was in town, Roger, Patrick and I went shopping for Patrick's upcoming birthday party at a large drug store on Ventura Boulevard. Patrick sat in the shopping cart as we perused the aisles. We picked up various sundries. As we were going toward the cashier, Patrick spotted a large samovar for serving coffee at parties. Having his coffee pot obsession, he immediately pointed and desired the samovar. "For me!" he said. Of course, it was too large and out of the question, so we said, "No," as we continued to roll along. He burst into tears, "My coffee pot! I want my coffee pot!"

Roger stood petrified as Patrick screamed, and said nervously, "I'll meet you at the car," as he dashed out of the store, leaving my mother and me to cope with our wailing son. Patrick was all worked up, and customers were staring at us, curious what the fuss was about. We managed to get outside of the store with our purchases, Patrick still in tears, but tired from the exertion. He fell asleep on the car ride home. In the back of my mind, I wondered if Roger was up for the challenges of everyday fatherhood and a second child.

The album *Crosby, Stills & Nash* had been released. Roger was well informed about David's activities, post-Byrds, and brought home a copy of the record. We were both very impressed at what they'd done when we listened. The harmonies were its strength, with timely lyrics. The three of them had all taken a leap forward. I knew Roger felt competitive to create a good album in response to Crosby's launch.

Terry Melcher had come back into our lives. He was to produce the next recording for the Byrds. We visited him in Malibu at his beach house, where he lived with Candice Bergen. I liked Candy: she was intelligent, sophisticated and beautiful, with a great sense of humor. She, however, did not want Terry to get involved in the lifestyle of the rock musicians he'd be producing. The two shared a beautiful little house, airy, feminine and furnished like an English seaside cottage. The only deviation from this sweet atmosphere was that in the living room, on the coffee table, was a huge illustrated book, *The Kama Sutra*, the Indian book of sex positions. The pages were dog-eared.

Terry was excited, on one particular day, to show Roger his new catamaran. He and Roger went out to sea in the late afternoon, while Patrick and I played on the beach. Candy had left earlier for an appointment in her tan Mercedes convertible.

Patrick and I watched as the catamaran sailed off into the horizon, out of sight. Time went by, and the sun was setting. Roger and Terry were nowhere in sight. I was frightened: where had they disappeared to? Had the winds taken them far out to sea? Patrick had no idea of my growing worry as he continued to play in the sand and waves. It began getting cold as the sun receded, and the wind picked up. I feared I would never see Roger again.

Finally, on the horizon, there was a speck in the distance. I prayed this was the catamaran returning. Sure enough, as the craft drew closer, I saw that it was Terry and Roger. I sighed with relief, and my concern melted away, yet I shivered with the chill in the air. Another day that I was not prepared for the cold weather!

"I was so worried! I'm glad you're all right," I shouted over the roar of waves and wind, as they pulled the boat onto the shore, now that it was nearly dark. They were both laughing and windblown. "We had a great time!" they said. We all went inside to get warm. Patrick hated to leave the shore – he loved the water.

Terry took us to a nice Italian restaurant on the coast highway. Shortly after this experience, Terry and Candy moved to Benedict Canyon, away from the beach house, which belonged to Terry's mother, Doris Day. Terry must have moved for proximity to the Columbia Studios. Long hours in the recording studio ensued, and I think it put a strain on his relationship with Candice.

I listened to the rough mix tapes that Roger brought home after the recording sessions with Terry and the Byrds. 'Jesus is Just Alright' was a song that Terry had bought the publishing rights to. I thought it was the strongest. I noticed an effort was made to include strong harmonies in the wake of Crosby's debut record with Stephen Stills and Graham Nash. I was hopeful that with the backing of this new movie, *Easy Rider*, the record would be a success. It was a big hit in America, restoring the Byrds to good record sales.

My pregnancy was progressing. Susie White, Clarence's pretty wife, and I were pregnant at the same time. It was a perfect friendship: she would visit with her daughter Michelle, who was close friends with Patrick at this point, and they would play in the sprawling backyard. Because our husbands were both on tour most of the time, we offered each other companionship and support. Susie was very philosophical about her stretches of solitude, and had taken on the financial tasks in the relationship. She and Clarence had been married a long time, going back to Kentucky. I remember with warmth her soft Kentucky accent and kind smile.

My brother Marcus and his young family would occasionally visit at this house. His children were close in age to Patrick. We had birthday parties for the kids – our home was an ideal space for children to run safely, hide and play – no traffic anywhere. Even when Roger was gone, I didn't feel my life revolve completely around his schedule, I was embracing life in this wonderful home.

Roger was touring in West Virginia when I heard on the evening broadcast about the ghastly and brutal killing of Sharon Tate, who had been pregnant. This news was profoundly disturbing; I was alone in this house with Patrick, in nearby hills, pregnant myself. I felt frightened that there was a killer on the loose in the Hollywood Hills... how could I protect myself? Roger had a gun in the house, a Walther P-38; he used it for target practice on occasion in the back yard.

We had neighbors, an older couple named the Robbins. Le Roy was a soundman and amateur photographer. He had coincidentally worked on *Easy Rider* as the location sound recorder. He and his wife, Florence, would have cocktails every evening at four-thirty before dinner. She was from New Mexico, and made Mexican food in a different style. The enchiladas she prepared were flat corn tortillas instead of rolled. They had a lot of Native American pottery and artifacts, and old toys that their grown son had left behind, which Patrick would play with when we'd visit. I was grateful to have them nearby in the wake of this strange and frightening development.

When Roger returned from his tour, Terry told him that the murders had taken place in the house that he and Candice had once lived in, *before* they lived in Malibu. This coincidence was chilling. I didn't feel safe in the hills unless I knew I had someone nearby, because my pregnancy made me feel more sensitive and vulnerable. I felt uneasy that the ugliness of some crazed mind was creeping into our idyllic life.

Everyone in the Hollywood community became paranoid during the end of summer 1969. People no longer would welcome strangers into their homes for parties: the sense of freeness and openness of the Sixties in Los Angeles forever changed. Peace and Love were no more. Fear and Paranoia gripped our collective psyche, along with the vivid images presented on the evening news of the Vietnam War. I'll never forget the horrendous wail of a young, wounded soldier calling out for his mother as he was carried away on a stretcher to a helicopter. I wondered about the kind of world in which my children would grow up.

With Roger's constant touring, my connection to him was a nightly phone call, where I could communicate how things were going, and how much I missed him. The morning of October 25, I called my brother Marcus to take me to the hospital: I was in labor. Roger was on tour, and I gave birth to our son early that morning. He weighed a whopping ten pounds. Patrick stayed with Marcus and his children while I recovered in the same hospital where Bobby Kennedy had been brought, the Good Samaritan.

We had a beautiful baby, a perfectly happy and healthy child. He stood out in the nursery, being so large and hefty. Roger came to the hospital and picked me up in Sidney, the black Cadillac. Roger loved his new son.

Because we didn't have our son's Subud name yet, his birth certificate read 'Boy McGuinn.' We brought him home, where

Patrick was visiting with Dorothy. We placed Baby Boy McGuinn on Patrick's lap and he looked with wonder as he said, "Who gave to me?" We all laughed with joy. Having children brings sweetness and innocence into the home.

'Ballad of Easy Rider' was a hit on the airwaves. It was a beautiful production by Terry, which was different from that of the movie soundtrack. Roger had informed me of another personnel change in the Byrds: bass player Skip Battin was replacing John York. We drove to Skip's Laurel Canyon home. He had a wife named Jackie and a teenage son. She served us Laughing Cow cheese and walnuts. They seemed like a real hippie couple.

Based on all the touring ahead, I was beginning to worry about all the different personnel changes. I knew that Roger had to uphold his commitments, but I felt that if only they could get a permanent lineup, things would run smoother. Clarence's guitar playing was at the forefront of the band now, and Roger's twelve-string had become the rhythm guitar, which was a shame.

One day at a rehearsal at the warehouse where they kept their equipment, the band was working on a song, and Roger was playing his twelve-string quietly in the background as Clarence took lead. I stood in front of the band listening, and during a pause in the loud music asked, "Roger, can't you play the Rickenbacker as you did on 'Bells of Rhymney?'"

Roger looked at me fiercely, and in one sweep of his hand, unfastened his guitar strap and thrust the Rickenbacker toward me and said, "You wanna show me what you mean?"

I could have sunk into the floor. Everyone stood, shocked. I could see the equipment manager, Jimmi Seiter, smirking, thinking that I'd been put in my place. I realized my words were to be silenced and that my place was supposed to be at home with the children. My feeling was that I had spoken out of place, and put Roger in a position where he realized that his guitar playing was no longer dominant in the band.

This incident seemed to signal a shift in our marriage. Roger drew more into his fraternity of long haired, drug-curious, party boys, ready to tour consistently and gain access to all the pleasures the road life could offer.

147

A young couple from Subud showed up at our home one afternoon. On the piece of paper from Indonesia they gave to me was handwritten, "Henry." This would be the name of our baby son. When Peter Fonda discovered our son's new name, he asked, "Are you going to call him Hank? That's my dad's nickname."

The Rolling Stones were performing in Los Angeles for the first time in a while on November 8. Roger had gotten passes for us to see the show. I reluctantly hired a babysitter for Patrick and Henry. Roger and I drove the smooth ride to Inglewood's Forum in the Cadillac. It was a quiet journey.

Before we descended into the large backstage loading area, I could see ahead of us, down below, a frantic Gram Parsons, dressed in a white top hat, white satin suit, and a long flowing scarf, banging on the backstage metal door, going from one door to the next, desperately trying to get inside. Roger and I quietly drove by in the Cadillac, unnoticed by Gram. We parked and got out of the car. I felt a sudden unease as we approached the security guard, gaining quick admittance backstage.

I don't recall any backstage interactions; we were promptly seated in the front reserved row of the arena. Soon, we saw Gram, in good spirits, sitting nearby. I couldn't stop thinking about my young sons at home, as the concert was soon to begin. The feeling of unease continued as my breasts engorged with milk, since I was breastfeeding Henry, only two weeks old.

It was just too soon for me to be away from Henry. I turned to Roger suddenly and said, "You know, I think I'm leaving. Can I have the car keys?"

Surprised, Roger fished for the keys and handed them to me. I asked, "Are you going to be able to get a ride home?"

"Oh, sure. I'll manage. Are you going to be able to find the car?"

"Sure, I'll manage." I said in reply. I walked back to the car, grateful that I wasn't going to be sitting listening to a loud concert. It was becoming redundant, and my children were more significant to me.

I returned home and dismissed the babysitter. Henry was just beginning to stir as I walked into the bedroom. I loved holding him; he was a peaceful child. I fed him and we all went to sleep. Later, Roger came in with a batch of friends, and started playing pool. The party had begun. I got up and put my robe on to see what the commotion was. "You missed a great show," Roger said as he chalked his cue stick.

Christian Marquand and another Frenchman were preparing to play a round or two as they smoked cigarettes. "Come and join us, Ianthe!" they said. I smiled, "No, I'm going back to bed." It was dawn before Roger came to bed that night. He was becoming increasingly nocturnal.

That morning, I woke up to make coffee and I noticed in the living room a small red pill on the floor, next to one of the rattan chairs. I picked it up and wondered who had dropped it. This set off a new fear – what if Patrick had found it first, and thought it was candy? I shivered at the thought. Roger was changing, and not for the better, so it seemed. He slept all day. This became his pattern. In an effort to wake him before the afternoon set in, I began making him a tray, serving breakfast in bed. This usually was a pleasant awakening for him. I'd serve him omelets, French toast, or pancakes with hot coffee. He became accustomed to this.

Crime investigators uncovered Charles Manson's involvement with Sharon Tate's murder. Terry became even more paranoid, and decided to look for another place to live, now that the Byrds recordings were completed. Afraid of being alone, he asked Roger to accompany him on his search. Roger took Terry on drives in the Cadillac. I accompanied them on one such weekend trip, caravanning in Porsches.

Terry's handsome friend, Mike, a young Hollywood hopeful, had a blue Porsche, which Roger drove. Terry was passenger. I drove with Mike in our mustard 911-S. We stopped at every bar along the way. Terry needed a lot of sedation, valium and gin. We eventually wound up in the Riverside mountain range, above the town of Hemet.

Terry met the real estate person, as we all toured the new house – it was a two-story, all-wood Swiss chalet-type log cabin, and remote as could be. Terry was seeking isolation in the midst of this terrifying episode; plus his relationship with Candy was dissolving. We felt supportive being with him. Recording for the next album was set to take place in New York City.

My mother came to town for Christmas and we celebrated traditionally with the family. Mom and Dorothy loved spending time with Henry. There was no big tamale bash this year. The Byrds were performing shows during Christmas and I was glad Roger was close to home. The year quietly concluded.

1970 - Three is a Crowd

Roger, early 1970

A young man named Jackson Browne came to visit us on Alomar. He carried an acoustic guitar. Roger had seen him perform at the Troubadour and had invited him over to share some songs, which the Byrds were possibly interested in recording. Clarence and Roger were drinking coffee and eating my home baked banana bread in anticipation.

I was struck by Jackson's fresh talent and innocent good looks. He took out his guitar and played several of his beautiful, melancholy compositions, including a song called 'Jamaica.' Clarence said that he liked the song and that it should be on the next album, and Roger agreed. They invited him to a charity concert they were performing for the New Ash Grove, recovering from a recent fire, that weekend.

At the show, Chris Hillman showed up, and told me about the harrowing time he and Gram had just experienced at the Altamont concert, where a biker had stabbed someone in the audience. The Flying Burrito Brothers had opened for the Rolling Stones. My friend, Berta, was there at the Ash Grove with Jackson Browne; apparently they knew each other. In between sets, the three of us took a walk around the block during a full moon night.

There was a corona around the moon, and it was shockingly vivid. The three of us started singing, "Corona, corona!" to the tune of 'Corina, Corina.' We all laughed. Jackson was so friendly and sweet. His demeanor reminded me of when Roger was a struggling artist, and I realized that Jackson was at that beginning stage in his career. I was struck with a feeling that Jackson was going to be successful.

The Byrds did a rock set that was received very well. As usual, Clarence's guitar playing was an audience pleaser, and he had an air of homecoming at the Ash Grove, having played there so often before.

Travel plans were underway for live recordings that were to become a part of the next album. Susie and I were planning to join our husbands on the trip to New York, and I thought it was going to be fun, seeing a new side of New York City with Terry, who was producing the recordings. Patrick and Henry would stay with their grandmother in Tucson.

Terry was booked to stay at The Plaza Hotel near Central Park. Roger and I, as usual, would stay at the Gramercy Park Hotel; Susie and Clarence were staying there as well. We flew to New York at the end of February.

The Byrds were to perform at two venues on two nights. The first, Queens College, went well. Susie and I arrived that day. The next night, the Byrds were performing at Felt Forum in Madison Square Garden. I rested up for this show.

Roger came in late that first night, excited about the results of the Queens show. He said the recording was strong enough for use on the live album.

The next day, Terry invited Roger and me to the Plaza Hotel for Sunday brunch. Roger and I both ordered eggs Benedict and screwdrivers. Mike, Terry's handsome friend in the blue Porsche, also joined us. Terry suggested we all get together after the Forum show to listen to the recording at his hotel that night.

The show sold out. Roger and the band went to do a sound check. Susie and I had a light dinner together at the Gramercy, and took a cab to the Forum.

New York was always exciting and full of many characters. There was lots of security at this show. Terry was busy with the engineers setting up the microphones and equipment for the recording.

The Byrds took the Forum stage to enthusiastic response. Susie and I remained backstage. During the show, in the dressing room, she confided in me, "I was taking out Clarence's cape from the travel bag, and I saw lipstick and smelled perfume on it. I think he was with a girl last night."

Shocked, I said, "Are you sure?" Their marriage seemed so solid; I couldn't believe Clarence would stray. Susie nodded solemnly. "I'm going to get to the bottom of this as soon as we have some time alone."

I felt uneasy during the rest of the show. If Clarence would cheat on Susie, and they seemed so stable, Roger, with his recent unkind behavior toward me, raised my suspicions about his fidelity. Our days at Subud had ended: with Roger's constant touring, and my raising the children, we rarely had any time to drive all the way downtown for Latihan practice. I felt that this lapse was significant.

After the show, Roger and I took a cab to Terry's hotel as planned. When we arrived at the large suite, Terry's friend, Mike, had another friend, a handsome man with blond hair, stretched out on the sofa, apparently passed out.

Terry threaded up the tape machine to listen to the playback of the show, and we started to listen to the music. There was a knock at the door. Room service arrived, with a bottle of champagne and Terry's favorite, a bottle of Tanqueray gin. Terry tipped the server. No sooner had room service left when there was another knock at the door.

Terry opened the door, and a woman in her thirties, resembling Edith Piaf, dressed in all black, with bright red lipstick, said, "I'm looking for Mr. Stern." Terry let her in and said, "Mike, there's someone here for you." Mike shouted from the next room, "I'm not expecting anyone!"

Mike came out from the bedroom and saw the woman. She said, "Well, I was told to come to this room," when she saw Mike. Everyone looked at each other curiously, except for Terry, who had a twinkle in his eye. He took Mike by the arm, led him to the corner, and began a quiet conversation.

The woman stood uncomfortably in the middle of the room, as Terry and Mike whispered. Roger politely asked the woman, "Would you like a drink?" indicating the booze. The woman shook her head, no.

"Are you kidding me? Terry, how could you do this?" Mike erupted from the corner.

"C'mon Mike, you know. You were complaining about it. I got the number from one of the bellhops." Terry laughed.

"Damn you, Terry. You'd better fix this." Mike shook his head with anger, disgusted, and strode into the other room.

Terry took out his wallet and pulled out some bills, saying to the woman, "I'm sorry, my friend changed his mind."

The woman, indignant and humiliated, took the money and started stuffing it in her pocketbook. She crept out quietly. The door shut. Terry burst into laughter.

The young blond man, still passed out, lay quietly, not wakened by the commotion. Terry, in a whimsical mood, took the bucket of ice from the champagne and splashed it on the sleeping beauty, upon which the boy leaped from the sofa, gasping, "What the hell's going on?"

Terry started laughing, "It's time to get up." When Mike came back and saw the ruckus, he went and grabbed a towel from the bathroom, handing it to the young man.

"Okay, you'd better leave," Terry demanded. The young man grabbed the towel, wiping his face and hair, then threw it on the ground, accepting his jacket from Mike, and slamming the door behind him.

Mike stormed back into the bedroom after the young man left. Roger and I, innocent bystanders, were bemused and embarrassed by all of the drama that had unfolded. Terry flopped into the chair and nonchalantly poured himself a gin and tonic, seemingly unfazed by all of the preceding events.

Roger said, "Well, I guess we'd better go." Terry smiled, "We can listen to the tape later." It was evident that Terry had a dark mischievous side that could be frightening if you were on the receiving end.

While we were in New York, Roger was supposed to record some tracks with Bob Dylan. Clive Davis, along with Bob Johnston, Dylan's producer, was to organize the session time at Columbia's studio in Manhattan. The idea of the session loomed, but Roger and I didn't know what was happening, and by the time everyone else was readying to leave the hotel, we still hadn't heard. Half of the guys were out of New York. Roger and I waited and waited at the hotel. The call never came, and we finally left New York City. When we settled back in LA, we received word that Dylan was angry that he'd had to find other musicians to record with him. It turned out that Bob Johnston was partly responsible for the misunderstanding. Another missed opportunity.

After Larry Spector was fired by Roger, Eddie Tickner and Jim Dickson eventually came back into the fold. Billy James handled the publicity. Now that the live music portion of the album was recorded, Terry and the Byrds went back in the studio, recording more for a proposed double-album. It was an ambitious project, and I only remember hearing the rough mix tapes the following day, or sometimes at night, when Roger would come in late, and play a game of pool while listening to the day's recordings. Ever since the incident at the rehearsal, I'd become less outspoken about the music that Roger made.

I liked Jacques Levy's co-compositions with Roger; I thought they were powerful songs. In general, I just didn't feel that Clarence had a strong enough voice to carry off some of the songs, and I was in no way interested in Skip Battin or Gene Parsons' music. The visual component of the 1965 first-edition Byrds, with good looking, lean young men, had given way to bearded, grizzled mountain men. It wasn't an attractive visual experience.

I knew that Roger had to persevere, and I knew he thought the music was strong, because this edition of the Byrds was able to perform on stage like never before. They just had to keep playing those old songs, which seemed misaligned with these new personas. It was something John York had no interest in doing, and he left, and

155

I can understand why. In my opinion, the creative thrust of the band was sorely lacking.

Roger had become a more aggressive performer on stage. Whether it was drug-fueled or had to do with Clarence taking the entire guitar spotlight, Roger felt compelled to be a stronger stage presence. I found this shift in his personality insincere; it was far removed from the man I met, and fell in love with, the graceful young man with the halo at the Ash Grove.

Susie told me that she had spoken to Clarence, and he had denied any extra-marital affair. She took his word for it. I was grateful that Roger had not given in to groupies. There certainly were many younger, sexier women ripening and emerging on the scene.

One afternoon, Jimmi Seiter stopped by our house on Alomar with a young woman in tow. I'll never forget her tight gray T-shirt displaying enormous breasts, with Mickey Mouse emblazoned across, tight jeans, and long, curly black hair. I thought she might be Jimmi's girlfriend. She didn't say much, taking a seat at the table.

Roger and Jimmi talked shop. I didn't think they were staying long. Jimmi introduced her, "This is Linda." She smiled and Roger nodded, his eyes transfixed on Mickey Mouse. I didn't feel the least bit insecure – Roger loved me, and we had two beautiful children, whose presence could be felt in the house. The Tiffany lamp that hung over the table in the living room hovered over Linda's head. She looked up into the lamp, with a bored, childlike gaze.

Roger enjoyed the distraction no doubt, because at one point, he was interviewed by Ed Ward, a journalist from *Rolling Stone*, and I asked Ed what he thought the difference was between Roger and Zubin Mehta, the conductor for the LA Philharmonic Orchestra. Ed said, "Roger is more domesticated."

Roger came home one afternoon, holding an album in his hand. "I just ran into David. He gave me a copy of their new record." I looked at the cover: *Déjà Vu* by Crosby, Stills, Nash & Young. Roger placed the LP on the turntable, curious. The opening notes of 'Carry On' were arresting, and we both sat, listening to the entire first side, without interruption, mesmerized.

It was a powerful listening experience, not only because of Roger's state-of-the-art McIntosh stereo: Crosby and Nash's high harmonies filled the ceiling of our home. By the time Neil Young's

'Helpless' came on, it pushed Roger over the edge, and a tear streamed down his face. He was deeply moved by Neil's plaintive delivery and beautiful songwriting. Roger was speechless, in tears. I'd never before seen Roger respond so humanly, so emotionally. Listening to the entire album was transcendent for both of us. I think Roger may have truly questioned the direction of his own music.

In May, Roger and I went to a screening of the Beatles' *Let It Be*. Robert Redford and Paul Newman hosted the event, taking place at a private club called The Factory, across the street from Barney's Beanery on Santa Monica Boulevard. It was a very exclusive group: Lou Adler, Michelle and John Phillips among others attended.

After the screening, John Phillips invited Roger and me to his mansion in Holmby Hills. He and Roger were old friends from the early days in New York City. We drove in the Cadillac, following John's car going west, and pulled into the regal manor. When I saw this mansion, I was surprised at how humbly Roger and I lived by comparison in Sherman Oaks.

Inside, John had an immense recording studio built into one of the rooms. It certainly caused more envy on Roger's part – this studio was even more well-appointed and technologically state-of-the-art than Michael Nesmith's. Michelle was friendly to Roger, but not to me. She offered us drinks, and John pulled out a fat joint, which we shared in the studio. Roger and I drove home, quietly.

That June, Susie and I were again to join the Byrds on a European tour. It was on this tour that I came to realize how much the band was indulging in alcohol and substance abuse. Both Susie and I were shocked to discover that pills were commonly used at any given time of day. We flew to London, first class, in a Boeing 747, my first time on such a luxurious airliner.

The city of Frankfurt was clean and industrial. The venue was in a stadium, where there were concrete slopes leading to the stage on a playing field. Sadly, I couldn't shake the feeling of old 'Nazi' vibes from World War II: I was very sensitive to the images I'd seen in old newsreels. The Byrds performed that afternoon to a large crowd of young people, who gave an enthusiastic welcome. A highlight for the audience was the a cappella rendition of 'Amazing Grace.' Roger, Clarence, Skip and Gene's voices blended perfectly together and it was a moving, spiritual song to close the loud rock show.

We arrived in Amsterdam and stayed at a hotel with a tiny staircase that led to the second floor. The doorways were so low that Roger had to stoop in order to get through without bumping his head. In those days, he stood at six feet. The quaint, colorful buildings lined the cobblestone sidewalks.

That evening we attended the film premiere of *Woodstock*. It was an impressive documentary. I reflected on my disappointment that the Byrds hadn't performed at Woodstock. The exposure would have helped their status in rock history.

We met the promoter, a young man named Barry Vissor, at a nightclub. He was thin and sallow-faced, with long hair and American hippie attire: a wrinkled shirt and jeans. I was shocked to see some hashish the size of a sugar cube sitting on one of the tables. Marijuana was legal and sold in 'hash clubs.' Barry took me, Roger, Susie and Clarence sightseeing, and we passed through the 'red light' district, where scantily clad girls in lacy blouses and miniskirts sat in storefront windows peddling their wares. Prostitution was also legal in the Netherlands. Tulips and windmills aside, it was a very advanced country for its small size, and I admired this.

The music festival in Rotterdam included Santana and the Jefferson Airplane. Grace Slick invited us to a small trailer she shared with Paul Kantner on the grounds. She'd been drinking and we all smoked some very strong pot. It was a tight fit, but the four of us sat. Smoke swallowed the humidity and light from the one light bulb. Paul and Grace complained about the bad weather. The wind and rain were so severe it was surprising the audience remained for the performances.

Roger braved the rain, and once on stage got an electric shock when he touched the microphone with his lips. As I recall the crew placed rubber mats under the equipment to prevent continued shocks. It was an endurance test for both performers and audience.

During the time in the Netherlands, Roger seemed aloof. He would ignore or question anything I said. His drinking began in the morning, after a night of drinking, and I felt afraid for him. I couldn't understand what he was going through.

We flew back to London, staying at an upscale hotel, and that evening Roger said he was going to take a bath. This was unusual, because he usually showered. He had been drinking. After he had been a long time in the bathroom, I knocked on the door.

"Roger, you okay?"

It was quiet... no response. I opened the door and peeked in.

He was in the tub... passed out! "Oh my God, Roger!" I cried. I rushed into the white-tiled bathroom. I grabbed him by the arm and tried to sit him up. He was slippery wet and I couldn't get a good grip. I pulled the stopper and the water drained. I shook his head and he opened, then closed, his eyes.

"Roger! Roger! Wake up! Come on, help me!" I felt terrified and desperate. I got a towel and put it on his shoulders. If he had been shorter, and the tub larger, he would surely have drowned. I pulled his torso over the edge of the tub, and he finally came to. "Help me, Roger!" I cried, "You've got to get out of this tub!"

He staggered to his knees and placed a hand on the edge of the bath, then with his other hand on my shoulder he was able to lift himself out of the tub. I got another towel to dry him off as he stumbled into the bedroom and fell into bed.

"Oh, Roger." My tears were falling hot on my cheeks. "What's the matter?"

"I took two Placidyl," he whispered. This was a sedative with euphoric side effects. I covered his naked body with the blankets and dried his legs. I knew something was terribly wrong. I couldn't understand why he wasn't sharing this with me. I got into bed next to him. I tried to put my arms around him, but he pulled away. I felt saddened. He began to snore, something he never did. I stayed up staring at his back, making sure his breathing didn't stop. I eventually fell asleep, lying beside him, the ambient city light filling the room.

In the morning, Roger woke up as if nothing had happened. There was a silence between us. We ordered room service and he got a call from the road manager about the pickup time for the airport. My thoughts were still processing the night before. I dressed and packed. We later met the group in the lobby and there was silence between Roger and me. He went to the bar with Clarence and I followed.

"Please Roger, don't drink." I said softly.

"Leave me alone," he ordered. I stopped and turned to face Susie, as she shrugged helplessly. In the jet to Los Angeles, Roger was superficially polite and animated with me – travel always made him happy. But something was wrong between us.

Returning to LA was a relief. Road tours are not meant for mothers who miss their children. My days as one of the gang were over; I was officially a stay-at-home mom now. I'd brought gifts and toys for Patrick and Henry, who were happy to see us. I was exhausted from this trip, and from the questions I had about Roger's behavior. I was grateful to have my mom there for a few days while I recovered from jet lag.

Europe was soon forgotten and Roger and I fell back into our mutual roles. He had become civil again. I credit Patrick and Henry for that.

Because we continued to have so many visitors at the house for Roger's interviews, I thought it was time to renovate the decor and update it, since it still had 1960s flowered wallpaper in the bathroom that my brother Marcus had put up and a green 'high-low' carpet in the billiard room.

Peter Fonda had a friend, John Hamberlin, who recommended a young contractor/carpenter by the name of Harrison Ford. I had some projects around the house, remodeling the kitchen, painting, and carpet removal that were pressing.

That late summer day I was ascending the path where there had been an old tree house. Harrison and Hamberlin arrived in their car and approached me. Young Harrison had a striking, handsome face, and I felt an instant attraction to him. He was muscular, polite and soft-spoken, wearing Levi's jeans, a blue denim work shirt and construction boots. He was the polar opposite of Roger, with rugged features and a sense of earthiness. I showed them in and described the work involved.

They were going to put Mexican tile on the counter top and a brick facade in the kitchen, and strip carpet from the billiard room, which turned out to have a beautiful wooden floor underneath. The stove had to move into the garage for the duration of this work. Roger did not like the idea of what the project involved, and said once, "I'm a Cancer, my home is important to me. This work will disrupt our home." He did like the idea of an electrical strip, the length of the wall, to plug in all of the electronic toys he had acquired.

The remodeling began in earnest and the workers came in and out of the house. Estimated time and money were variable. Eddie Traubner, Roger's new accountant, would complain, "This Harrison Ford keeps wanting more money. What is he building, another addition?" I was hoping the house would be completed before the holidays, but that was not to be.

During this time, I found out Harrison was a struggling, out-of-work actor who had taken up construction work to support his wife and two sons. He had a crew of men helping him and he would find subcontractors to do whatever he and his crew couldn't. What was very strange was discovering that he and Roger were both born in Chicago, and on the exact same day and year: July 13, 1942!

One afternoon I came home from shopping and found Harrison stretched out, lounging in Roger's black leather chair, looking at the panel of televisions on the mantel. "One day I will have all this," he said with a sweep of his hand. He got up from the chair and left the room. No need to state the obvious, as my son Henry would later love to point out.

I took up reading *The New York Times* on a daily basis, which always proffered bad news in those days. For some reason, I felt compelled to put a picture of Ethel and Julius Rosenberg in our guest bathroom, clipped out from *The Times*. "Something's going on with Ianthe," I overheard Roger say to one of our guests. "She's got a photo of the Rosenbergs in our bathroom. What kind of statement is that?"

Politically, I was becoming more aware of the strife in the country. I did feel that since I was staying home with the kids, I was being a dutiful wife, yet I could feel that Roger was disconnected from wanting to be a parent at home with his children, that he would rather be with his band of bad boys. That undercurrent never went away.

I knew I was a different person: I was now a mother with two young boys. Their toys, records, children's clothes and furniture were all over the house. I was living in the Valley, a Los Angeles suburb. My friendship with Karen had fallen into the background, and I only occasionally saw my brother and his family. In general, I was very secluded in my feelings. Sometimes I felt that Susie and I were the only ones who understood each other's sense of reality.

Harrison Ford's presence, and the bustle of the work, was a comforting distraction. I will always remember him in a tight white T-shirt and jeans as he worked. He had become the daytime presence. Roger was in and out, and couldn't stand the disruption from the renovation process. At one point, Roger punched the front door with his fist, breaking one of the panes of glass. He had wanted to go to Jimmi Seiter's, but I had reminded him that we had to visit his parents that night. Later, I learned that he had a new nickname for me... I was no longer 'The Bonnie.' Roger now called me 'The Warden' behind my back.

Chris Hillman, who'd maintained contact with Roger and me, and knew of the strain between us, attempted a lighthearted drive in the country. He and his new girlfriend, Jeannie, invited us to go for a drive to Joshua Tree, two hours outside of LA.

Me and Roger in Chris Hillman's kitchen, 1968

Roger begrudgingly agreed, as long as we could take the Cadillac. Chris and Roger sat in front; Jeannie and I sat in back. The drive was quiet most of the way. We drove through the beautiful monument of Joshua Trees and boulders. Jeannie and I got stoned in back, and laughed most of the way. Roger was annoyed, and Chris' gesture fell flat. We drove back to LA tired and carsick.

Days later, I went to get my driver's license in the Valley. I saw Ry Cooder in line at the DMV. After warm greetings, he observed, "I can't believe what the Byrds have done to Clarence White. His character has changed so much. All that drug use is really destroying his talent."

"I couldn't agree with you more... that's what the rock business is all about. Corruption." I said.

It was my birthday on November 3, 1970. The work on the house was still going on and seemed to be dragging. Roger was always on the road. I needed to talk to him. I had never felt more distant from him. I called Nancy Kubo in Boston at her work. She had seen Roger at a Boston gig and I wanted to ask what her feelings were, when she saw him. Her workmate informed me that Nancy had left, and was in New York.

I looked at the itinerary and found the Byrds' hotel number. I had a sneaking suspicion, and I called and asked for Mr. and Mrs. McGuinn's room. The line was connected and the phone rang – Nancy answered! I couldn't believe my ears.

"Is that you, Nancy? Where is Roger... let me talk to Roger."

"Oh, um, Dolores... let me get Roger," she muttered.

Roger came on the line, soft-spoken, "Oh, hi Ianthe, we were having this, um, meeting. Oh hell, well I guess you caught me."

"It's my birthday, why didn't you call?" I slammed the phone down as my heart sank to my stomach. I looked up as Harrison walked into the living room.

"I just spoke to Roger. He was sleeping with my friend, Nancy, on the road," I heard myself saying aloud.

"Well I'll be," he answered, a sincere look of surprise on his face. The pain became unbearable, and I lost composure and burst into tears, running to our bedroom. The boys were taking a nap. I must have woken Patrick, and he came into the bedroom and asked, "What's wrong Mommy?"

"Nothing Patrick... everything is all right," I said, holding back sobs. He looked at me quizzically and said, "I hear the baby waking up." I wiped my eyes and we went into the nursery.

I called Mom and told her the story. She listened quietly, then finally said, "Dolores, if you want your family to stay together, you will have to forgive him and let it go." I was crushed: how could he be with Nancy, my friend? And how could Nancy betray me?

Both of them called that evening. Nancy apologized. "There's honor among thieves," I cried to Nancy, my voice quivering, as she handed the phone to Roger. Roger seemed empathetic, and asked me to meet him at the airport when he came back to LA in a few days. I couldn't believe the hypocrisy: they were still together in their New York hotel room, and had the nerve to call me, deepening the pain and betrayal I felt. I agreed to meet Roger at LAX, and said goodbye. From sheer emotional exhaustion, I fell asleep that night.

At the airport a few days later, Roger strode off the plane, looking not the least bit guilty or sheepish for fucking my friend. I went up to him with Henry in my arms and Patrick next to me. "Hi Patrick," he said and picked him up, and put his arm around my shoulders. "Some birthday present," he uttered, unfazed. There was no apology.

I tried to be strong and cheerful during Roger's time at home. We went through the motions of civility, but I could see the change in him. He was distant and disengaged with anything to do with the kids, the house, and me. My only friend was Susie White. Karen had moved to Vancouver with her new husband Michael. I shared news of the Nancy Kubo incident with Susie, and I sensed she already knew about it, probably from Clarence. It was one of those things that everyone knew about, but me.

During the remodeling, Harrison found James Taylor's *Sweet Baby James* album, a promotional record sent to Roger by Warner Brothers, lying around in a pile of other unopened records. Harrison quipped, "You should play this, it's good listening." He opened the shrink-wrap and put the disc on the turntable, and I didn't stop playing it for the rest of the week. James Taylor's deep voice offered consolation and empathy, and the poetry of his lyrics had an understanding of my inner pain.

Roger seemed disturbed when I listened to *Sweet Baby James*, but I didn't care. Roger always had his way with the music and the movies we watched, and I'd always catered to his will. I felt rebellious, and that I deserved to express myself with the music I enjoyed. Roger had already stifled my joy of reading books – for some reason, he didn't like me to read. He said that I assumed the character in the books I read, which threatened him.

Days later, Harrison discovered there was evidence of termites in the back bedrooms. The house would have to be tented and fumigated. Everything had to be removed from the kitchen and once we returned, kitchen equipment would have to be washed, because of the chemical residue.

I look back and think that our house on Alomar had become such a hub – day and night, visitors, journalists, musicians, all of whom would smoke or play billiards, require beer or pot, and in my mind, I must have felt tired of the constant barrage of humanity in our home. Now with the termites, it was as if the house was being purged of everything.

Perhaps my desire to renovate the house was also a way of reclaiming privacy. But it affected Roger, who was now spending most of his time at Jimmi Seiter's crash pad in the Valley during the renovation, when he wasn't on tour.

Harrison made plans to tent the house on Thanksgiving weekend, while we would all be away. Roger was on tour, and would wind up having Thanksgiving dinner with Skip Battin's parents in Ohio, after playing a gig in Cleveland.

My mother invited Roger's parents to Thanksgiving dinner in Tucson, and we all decided to drive together in the Cadillac. Jim Sr. drove. Dorothy loved the smooth ride. I sat in back with the kids who slept most of the way.

My mother prepared a delicious meal, and had many friends over who enjoyed seeing the boys, including my brother Larry and his lovely new girlfriend, Madelyn. She would become a dear friend to me.

At the end of the Thanksgiving weekend, it was time to head back to LA. With the house still in recovery from the fumigation, the boys and I would stay at Dorothy and Jim's near Burbank.

Roger would stay at his road manager's house in Van Nuys. Roger had just returned from the two-week tour with the band. I wanted to be with him; I needed a hug, a kind word and some reassurance after being separated.

The drive back to Los Angeles took eight hours. It's an exhausting journey through arid desert terrain, and treacherous wind storms in

Palm Springs. All I could think about was getting the house back in order so that Roger could come home. We arrived on Sunday afternoon. I called him at Jimmi Seiter's to let him know we were back and staying with his parents. Roger seemed distracted and made no effort to visit us.

On Monday, leaving the boys with my in-laws, I drove downtown to pay a traffic violation that was due that day. Raw, still tired from our trip, I drove mechanically down the Hollywood freeway. The smog and exhaust clouded my head and burned my eyes. The four lanes of commuter traffic kept a steady, slow tempo. Occasionally, a single car would rally out and merge into a different lane, as if this act might speed up the pace.

Downtown Los Angeles appeared ominous. The off-ramp proved less of a release from the grip of the traffic. The car and I seemed to shrink in size as we maneuvered into the steel canyon. A humbling feeling of being small and insignificant seized me.

I parked the black El Dorado. It took on a life its own – sophisticated, aloof. I crossed the street to the Motor Vehicles building. Two black Muslims were guarding the entrance, selling newspapers.

"*Mohammed Speaks*?" one of them offered.

"I've got to pay my ticket."

They parted and let me through. The line was brisk, and I paid forty-five dollars for speeding and failure to yield. I walked back out into the glaring sun.

"Want a newspaper, Miss?" His white teeth dominated his face. Suddenly, he looked at me. It was a deep stare that penetrates the soul.

"God Bless you and help you," he blurted out. It scared the hell out of me. His piercing scrutiny shattered my composure. I fumbled through my purse in an effort to avoid his eyes. What had he seen?

"Is this enough?" I asked, handing him some coins.

"Any amount is fine."

Clutching my paper, I rushed to the car. It was steaming inside. The steering wheel felt hot and greasy. Was this November? I had a sense of foreboding. I drove back into the Valley, immune to everything around me.

Jimmi Seiter rented a sprawling house with a swimming pool; it was a perfect party place. Besides being road manager, he took care of the band's pharmaceutical needs. We shared a mutual dislike of one another. I walked into the kitchen. There were four or five roadies sitting at the table drinking coffee, nursing their hangovers.

"Is Roger here?" I asked. They all looked at each other with uneasy delight and pointed to the hall. "He's in the back."

I followed the hallway and it led into a bedroom flooded with sunlight and cluttered with clothes, electronic equipment, overflowing ashtrays and empty bottles of booze.

Sleeping on the edge of a twin bed was Roger, and next to him, against the wall, was a naked female body with long tumbling black curly hair. I was stunned.

"Roger?" My voice emerged as a squeak.

He woke up. "Ever get the feeling it's going to be one of those days?" he asked.

She feigned sleep. Roger pulled the sheet over her tenderly. There was a headboard with empty bottles of beer, Southern Comfort and cola cans. I picked up an unfinished bottle of Heineken and held it over her head, as if to douse her with it.

"Don't... please don't," he whispered.

"Why, Roger?" I placed the bottle down. I felt beaten. Roger got out of bed, put his clothes on and steered me into the kitchen. I was numb. Everyone was quiet, anticipating an explosion. They looked at each other, then at me, with smug and contemptuous stares.

Linda finally had the courage to get out of bed. She came into the kitchen with a shy, guilty expression. She still wore the gray Mickey Mouse T-shirt. The roadies were still at the table sorting out pills of different colors. Seiter said casually, "This one is the Prelude, these are the Dexies, and here, the LSD." With that, I snatched up an LSD tab and swallowed it without any water. Someone got a glass and filled it with tap water. "Here, you better drink this."

The rest of the day was a blur.

I think Roger called his parents and said I would be late.

The three of us sat by the pool and talked. She said she didn't want to break up the family. He told me that he loved me, but was "in love" with her. I begged Roger not to leave us. I told him I would wait until he got Linda out of his system. I knew it was a passing fling. I told him I would do anything he wanted. With that he said, "Why don't the three of us get in bed together?" I was taken by surprise; I certainly didn't mean it that way.

"Okay," I said, fueled by the acid that was taking hold and the vodka and orange juice I was drinking.

We went into a bedroom with a double bed. Roger ripped off his clothes and started to undress Linda tenderly. I scuffled with my own clothes, and plopped into bed waiting for them to stop necking. I felt naked to the core under the thin, dirty sheets. The pillows were propped up and Roger smiled like a Cheshire Cat. I moved over for them. Roger in the middle, we all hugged. I was confused. This didn't feel right. Roger was my husband. Why was I sharing him with this bimbo?

I pushed my way into the middle, trying to separate them. Her huge breasts appeared in my face, slapping my cheeks. I rested my head against her chest. I was so tired. The LSD had turned me into a small child; I took a nipple into my mouth and sucked... I had a sudden urge to bite the breast. I spit it out, the taste of lotion overwhelming my taste buds. I shoved her away. Roger had been kissing my neck and wrapping his legs around both of us, while caressing her face. It was a terrible entanglement. When I shoved Linda, he had seen my anger flare, and as I sat up, he slapped my face.

My ear rang with the impact. I was dizzy. I extracted myself from the disgusting duo and started to put my clothes on, the tears falling nonstop... I used the edge of my blouse to wipe my nose. Roger and Linda remained in bed, as he consoled her with a smattering of kisses. I staggered out, and grabbing my purse, stumbled to the Cadillac. I hated myself for being so stupid, and being a part of Roger's disgusting whims. He was another person. I felt I needed a long hot shower, and even this would not clean the filth I had experienced.

I drove to Roger's parents, still feeling the effects of the LSD. Now what? I would have to face my sweet, innocent children. I felt unclean. I rushed into the house and slipped by Dorothy and the boys. Jim took one look at me and stood back. I went into the guest room and turned on the hot water in the shower. I stripped and lathered my thinning body with soap. I stood under the beating water until it got cold. I dried myself and went out to face my family, hoping to hide my shame.

I saw Jim Sr., and numbly I told him I'd caught Roger with another woman. Jim patted me on the shoulder and said it would be all right. Dorothy never found out.

The next day was spent washing dishes and cleaning the house. The boys and I went home to what had once been a refuge. It seemed empty and isolated that evening. I fed them and put them to bed. Roger never came home. He may have called to say he was going on the road, maybe the road manager called.

Trying to sleep was useless. I walked outside into the night. The moon was bright and the lights in the Valley flickered in the distance.

"Why?"

Tears filled my eyes. "Why, God, why me? Why my little family?"

"I can't do this alone. What am I supposed to do now?" I looked up, searching the night sky. "Please help me..." I said aloud.

There was quiet. A soft stirring, then a short cry came from within the house. It was Henry. The answer had come, and was clear. The stillness resumed as I gathered myself and knew my fate. My sons were all that mattered.

Roger eventually came home a few days later. He looked me in the eye and said, "The house looks nice." There was now an echo in the billiard room, because the carpet had been torn out. It had battened the acoustics in the room that was now painted gray.

It was evident that the house was no longer the hub; people were avoiding the bad vibes of Roger's infidelity and my hurt. Susie brought Michelle over a few times, and we talked about the future. The band had solid tour dates going forward. A lot of money was being generated. Susie handled the accounting.

I confided in Bob and Cheryl Hippard the turmoil of my marriage. They were very compassionate and suggested I start thinking about my interests; what the future might hold without Roger. The thought was paralyzing. I emphasized to them that I wanted to keep our marriage together, and that I would be willing to let him have his fling, and not separate. They listened, but I think they knew that would be impossible.

That Christmas, my mother, Larry and Madelyn all came to visit Los Angeles and we had a quiet gathering. Roger made some brief appearances and was aloof toward them. Madelyn was shocked at his behavior. She said to me, "Just leave him, Ianthe. You're punishing yourself being with him."

It was true, because that Christmas, I hit the bottle with Smirnoff Vodka on the rocks or with orange juice in the afternoon. The anesthetic effects were a marvelous tonic for a broken heart. Roger was indifferent toward me; he did not seem to care what I did.

Interestingly, Roger gave me a Minolta 35mm camera for Christmas, like Linda had. She took a lot of pictures apparently. Maybe he figured I had to document the boys.

On December 27 there was a Byrds' concert at the Santa Monica Civic Auditorium. Roger and I drove the Cadillac, both of us in silence the whole ride.

Backstage, I thought I saw Linda, wearing big horn-rimmed glasses and a white dress, taking photographs. She was probably with Jimmi Seiter.

It was with a bittersweet sense of reunion that I saw Terry Melcher and Ry Cooder, old friends. They were kind and welcoming. Terry mentioned upcoming recording sessions for the New Year. It was a real rock 'n' roll grind: recording, touring, recording.

Roger had been drinking and again had taken center stage, feeling prideful. He had become almost a caricature of Bobby Darin with his sense of showbiz swagger. It was a sloppy, loud performance. Afterward, everyone self-congratulated each other backstage, and said their goodbyes. New Year's Eve was coming up. Susie and I made plans to spend time together, with the kids.

On the quiet drive home with Roger, I mentioned seeing Linda in her virginal white dress backstage. "You're seeing things," he said, coldly.

1971 –Earthquake:
God's Answer Pick Up and Dust Off

Roger pensive

I spent the beginning of the year getting the house together after the renovation was completed. I had asked Harrison Ford to build a piece of furniture for the boys' room, a type of bookshelf/desk where toys and books could be stored, and that would provide a counter space for them. He and his friend Tom brought it in one day, completed. It just barely fit into the nursery. It was a large pine bookcase that grazed the ceiling. The lines were simple and it was put together with wooden dowels. I complimented Harrison on the workmanship.

Roger was on tour yet again.

On the morning of February 9, it was still dark, when the sound of the sliding glass doors and windows rattling, combined with a low roar that felt like the depths of hell were being let loose, woke me. As I jumped out of bed to get the kids, adrenaline shot through to the tips of my toes and fingers.

Running to the doorway of my bedroom took an eternity; it felt as if I was running on a conveyer belt. The floor was moving. The house started shaking and creaking. Things started falling, crashing as they hit the floor.

I reached the hallway that separated the two bedrooms. Patrick was there. I touched his head and asked him to wait for me as I stumbled along to get Henry out of his crib. The hanging lamp in the nursery was swaying quietly in the midst of the clamor.

The safest place was outside. I didn't know whether the gas pipes would explode. With Henry in my arms and Patrick's hand in mine, we seemed to float outside. The lights went off and on as if some mysterious person in the chaos had the courage to remain inside and warn us.

Once outside, I put the kids on a wicker swing hanging from one of the trees. It was dawn. I looked below; there was, hanging over the city, a gloomy curtain of dust, mist and smog.

Patrick said he was cold, so I went back into the house, got some blankets, and for some unknown reason an oil lamp. Things were quiet now and Patrick kept asking, "Who shook our house, Mommy?"

I was in a daze. I told them to wait for me as I gave them a push on the swing.

The mess inside was incredible. Roger had six televisions mounted on the mantel. Three of them were on the floor, shattered. All of his equipment had fallen. It had been precariously placed. I couldn't walk in the kitchen; the refrigerator and stove had come out a foot, blocking entry. It looked like someone had gone wild and thrown everything movable onto the ground.

The jars of honey and syrup were broken, mixed in with the flour, oats and cornmeal, to add to the chaos. I couldn't get any food for the kids. I couldn't even venture into the kitchen with all of the shattered glass. The Mexican tile that Harrison had carefully placed over the drain board had acted as a breaking point for anything that fell from the cabinets.

The billiard table had swiveled on the newly varnished hardwood floors, cockeyed. I thought of all the hard work that Harrison and his crew and I had done to get this house in shape, and the cosmic message of impermanence that this earthquake sent.

As I looked out the windows, I saw the kids. I never felt more alone in the world. Tears welled in my eyes, and I choked them back.

Another tremor rumbled and I ran out wildly and put the kids in the Porsche. We drove to my brother Marcus' home. As the sun rose, I saw the devastation in the roads and people's houses, looks of shock, sadness and bewilderment on their faces as they stood outside their homes. I could hear the sirens of ambulances in the distance.

Traffic lights were blinking ominously on Ventura Boulevard, and there was a dusty haze everywhere, like the ground was trying to rise up from under the asphalt. Two hundred tremors were to follow in the coming weeks.

At Marcus', Barbara was mourning the one lamp that was broken; everything else was in place. They offered me some coffee – their electricity was fine. Shell-shocked, I sipped the hot coffee and told them of the destruction at my Alomar home. They were sympathetic. I left the boys with Barbara and their kids, and Marcus and I returned to the house to check things out.

It was days and days of clean up. Our neighbor, Mr. Robbins, came by and said they had some things fall out of their kitchen as well, but he shook his head when he saw all of Roger's broken televisions and the general mess that would have to be cleaned.

Roger never called to find out how we were. He told me later he assumed we had survived. I asked when I'd see him; he suggested I come up to New York to attend the Carnegie Hall concert on February 17.

I took the boys to Tucson to stay with my mother, and from there flew to Vancouver to visit Karen. Her mother had told me that Karen was pregnant, and in a psychiatric unit at the University Hospital in Vancouver after having a nervous breakdown. This was disturbing news for me.

I took a cab from the airport to visit Karen in the hospital. I was heartbroken to see her in this state. Although she was happy to see me, she said that she was afraid of having the baby, because she didn't feel capable of caring for it. She had been having visions of bursts of fire. She appeared calm, but was sedated with medication. When she asked how I was doing, I told her about the breakdown of my marriage with Roger. She and I commiserated in our sorrows.

The area where we were sitting had a large stone fireplace. Someone had carved in one of the stones, "Please get me out of here." There were other desperate messages scratched into the rocks. I felt deeply saddened by this visit with Karen. The atmosphere of Vancouver itself was somber, gray and drizzling the whole time I was there. I stayed the night in a strange hotel, and her husband took me to the airport the next day.

I flew to Boston to see Jet Thomas. Since the incident where I discovered Roger and Linda together, I had sought solace from Jet's kind words and understanding. I planned to stay at his apartment in Cambridge, and then fly to New York to meet Roger. Right before bed, I happened to glance at the Byrds' itinerary and noticed that Roger was performing in Lowell, Massachusetts that very night.

Without telling Jet, I dressed up in warm clothes and impulsively got in a cab and asked the cabbie to take me to Lowell. "Are you sure, ma'am? It's gonna cost you," he said.

It was the middle of the night and snowing. I said, "Yes." I don't remember how long a drive it was, but I felt determined to see Roger.

The cab pulled into Lowell some time later, at the motel where the Byrds were staying. I went to the front desk and told them I was Roger's wife, and showed my photo identification to prove it. They acquiesced and gave me his room number.

The lights were on in the room. I knocked on the door, a secret knock that Roger had devised, so band members knew it was someone in the group. Roger opened the door, and I saw behind him a young teenage woman with scraggly brown hair. I felt enraged.

"What the hell are you doing?" I yelled at them.

"Oh, hi Ianthe," Roger calmly said.

"Get the fuck out of here, who do you think you are!?" I shouted at the young woman. Roger's Halliburton suitcase was propped open next to the front door, and when I walked by it I saw a pair of pink lace bikini underwear, a bra and other female undergarments. I grabbed the articles and began tossing them outside on the snow.

Jimmi Seiter, hearing the commotion, rushed into the room, and took the girl with him. He sneered at me as he caught the girl's jacket that Roger threw at him. I took a seat on one of the double beds. Roger took a seat opposite me, gazing at me analytically. I started crying. "Well, three strikes and you're out, right Ianthe? I guess I'm out."

"Roger, what about us? What about the kids and our family?" I said between sobs.

"Well, right now, I can't think about that. Where did you come from? How did you find me here?"

"I was at Jet's and I was planning on flying to New York to see you there. I saw the itinerary."

"Well, let me drive you back to Cambridge."

Tears streamed down my face most of the way as Roger drove us in silence back to Jet's in Cambridge. It was dawn when we arrived. Jet opened the door and was surprised to see me – he didn't know I'd ever left. Roger didn't step out of the car; he turned around and drove away as Jet let me in.

When I relayed the story, Jet was speechless but told me to try to get some sleep. I lay down, my thoughts swirling with confusion and anger. A few hours later, Jet served some hot tea and English muffins.

"Why don't you go to the pool for a swim?" He suggested. Harvard was now co-ed, and had a heated indoor pool. Later that morning I went swimming.

After the swim, I went to the locker room. I saw myself in a full-length mirror – I was stunned – I could see the back of my body. The skin on my buttocks was hanging loose. I weighed myself and I was eighty-eight pounds – I had lost thirty pounds in three months from stress and worry. I knew I couldn't have Roger see me nude in this physical condition. I frightened myself.

I rethought my trip. I was planning to see Jacques Levy, so I flew to New York, and stayed with Jacques, who lived near Soho on LaGuardia Place.

"Oh, you poor kid! What's happened to you?" Jacques said when he saw me at the door. His girlfriend, Kathleen, made dinner for us. We talked. I explained to Jacques the events of the past three months. Jacques listened thoughtfully.

"You really need to get yourself together, Ianthe. It sounds like Roger has certainly made a statement that he doesn't want to be with you, and you have to face that. You have to get your life in order, and decide what your future is going to be without Roger."

He didn't mince words. It was obvious to him that my marriage was over. Jacques and Kathleen were going to Roger's show in a few days. I called Roger on the road. "I guess I'm going back to Tucson to get the kids, and then I'll be going back to Los Angeles. When will I see you?"

Roger was quiet for a moment on the other end and then said, "Well, I'm glad you're going back. By the way, you're fired."

I was speechless as he hung up on me. After that, he probably put in a call to Linda to invite her to the Carnegie Hall concert. I heard from Jacques, later, that Linda was there. The Byrds went on to tour Europe from New York.

In Los Angeles, the aftershocks continued. Dorothy and Jim McGuinn had decided to give up on their house in Los Angeles and move to Tucson. Their house had been severely damaged by the earthquake. It was such a sudden decision to move that I was surprised. It seemed everyone in LA had the same idea. There were several houses put on the market, and yard sales everywhere.

Harrison Ford stopped by the house. He asked Patrick and me to join him, and we drove in his pickup truck to his home. His wife, Mary, and two sons were baking cookies in the kitchen. Patrick was asked to help them.

Harrison showed me his black and white glossy 8x10 actor's head shot. "This is what I used to look like, when I was trying to be an actor," he said, handing the photograph to me. He wore a tweed sports coat and necktie, his hair parted on the side. I told him that Bob Hippard had encouraged me to join the Actor's Studio. "You don't want to do that," Harrison quipped. His wife joined in, "Yeah. And you don't want to be hanging out at the bars, like all the other Hollywood divorcées."

We left the house, and next door, they were having a yard sale. There was a red, tin tackle box, which I bought for a dollar. I gave it to Harrison, and I said, "Here, so you can put all your money in." "Thanks!" he said. He drove us home.

One afternoon, I was sitting in the kitchen having some hot tea when Roger suddenly appeared, walking by the bay window. Surprised to see me, he waved as he walked past. I stood by the door as he walked in.

"Hello Ianthe, I've come to get a few things." He proceeded to the back of the house. Patrick saw him walking down the hall and said, "Hi Roger!" Roger was friendly and picked him up. He collected some clothes from the bedroom, and after looking around decided not to take much else. Patrick had called his father Roger, instead of daddy, from the beginning.

"I'm sending someone for the pool table and the Moog," he said. "I'm going to leave you the Porsche, and I'm going to take Sidney. I know you like the Porsche better."

"So, this is it, Roger?" I said calmly.

"You need to get a lawyer, and file for divorce," he said coldly.

I resisted by saying, "If you want a divorce, Roger, you should get it."

"I've been faithful to you all these years. And when I was young, I had the opportunity, I never took it. So, I thought this is my last chance."

With that, he kissed the boys on the head, took the keys to the car and fled. Roger left no room for communication or reconciliation. It was all on his terms. I felt empty and scared for my little family's future. This dissolution had been coming for so long, that when it finally happened, I just felt numb.

I called my mother and said, "It's over."

Mother suggested I get a young girl to live in and help me with the children. "You're going to need help," she said, giving me the name of a woman in Tucson, who might know someone willing to move to Los Angeles.

I made dinner for the boys, realizing this was to be the future of my family: just the three of us. It broke my heart. I called Jet and gave him the latest update. "You've got to be strong, Ianthe, not only for yourself, but for your children. I have a very good friend who's a student whose in-laws live in Tucson. The Bakers. You should look them up." This was no consolation for me at this point.

The boys and I went to visit Bob and Cheryl Hippard. "You just missed Roger," Bob said. "And I hate to tell you this, but he's in love, Ianthe. What are you going to do?"

I said, "Roger wants me to get a divorce. But I refuse to. I think he should."

"Either way, you're going to need a good lawyer," Bob said. He gave me the name of a law firm in Beverly Hills.

Cheryl said, "You've got to start doing something for yourself, Ianthe. What about the classes at Actor's Studio? That should help you gain your confidence back." We drank some coffee, and I resolved to take everyone's advice and move on.

The Actor's Studio was a large gray building off Hollywood Boulevard, in an upstairs loft. They seemed eager for new members, and they accepted me, after I paid a fee and had a mug shot taken. The instructor Peggy Feury, a thin, wiry woman with wild blonde hair, assigned me to an acting partner, a beautiful young woman with blue eyes. On the first assignment, my partner would talk to me, try to elicit a response. The instructor wanted me to remain emotionless.

The exercise was easy, but one of the instructor's comments was, "Never walk out. Once you walk out, it's the end. There's no going back." I always felt that was sage advice, and that Roger had walked out on me.

In the class we did "Me Me/ La La" vocal exercises and I found myself meeting a young man, Arthur, who would become my study partner. He had a scene, but I was just helping him with his lines that week.

It takes courage to get up in front of people and bare your soul and body, but the acting classes did strengthen me in that the instructor offered helpful advice about body language, how to carry oneself, and how to find one's inner power. "Use it!" she would shout. "You've been hurt? And who hasn't? Use it. Articulate it."

Susie was checking on me, and knew I was suffering. I'd been drinking. She mentioned that Roger and the guys were recording that night at the Columbia Hollywood studio. I got into my head that I wanted to see Roger. My acting instructor's advice resonated with me, and I felt that I should make an attempt to reconcile with him.

I drove down to Hollywood and walked into the control booth at the recording studio. Linda was there, lounging on the couch, dressed in a skimpy outfit. When she saw me, she stood up suddenly. I sternly told her, "You bitch, don't you know what you've done?" Roger stood up to guard her. Everyone in the control booth – about ten people – stopped and held their breath.

I then kneed Roger in the balls, and he bent over, groaning in pain. Roger dashed to the other side of the control panel, fearful. Linda tried to follow Roger, but I grabbed her by her hair, and started pulling her down toward the floor. She started screaming in pain. The onlookers gasped in shock.

Letting go of Linda's knotted hair, I grabbed a nearby empty wine bottle, and I strode toward Roger, brandishing it. Roger backed away, terrified of my wrath.

Terry remembered later that the bottle was broken, but I can't recall that.

Suddenly, Terry grabbed me by the waist and turned me around, lifting me off the floor and out the door. The bottle fell out of my hand, crashing on the floor. As I was being carried away, back-up singer Merry Clayton, who'd witnessed the whole ordeal, said, "Honey, you ain't gonna keep your man by doing that."

In the hallway, Terry set me down, as I started sobbing uncontrollably and leaned against him. He patted my shoulders and gently held me. "C'mon, Ianthe, let's go have some coffee."

He took me to a little bar across the street on Gower. We ordered black coffee. Terry said in his soft voice, "You know, relationships are temporary, they're not meant to last. Humans are primates, they're not monogamous." This was little consolation for the pain I felt pulsing through my entire body, and the sting of dried tears on my face. I thought of Terry's pet monkey, at home in his cage, all alone.

"Let me get you a cab home. I'll call you in the morning and see how you're doing."

"I can drive," I told him.

The next day, Terry called and said he'd made an appointment for me to see his psychiatrist in Beverly Hills. I went and met an odd man in his forties, wearing a bow tie, who listened quietly as I lay back on a leather sofa, describing my situation. He finally said, "I'll make an appointment for you for next week."

I was only there for one visit after I got the bill. One morning, I was feeding the boys breakfast when I received a call from Eddie Traubner, Roger's accountant. He said, "You need to get a lawyer to take care of your interests. Roger wants a divorce. You can come to my office and get a check if you need money. The joint checking accounts have been closed."

The next day, I drove to Eddie Traubner's in Century City, bringing the boys with me. He looked at me with dismay and said, "My dear, I can't believe what's happened to you." He was referring to my gaunt appearance. "I must address the amount of money you and the boys are going to need. What do you think your expenses are?"

I had no idea. I had no sense of what our monthly expenses would be. He came up with a figure. "Do you think one thousand dollars a month would be okay? You're going to have to open a bank account. I'm sorry this is happening to you. But you must look after the boys' future... and your own. Did you ever have a career?"

"As a waitress..." I whispered. All of Eddie's words were like a wake up call that my domestic life was no more, and that I would have to fend for myself. The days of parties and serving beer, or coffee and banana bread, to all of our guests were over. Going to the market, not caring what the total cost would be, was also in the past. I had to develop my instincts again, my savvy of living on a budget, but now with two children. I felt completely lost, unloved, and depleted.

Eddie wrote me a check for one thousand dollars, to last the month. "Let me know when you find a lawyer," he said, patting me on the back as I walked out the door, dizzy with all the changes I had to process.

I got home and had a vodka and orange juice, as I carefully looked over the check, studying Eddie's penmanship. This was to be the future: a monthly check from an accountant, to substitute for Roger's absence, as a parent, and a husband.

Elizabeth was a teenage Latina from Tucson that my mom recommended. Unbeknownst to me, she was pregnant and had left her parents. I showed her around the house and oriented her. She seemed competent, clean and friendly. She slept in the boys' bedroom.

The arrangement seemed to work out at first. I attended my acting classes and ran errands, and Patrick attended day care. I decided to go shopping for clothes in Beverly Hills. I'd never spent any money on my own clothing, and nothing fit me anymore.

One morning when I returned from the market, I heard Henry crying. I went to the bedroom to pick him up. He had a black eye! I was appalled. I asked Elizabeth, in Spanish, what happened. Upon seeing her, it appeared that he'd bitten her on the cheek. She refused to tell me what happened, but she did say that Henry bit her.

This was shocking to me because Henry had always been a sweet, calm child, who slept throughout the whole night and hardly ever cried. He would awake cheerful and rested. I was furious at Elizabeth, and told her that she would have to leave. Elizabeth had been in touch with my sister-in-law, Barbara, who soon made arrangements to hire Elizabeth as a live-in maid. Good riddance, I thought.

I called Dr. Fleiss and took Henry to be examined. He said he didn't think there was any severe injury. He asked, "How are things at home?" I felt awful, and I burst into tears when I relayed all of the horrible events of the past few months. He was sympathetic.

After Elizabeth, I decided to forego a nanny, and only hired part-time babysitters for the boys. I continued to attend acting classes, and I felt more confident in my new wardrobe of clothes.

I went to the Ash Grove one night, needing a night out. The club had added a second story and a balcony, after the renovation. I was going up the stairs to look at the view from the balcony, when I saw Harrison Ford coming down the stairs, wearing jeans, a white collared shirt and a cowboy hat. "What are you doing here?" he asked.

"What are *you* doing here?" I answered.

"How are you and Roger getting along?"

"Roger moved out. I'm alone with the boys." I said.

We stood in the stairwell, facing each other for a moment. He took a sip of his beer and said, "This is no place for you to be hanging out. If any place, you should be hanging out in Beverly Hills. There's some clubs there where you could meet interesting people."

I thanked him for his concern.

"By the way," I said. "Thanks for making the boys' bookcase. It is so well crafted and looks great."

"Ianthe, stop saying that. Tom made it!" he retorted. I was surprised at his vehemence. I shrugged and we went our separate ways. I drove home in the Porsche and checked on the boys, dismissing the babysitter that night. I was tired, and went to bed around midnight.

Around two in the morning, I awoke hearing footsteps on the flagstone walk, and then a gentle knock on the front door. "Ianthe?" I heard a voice softly call.

At first, I thought Roger was returning. I got out of bed. "It's Harrison, can I come in?" I was very surprised and cracked open the door to see that it was him. Then I let him in, without turning on any lights. I smelled alcohol on his breath; he was clearly drunk.

"What are you doing here?" I asked, perplexed. He put his arms around me. "You know, I've been wanting to do this since I met you." He gently kissed my cheek and my forehead. I was overwhelmed with joy that someone was attracted to me after all of the rejection and negativity that Roger had shown.

I squeezed Harrison tightly around the waist and held him. He squeezed me tighter, and knowing every square inch of the house, took me by the hand and led me into the bedroom. He fumbled a bit, removing his cowboy boots, and put his clothes in a pile on a chair.

He was naked, and approached the bed, gently pulling my nightgown off over me. He had a stunning, beautiful body, fit from all of his manual labor. We got into bed and held each other, kissing passionately, his kisses tasting like beer.

We made love, awkwardly discovering each other's bodies. I had never felt a more firm, masculine body. His strength was easy to surrender to. I, too, had felt the strong attraction the day I met him, and had envisioned us making love. I didn't want this to be a one night stand, but I knew in the back of my mind it would be. I realized my body was diminished with drastic weight loss, and I felt that I was no longer the person he found attractive. In any case, he was married. He moaned gently in my ear, breathing heavily, quietly laying on top of me.

He rolled out of bed and slipped his clothes back on without saying a word. He left the room, muttering, "I'll see you around." The house door closed. It was the last time I ever saw Harrison, except on the movie screen.

Some nights later, I was at the Troubadour, again solo, seeing a performance by Jackson Browne. I'd dropped by backstage to say hi and wish him a good show. He knew about my breakup with Roger.

On stage, Jackson put on a compelling, sensitive show. He was becoming a great artist, and the audience loved him. At one point he opened up one of the songs, introducing it and dedicating the song to "Wendy and Ianthe McGuinn." I can't remember which song it was, because I was so startled by this dedication. It disturbed me: Wendy was a groupie who had been involved with members of the Association and dated David Crosby for a while. I didn't want pity and I definitely did not want to be associated with Wendy. I sensed that was the message Jackson dedicated in this particular song. I felt self-conscious about what I should reveal to people from that point forward.

Backstage, after the show, I saw Jackson, sweaty with a towel around his neck. He said, "How did you like that song?"

Without a pause, I said, "Please don't ever say my name on stage again." He was startled, and I spun on my foot and walked down the stairs. I never saw him again, but during the 1970s, I bought Jackson's records, and enjoyed listening to them. Decades later, when he was accused of domestic violence, I found it hard to think of him as the innocent songwriter I once knew.

Maybe I was burning all of my bridges? I was in touch with Chris Hillman who was still involved with Jeannie. She was a petite blonde, very friendly and energetic, a beautiful companion for Chris. They lived in Venice Beach, and they invited me for a bonfire gathering that weekend, celebrating Earth Day. I wore jeans and a T-shirt, and made my way to Venice Beach in the Porsche. Before the party, Jeannie said she wanted to take me to a boutique that sold antique clothing off the promenade. We strolled into the store and saw many interesting dresses, some owned by former actresses and Hollywood starlets. I bought a long brown velvet coat. Jeannie bought a lacy transparent blouse. The owner of the boutique, resembling Mephisto with a lean goatee and long dishwater blond hair, grateful for the business, asked us if we wanted to share a joint with him. Jeannie giggled, "Yes!"

The three of us went to the back office, which was very ornate with heavily upholstered Victorian furniture and long dark-colored velvet drapes, lampshades with orange stained glass, and a fainting couch. It was a dramatic scene, and I wondered if this was the site of many a seduction. We smoked the joint. As the marijuana took effect, he said, mischievously, "In case you didn't know, this has been laced with Angel Dust."

I'd never heard of Angel Dust, but Jeannie had, apparently, because she said, "Uh oh, we'd better start heading home." We gathered our purchases and quickly left the shop.

The sun was setting when suddenly the PCP hit me. It felt as if I was walking on air – there was no sensation in my toes. We got to the event where Chris was performing. Michael Clarke was there. I hadn't seen him in years. He was happy to see me and said, "I hear you and Roger split."

"Yes," I confirmed as I gazed at the huge bonfire nearby. People were gathering around the fire dancing, drinking and partying. It was a wild beach party, a bacchanal. People spoke about pollution and saving the ecological environment. Somehow, with the PCP influence, I began a mantra, "Evolution, Pollution, Solution..." which made perfect sense to me at the time, as I repeated it constantly.

As the evening wore on, Michael and I started walking along the beach, away from the crowd, in the dark night. The moon was out, reflecting beautifully on the ocean. Michael put his arm around my shoulder, and leaned down to kiss me, a brief affectionate kiss. I felt as if I was kissing my kid brother – but I appreciated the attention and kindness.

We sat on the sand and felt the breeze, sharing a beer. "Yeah, I could live up there, in your house on Alomar..." as he grabbed me and lay me down on the cold sand, ready to make love. We started necking on the beach. I heard passers by coming along, commenting on our embrace, and I said, "Michael, we'd better stop."

Michael and I straggled back to the party. I don't remember driving home, but I must have, because I didn't stay the night with anyone. The boys had a babysitter that night.

After this encounter, I started to realize that I was behaving self-destructively. In my grief, I was self-medicating with booze, pot, and one-night stands. This wasn't how I wanted to live, and I wondered how I could still maintain a life in Los Angeles. I was doing exactly what Harrison Ford's wife had warned me against.

I called my mother. She said that she could offer support with the boys if I brought them to Tucson. I prepared for the trip, packing the boys' clothes and toys.

We drove that night, and I became so sleepy, I pulled over on the highway so that I could sleep a little bit. We were all rudely awakened by a bustling freight truck, sixteen-wheeler, which shook the road as it rumbled by. Patrick was terrified, and screamed, thinking we were in the midst of another earthquake. The post-traumatic stress of the earthquake still resonated for all of us.

Pulling into Tucson at dawn, I was relieved to see my mother, and have a nice hot meal. She saw me and said, "Dolores, I can't believe how much weight you've lost. You'd better come back to Tucson to stay for a while and get your health back."

I was beginning to agree that Tucson was a better place for me and the boys, in the wake of Roger leaving us behind. His parents had already moved here, and lived in an apartment near the airport, all of their belongings in storage. I decided I could rent out the house on Alomar while I recovered in Tucson.

After a week, I drove back to Los Angeles in the Porsche, leaving the boys with Mom. Upon return, I called Eddie Traubner and let him know that I was going to rent out the house, which he said would be okay. I started packing and getting everything ready for a move-out.

Karen was back in Silverlake, living with her mother, after leaving her husband and child in Vancouver. I had started practicing Tai Chi a few months prior, on Saturday mornings in the park. I invited Karen to join me that weekend. She enjoyed it. On the drive home, I couldn't believe it when she told me she didn't want to live anymore. When she said that, I was frightened by her words. I went on with a bunch of platitudes, that didn't have an impact. I loved my dear friend; she and I had been through some very tough times together. She had voiced her dissatisfaction with life to both her mother and psychiatrist. She seemed resolute. It saddens me now, realizing this would be the last time I would see her alive.

I got a call from Karen's mother one morning a week later as I continued to pack. Karen had hanged herself on Mother's Day. I was devastated. Karen's mom said that her daughter's face had the most peaceful expression that she'd ever seen. I couldn't bear the loss, and I started sobbing with Barbara on the phone. Life's closures were happening all around me.

Terry Melcher heard that I was leaving town, and invited me up to his hideaway, which he'd purchased in Idyllwild, near Hemet. He'd become a recluse since the Manson trial. There were other people invited to a small gathering he was having that day. I was surprised to see Gene Clark. He seemed shy and we talked a little. There were other people I didn't know. The house was a rustic chalet, upstairs and downstairs, like a loft. Terry had furnished it with western, and with some Native American, influence. It was a quiet party: cocktails, music and some pot passed around. Terry played 'Sloop John B' on the piano, his signature song.

Guests were invited to stay the night. Most people, including Gene Clark, left. Terry asked me to join him in bed. We went up to his bedroom, and Terry, very relaxed from all of the booze and pot, fell asleep on his bed with his clothes on. I climbed onto the bed, still in my clothes, and slept beside him.

I awoke the next morning, and without waking him I quietly left and drove down the steep mountain in the Porsche, which would later be the site where he would have a terrible motorcycle accident. This was the last time I'd ever see Terry.

When I was back in LA, Jeannie called me and invited me to lunch. We went to a Chinese restaurant in Hollywood. We had Mai Tai cocktails and fried shrimp. It was a welcome lighthearted visit; she was so cheerful. She had an idea: we should go see Gram Parsons, and visit him at the Chateau Marmont, where he was staying.

It was early evening by then, and we drove in my Porsche to the Chateau. We pulled in, went to the front desk and asked what room Gram was staying in. They gave us the room number, and we went to see him.

Gram opened the door, in a heroin stupor, and was surprised to see us. Gretchen, Gram's new wife, was in the back room; she peeked out and looked at us briefly. We felt odd and uncomfortable. He said, "I hear you and Roger broke up, Ianthe. That's too bad."

"I'm moving to Tucson. Maybe we can get together some time soon before I leave, Gram."

Gretchen started calling out for Gram from the other room, ignoring us, making us feel unwelcome. We said our goodbyes. That was the last time I ever saw Gram.

I'd been served divorce papers from Roger. After I consulted the lawyer that Bob Hippard had recommended, I was told that divorce was not his specialty, and he recommended another firm. My first visit with this new lawyer was a rude awakening. Mr. Gerald Hodge asked me, "What assets do you have? Do you have any savings accounts, stocks or bonds?"

"No," I said.

"Furs or jewels?"

"No..." I replied.

"Property or real estate?"

"Well, the boys and I are currently at the house on Alomar that Roger and I bought."

"Any investment property?"

"No," I answered.

"And what about automobiles? A Rolls Royce?"

"Roger left me with a Porsche 911-S. I still drive it."

He jotted that down on a note pad, with a slight sense of pity.

"It appears that you have virtually no assets, Mrs. McGuinn. Roger has agreed to the monthly one thousand dollars, but we will try to increase that amount. For now, what are your plans?"

I paused a minute. "I plan to rent out the Alomar house and stay in Tucson for a while to be with my family."

"It would be best if you stayed on in Alomar. Are you willing to do that?"

"Right now I'm alone, and the house is just a reminder of how alone I am with the boys, and I just feel the need to take a break. Not only that, the aftershocks and tremors are disconcerting."

"Well, it's your decision. But I'd advise you against it. Stay in touch."

Before I left, I asked him about setting up a trust fund for the boys, as part of the divorce settlement. He said that it would be part of the settlement, along with alimony and child support. All of which never materialized. The subsequent decade of living in Tucson took away any sense of urgency on the legal side, as Roger's earning power declined with a lackluster artistic output and slumping record sales during the 1970s.

With an empty feeling in my gut, I walked out of the office, realizing I'd never taken advantage of Roger, or the money that had flowed so freely in our lives during our married years. We'd shared everything: before Roger had money, I fed him at the Ash Grove. My tips were used for food and gas money... and I drove him and the Byrds everywhere. It seemed so unfair that Roger metamorphosed and left the boys and me just when we needed him more than ever.

Daddy Gus pulled into the Alomar driveway with a rental cargo truck, and he and I filled it up with our boxes with the help of my brothers Marcus and Larry. It was a sad feeling leaving the house, and I walked through all of the rooms, with my footsteps echoing loudly. I placed a beautiful black and white photograph Bob Hippard had taken of Roger and Patrick and me, pregnant with Henry, sitting in a rocking chair. It had an 'American Gothic' feeling, and my hope was that Roger would find the photo, where I left it on his worktable in the garage, and feel some sense of remorse. I always regretted leaving that photo behind, and not keeping the photo for myself, because I doubt Roger kept it.

I went outside to where the swing was, looked down into the Valley below, and thought of the many happy times I'd had with Roger and the boys here. Now, it was an empty house, and I was going to move back to Tucson. There was a sense of deep loss, but I knew it was the only practical decision. I needed my family's support to help raise my children, and recover my strength.

We finished loading, and it was time to make the long journey to Tucson, through the dusty desert. I drove the Porsche, listening to sad songs on the radio, which of course reminded me of the past.

Once in Tucson, Daddy Gus and I placed everything in storage. We lived with my mother, while Madelyn helped me find a place for us to rent in Tucson.

Sometime in November, the divorce lawyer requested I come out to Los Angeles for a consultation. I flew out on a Friday to stay for the weekend, leaving the boys with my mother. I rented a car at LAX and drove directly to the lawyer's office to sign papers and meet with him.

I got a room at the Chateau Marmont. Glancing over the divorce papers, I noticed Roger's current address in Malibu Beach. I sighed deeply, went downstairs and had an early dinner accompanied by a few vodkas.

After dinner, fueled by vodka tonics, I decided to venture to see Roger in Malibu. I drove down the Pacific Coast Highway as the sun was setting. I drove for what felt like hours in the Malibu hills, on dusty dirt roads, trying to find the street Roger lived on. It was seemingly hopeless, driving in the darkness with no sense of orientation.

Miraculously, I found Roger's street, noticing a security camera as I drove through the open gate. Other cars were there. I got out of the car and approached the front door, knocking.

Roger opened the door. He was utterly shocked to see me. "Wow," he said, widening his eyes. "Come on in."

I stepped inside, as Linda and the other guests, including Carlos Bernal and Jimmi Seiter, glanced up at me. "Look who's here," Roger announced. Jimmi Seiter said, "Oh no! *Ono!*"— which was a current cry of dismay, citing Yoko Ono's tyranny over John Lennon. Everyone laughed uncomfortably, a palpable tension in the air. My reputation preceded me.

Linda was silent. Roger said, "We're just having a friendly game of pool, Ianthe. Wanna play?" He handed a cue stick to me. I took it. Someone handed me a bottle of cold beer.

"Why don't you and Linda have a go at it. The winner gets me," Roger said mockingly, a smug smile on his face as he put his arm around Linda. Everyone laughed or groaned, as if at a sporting event.

"Roger, what are you doing? Don't you see that your children need you?" I stammered.

Roger said in earnest, "The winner of the pool game gets me. Why don't you play?"

Some of the people clapped in encouragement. I hadn't played pool in ages. Our old billiard table sat in the center of the large living room. Everyone present gathered around the pool table. Roger racked up the balls.

I found myself in the center of this surreal, neo-Roman display of decadence: playing pool for the man I still loved, as he tortured me to compete with his concubine.

Linda, having months of practice over the past year, easily shot several balls into the corner pockets. When I finally had a turn, I prayed each time I struck the ball. God was not listening; I seemed to miss all my targets, to the jeers and cries of the onlookers. I was disgusted by the cruel intentions of Roger, putting me on the spot like that. He had no sense of compassion.

Even if I had won the pool game, Roger would certainly have not come through with his end of the bargain. As Linda finished me off on the billiard table, her face glowed, and everyone cheered. I lost badly to Linda. "Well, sorry! You lose, Ianthe," Roger said with a gleeful shrug. People returned, unfazed, to their drinking and smoking, congratulating Linda.

I felt nauseated. I went into the bathroom and noticed a plastic Cookie Monster toy on the counter. What kind of life was Roger living now? I splashed water on my face and fought back the tears. How in the hell would I find my way back to the hotel, out of the winding dirt roads of the Malibu Hills?

"You know, I used to let you win at chess, Roger," I said to him as I mustered my strength to leave. Roger groaned. "That's mean. I always thought I was a better player."

I rushed to the door, not saying anything more. Roger ignored me as I left and returned to his friends, as if I'd never been there. As I passed the kitchen, I noticed how filthy it was. There was a stack of dirty dishes in the sink, and a strange smell of decaying food.

While I was there, I overheard Jimmi Seiter mentioning recording the next day at Wally Heider's studio in Hollywood with Jim Dickson. At breakfast the next morning, I decided I'd go to the studio, vowing no physical confrontation. I don't know what compelled me. I wanted revenge for Roger's cruelty.

It was evening when I reached the studio, and I noticed Roger's Cadillac parked in front. I had a brilliant idea: I still had a duplicate set of keys to the Cadillac on my key ring. I parked my rental car, and easily opened the Cadillac, which smelled of old cigarettes and booze, and was filled with Roger and Linda's dirty clothes – another signal of Roger's degraded state. I started the ignition on the car and drove it around the corner, to the next block. I locked up Sidney, the Cadillac, and then dashed back to my rental, leaving.

I decided I could only cause trouble in the studio, so I returned to the Chateau Marmont. Many years later, Jim Dickson relayed to me the confusion and alarm that my prank caused. It ended the recording session, and Roger, confused, thought his car was stolen, and called the police. The police easily found the car. Jim Dickson and I had a good laugh over it. He actually thought it was a pretty gutsy thing that I had done.

1972 -1975 –Rebuilding (A Family sans Father)

One of our frequent visits to Dorothy and Jim's, in Tucson after Sylmar
Earthquake, 1972

Back in Tucson, I was anguished to discover that Roger and Linda
married just two weeks after the divorce was granted in November
1971. Bob Hippard informed me they were honeymooning in Europe,
on tour with the Byrds.

I phoned Eddie Traubner in LA and asked if I was going to be
receiving the rent money from our house on Alomar. That's when he
informed me that I had signed a 'quick claim deed' when Roger
bought the house. This was on Larry Spector's advice, a guarded
secret he and Roger shared. My ex-husband was now selling our

Alomar property, and there was nothing I could do. There was no returning to our home in Los Angeles, and I had no recourse. Roger was just as unscrupulous as Larry Spector.

Eddie Traubner complained to me that my lawyer was asking for large sums of money for fees. There was nothing I could do from Tucson. I felt helpless. A month later, my lawyer only increased our monthly payment to $1,125.00 per month. This would stay in effect until the boys turned eighteen, and by that point, the money did not go very far.

There was never any alimony or trust fund established. It's almost criminal how the lawyers that were involved reaped the benefits of hefty legal fees. The case went from one lawyer to the next consecutive associate, incurring more fees and boxes of paperwork along the way, losing momentum and relevance as the years went by. It would take days, sometimes weeks, for me to get a return phone call from my own lawyer. Then that consultation would be charged. Roger's accounting team paid all the fees. Those monies should have been applied to the boys and me. It seemed no one could possibly divert it to us, as the lawyers milked this settlement negotiation throughout the decade.

Roger's father later told me that Roger had earned $1 million dollars one year, but had nothing to show for it. I imagined a significant amount had been wasted on drug use. I was disgusted, thinking that the boys could have used that money for college. We never owned a home during our years in Tucson. The instability of renting was an on-going challenge.

I enrolled in classes with a goal of getting a degree for a profession, and I took up journal writing as I recovered from the negativity of Roger, the earthquake and our Los Angeles exile. The boys and I rented a home on the rustic west side of Tucson. I bought two old, sweet retired horses for a pittance so that the boys could learn to ride. We kept them in an existing corral on the back of the property. One of the horses was named after the brand on its hide, "W.S."

Some journal entries follow.

Friday, January 21, 1972

If I write something, I might release a few of my hostilities, or at least understand what the hell is happening to my brain. There seems to be so much pressure – self incurred no doubt. I can't honestly say it isn't. I seem to be burdening myself with unnecessary worry and doubts. That is absolutely no way to begin a beginning, a middle or an end; I'm not quite sure what phase of life I'm in; confused.

This morning I was rushing around, trying to get the house clean before I left. Fed the animals, fed the kids, got dressed, got them dressed – chaos. Henry, in the meantime, is busy destroying any order that I've made – I was really upset. It seems I should have had a bit more restraint.

It all begins to accumulate; being alone with two boys isn't easy. I'm scared I won't have the strength they need. I don't know what I want, what my role is, or how to behave. I suppose I'll learn as time goes on; of course, I'd go quite mad without them.

Monday, January 24, 1972

It seems I just lost a bout with the city of Tucson. The structure of rules and codes has been upheld by a little old woman in a prim red dress who took forty dollars away from me for speeding 25 miles over the limit. However, I was fortunate since the officer that gave me the ticket could have charged me with drunk driving.

Christ – What am I doing? Things are materializing so badly. I'm juggling my time so that there is nothing but running around, half mad, afraid of being late, or there are huge lags where I seem to sit and wait.

I'm supposed to go to Los Angeles this weekend, but it seems like such a chore and easier to put off until next weekend. Money might not let me go for another month.

Believe it or not, I just saw Josie, the best friend I had in high school. It's been over twelve years since I've seen her. She's taking nursing, married Jonny, my old boyfriend, and has two kids. I wonder how she's categorized me?

Tuesday

I went to one of my psychology classes for the first time today, it was really lively. The topic that seems to creep up in most of the discussions that I've attended is our future. I haven't been to school for ten years, and therefore not much involved with younger people. Their concern is so strong. I felt guilty for driving a car, flushing the toilet and using Kleenex.

My mother has an old pedal Singer sewing machine, and she keeps telling me to take it after she dies. I think that's sort of morbid – but she has this thought that the power will run out and it'll come in handy. In fact, everything that is manual... she recommends I buy a generator.

Mother has a really strong survival instinct. It makes me kind of proud. I'm her daughter. She has this fantastic sense of right and wrong. She has a third eye, being able to pick up on anything that's wrong or about to go wrong. Then she can assimilate it and come up with some really helpful, constructive advice.

I've never known her to be lazy or idle. In the worst of times she carries everyone with her sense of humor, which I'm beginning to believe is her strength. Her cooking is fantastic.

Wednesday

Coming out of that English class, I dropped my books and then stumbled over my feet. It felt like a case of mental exhaustion. Tests have a way of affecting people in different – *Fuck*!

I've gone back, re-read what's in this journal – and frankly I don't like it. I don't know if I like me. I don't know anything.

I'm tired of saying, 'I.' I can't stand 'I'... There has to be a way not to use it. Maybe if I pinch myself each time it's used – substituting it with some other word like dumb-head, pin-head, bumble-head.

Each time this book comes out, some awful piece of trivia is shoveled out. How can dumb-dumb allow this to happen? There was always a question of values and high standards that seems to be a bit hypocritical right now. It's just not there. The honesty that I believed in seems to have disappeared – maybe it's old age. I'm 29 years old.

> There once was a lass who was twenty
> Left home in search of plenty
> The plenty she sought was not in
> Riches she thought – but in truth
> And brave deeds help others in need
> Instead she was handed a rock.

Thursday

Hideyo Kondo was a Japanese art student studying in the United States. His father worked for the American Embassy in Kyoto, easily arranging for Hideyo's visa.

Upon arrival to the U.S., Hideyo's sponsors had a party for him. In this family were a boy and girl about Hideyo's age. The night of this party, the young fellow introduced him to some girls. Hideyo happened to be sitting by the door, and not knowing the custom of standing when introduced, was advised by his host, after Hideyo had remained seated during the introduction.

Wanting to do his best in this country, he spent the rest of the evening standing and sitting any time a group of girls walked into the room.

Monday

I'm beginning to really dislike weekends. It's such a relief when a new week begins and I can get on a schedule. That's really strange, there was a time when I hated schedules or any kind of regimentation. It all corresponds with the positive and negative, or tension and relief – you can't have one without the other.

In some of the Anthropology classes one observes a cautious, almost guarded vocabulary. An aggressive word can become the brunt of a heated discussion. Being a Chicano is something to be proud of these days. Ten years ago he was culturally deprived, today you could get socked in the mouth for using that term. I think I'll change my name back to DeLeon.

When we were going to Mom's I happened to grind the gears and Henry said, "The car's pooping, Mom." It's going to be a year since Roger's seen the kids – that really pains me. One would think he could at least call. I'd like to punch him. Forget it, Ianthe, it ain't worth the worry.

I simply had to write. It's amazing the instant excitement I have for school. It really feels like something good. I feel, though, I'm losing a something. It's sort of like tapping all areas to find the right combination and suddenly, blam. You've got it and everything feels positive.

There was a poker game tonight and I cleaned the house. Actually, I felt sort of guilty. I'm feeling so cocky I'll have to stop!

Tuesday

I got really angry in my psych class today. There was a discussion on Indians and I was offended by the term 'they.' These people kept saying 'they' and 'them', referencing the Indians. I was furious. Suddenly I felt like an alien, as if I was a whole different person apart from these other people in the room. It was an awkward feeling.

That does it! I have to keep neutral. I'm getting so opinionated, it's disgusting. I can't believe anything I have to talk about has validity. It's incoherent, subjective and totally biased, usually gets me into trouble.

Wednesday

It was pretty clear today, some mornings are so smoggy they remind me of Los Angeles. I took Mom downtown and it seems to change every time I go there. There's little I can relate to. We lived across the Santa Cruz River, where the Desert Inn now stands.

Henry was mad at Patrick, and blurted, "Patrick's stupid. It's rude to say stupid, but I say it anyway."

Lately, they've been getting along pretty well, except when Patrick is busy with something and Henry wants to interrupt and play. Patrick becomes a big authoritarian and shouts, "Henry, go to your mother right now!"

There is something that strikes me as very male with that statement. It's as if he's too busy doing something important, can't mess around with Henry, but Mom isn't doing much, so go to her.

If he's five now, what will it be like when he's older?

Mom was telling me I should be glad to be alone and not have to wash, cook and keep a husband happy. But Christ, I feel I have two old men living with me. These guys might be small, but they have tempers and determined wills and tremendous standards. Frankly, I don't think they'll let me get married.

Married! Blat! The thought seems remote and unrealistic.

Thursday

It was still early, the kids hadn't come out of school yet. Damian, one of Patrick's school mates, had been let out early, he walked up to the car, showed me a fork and said, "Want to see my mom's underwear, I mean silverware?"

Somewhere, I heard that American girls expect their dreams to come true; that around the corner they hope to find the right person. What a delusion. We're all brought up with a Walt Disney vision of happiness-forever and all the time if that state doesn't prevail, we feel something's wrong. A friend was married ten years; one day her husband told her that he finally realized he was in love with her. She really became indignant and wanted to leave. She felt she'd wasted all those years on this fellow that didn't love her. It seemed petty. There's something that tastes sour in that kind of relationship full of compromises and toleration.

197

Friday

After re-reading this journal, I think I'll prescribe to myself a boyfriend.

I was remembering back to the time before the earthquake. I met a woman from Los Angeles that owned a flea market here in town. They were closing up their business because they think Tucson is a 'hick town,' and are hoping Florida will treat them better.

It happened that we were neighbors in LA and she couldn't have been happier, and yet she was disappointed; after all this time she met someone who knew the old place.

We chatted briefly and found her husband was in the film business before the Quake, and just talking about it gave her goose bumps. Which is literally true – I *saw* them.

I felt sympathetic as she looked around, saying they couldn't make it. I wished them a good trip and left, but not before she gave me their phone number and asked me to call them before they left.

The kids' snoring makes me sleepy; I guess there's no sense in staying up. Another night of quiet wait. I'm looking forward to going back to L.A. for a while. The traveling will do me some good.

Patrick stood in front of me, head drooping between his rounded shoulders, eyes downcast and forlorn. "Mommy, I'm a dumb person."

"Why do you think that, Patrick?" I asked, astonished.

"Well, I can't play in the mud outside, or with water, and I never get to eat anything."

"But Patrick, you were outside all afternoon making mud-pies, and you got your shoes all muddy. Then when you came in, you had your favorite dinner."

"Well, I'm dumb 'cause I don't get any punch that's in the refrigerator."

Tuesday

The instructor in my psych class is keeping his back to me. I wonder if it's because of my argument last week?

I've been talking to my old friend, Josie, who happens to be in my psych class and she leaves me with my head spinning. I guess one thinks he has problems and when he hears someone else's, things seem pretty simple.

Hell, I've had my share of misery and when it comes it's in huge doses. The only reconciliation is that it will end and if you're lucky, will leave you a better and stronger person. 'Great happiness is reached through deep sorrow.'

I just read something that forewarns anything bad that occurs 'as the devil would have it.' That's pretty good, I guess I could begin a lot of my stories like that. It gives me the image of some small red creature, cross-legged, hand over his mouth, chuckling mischievously whenever someone falls prey to his will.

I don't know, though, the level of evils in a person. Deception as opposed to stealing as opposed to murder. Mother has this thought that if something you're doing makes you feel guilty, cut it out.

This is all sort of morbid and is depressing me, so I think I'll stop.

Thursday

There isn't anything to say. Everything seems to be pretty much the same. It's really depressing. I baked some orange cookies for Patrick's Valentine's party. Reminds me to get Mom some flowers or candy. She likes that kind of stuff. To be remembered is a good thing for one's spirits.

I can't stand this haircut. I feel like a boy. Two fellows winked at me today – I didn't know if it was because of me or the Porsche.

Brando was great in that movie tonight. I hate heroes and don't believe in them. Don't remember when I stopped. Maybe living in L.A. Everyone and everything is so phony.

Even the apartments have glitter in the plaster and colored lights shine all night on the poor trees. I wonder if that has any effect on their growth.

Forgot my purse last night, so I'll have to pick it up in the morning. Can't write anymore, doesn't feel right.

Monday

I want to write something, but it won't come out. I really feel like talking to someone. I saw my father yesterday; we hadn't seen each other since I was fifteen. He looked as if he was taking good care of himself.

I heard people whistling, but couldn't figure out why. Sitting, wondering what makes people happy. There's no real reason, no real happiness, only fragmented bits of joy that keep us going.

Feeling miserably depressed, things seem so damn lifeless, stale. There is a lot of work I must get to. It's cold out here. My back hurts, the right side of my head is aching, I'm hungry, people seem unfriendly... the elevator keeps whirring as it goes up and down. People's footsteps up and down stairs, doors opening and closing, distant conversations, fluorescent lights, echoing, all echoes – I'm going mad, I can't stand this any longer, goodbye.

Tuesday

It's simply a matter of finding the right time and place and mood. I've found I can't force myself to write, it's frustrating and thoroughly unsatisfying. I had an instructor in high school who said, "If you can't spell it, don't write it." That's really inhibiting, a lot of people would never pick up pencils.

I had a hard day, yesterday. I can't believe I'm still the same person. I took Henry and Patrick to a friend's house. That's really strange I've only met her once before and I call her a friend. Her name is Marian Baker Kahn. Knowing Jet, Gram's old friend, brought us together so fast and bypassed a lot of orientation it takes two people to hash out before they know one another.

As I walked in this office, a secretary looked up expectantly; when she saw me she dropped her head and lowered her eyes. I felt I disappointed her. She must have been expecting some fellow. Never looking up again, I wanted to say something to reassure her. Hell, what do I care about her feelings anyway?

I wish there was a class that taught us 'How Not to Judge and Evaluate People.' It really bothers me that we have notions about what a person should have or be before he is even considered a human being.

It must happen at some point when we deal with people. I remember just looking for a job.

Thursday

The men outside Mom's house have been tearing and repairing the road for the last three months. This one fellow keeps following me with his eyes. He never smiles or frowns, just looks. It's scary.

My brother's in the hospital, knee operation. I hope he recovers all right. I was in the hospital for one week during the summer, it was miserable. I was lonely. The nurses were always feigning cheerfulness or interest. Their sincerity was questionable.

The sun is going down. This is the worst time of day, it's usually the time when I get homesick, lonely or depressed. This week has been gloomy and unproductive. I've got to get out of this ennui before it becomes destructive.

Monday

Yesterday was great. I left Patrick and Henry with Mom and went to the library to work on a paper, due next week. The Armory was hustling with the same brightness the sun gave. Artists had their wares displayed on the grassy lawn. Beyond this point rested quietly the Papago Village. It was really clean.

One area in the middle was sectioned off. There, an old woman sat weaving a basket. She smiled gently, showing uneven spaces between her beautiful white teeth. People came around and asked her about her baskets and the materials she used.

It was the only shaded area there. The rest seemed so hot as the oil drums that had been converted into grills to make flour tortillas. Four or five food stalls were set up. Here, hard-working Indian women withstood the heat. Stacks of mesquite wood diminished in size as the orders for tortillas and pop-overs increased.

Everyone was scrubbed and freshly clothed. People were amiable and gathered in small groups to chat and discuss the day's events.

It was twelve o'clock and the library didn't open until one-thirty. So I decided to eat lunch. I ordered a bean burro and a strawberry soda, and looked for a patch of shaded territory.

Lovers and families spotted the grassy areas under the trees. I decided to sit on a bench, lest I soil my white pants on the grass. There, the old people congregated. I sat next to an old man who promptly left. A couple of Witnesses sat across from me discussing the Judgment Day.

Birds chirped noisily. Kids' voices called out. Bits of Spanish and English conversations carried over. The sky was blue and puffs of white clouds mellowly floated across.

I felt lighthearted and good with all the activity. Somehow it reminded me of my girlhood. I nestled myself against the hard bench. It felt warm and friendly in spite of its seeming hardness.

A young fellow with a fiddle case was introducing an older man to his young friend. Before long the three of them situated themselves under a tree. Set up with banjo, guitar and fiddle, they began to play. It was elating.

Soon more musicians turned up and the crowd around them began to grow. My burro was gone and the rest of my soda had turned warm. A loudspeaker system screeched and sounded in the background. Someone kept blowing into the mic and repeated, "Testing." Satisfied, they announced the beginning of a fiddle contest.

The musicians continued playing. Everyone smiled, tapped their feet, and clapped gratefully after each tune. Then a fellow in a straw cowboy hat came over and said it was time to go on stage. The group folded and the crowd dispersed. I looked at my watch, it was one-forty.

The library had been open for ten minutes. I gathered myself together, ready to face anything.

Tuesday

I dreamt last night that I fought with a turtle. I had a stick and this giant pale green turtle would bite it and then I'd try to shake him loose. My only hope was to tire him and throw him on his back, but he wouldn't yield. Can't remember the rest.

Patrick, Henry and I went to the museum at the University. They really enjoyed the animals upstairs. Patrick was scared of the buffalo. Henry thought the bobcat was a kitty. The skeleton of a man was displayed near the animals. The assumption was that he had been eaten by the animals next door.

Patrick wanted to be an Indian, so that he could grow corn and put it in baskets. When I told him he was a little Indian, he responded, "No, I'm not. I'm not brown."

After arriving home, we went for a long walk in the desert (our back yard). Patrick and our dog Oz led the way. Henry, being so fat, found it hard to keep up. Oz scouted ahead, sniffed around and returned to assure Patrick. He in turn shouted to us to follow him, everything was all right.

We rested on a hill overlooking the wash. Henry and I threw loose rocks down the slope. Patrick picked dried flowers and informed us we didn't bring any food or water in case we should happen to get lost. Ozzie sniffed the air and trotted back and forth.

After everyone had recuperated, we ventured downhill. Oz reached the bottom first. Patrick wanted short legs so that he could get down fast. We sighted our house and Patrick reassured us we were safe.

Friday

I awoke yesterday somehow feeling it was going to be another of the same type of days. The water beating on my head during my shower didn't indicate anything different or unusual. Fixing breakfast and dressing the boys reinforced my feeling.

The final phase of leaving the house got underway. I fed the dogs and walked down to the corral to feed the horses. The five month old filly met me half way, as she turned I saw a four-inch gash on her neck. W.S. had bitten her. I cursed her as I got the wheelbarrow and trudged up the hill to fill it with hay.

Pushing it down with a load, I caught a glimpse of W.S. kicking Lady, the colt's mother. Her leg was held above the ground. They ate as I ran back to the house to get some peroxide for the foal. Lady still had her leg above ground. I went close and gently touched her leg. It crackled and I knew it was broken. I called the vet and when he came, they put her to sleep. It was a dreadful experience.

Monday

There's no reason for my feelings of isolation. Sunday we had a grand picnic with Mom and Daddy Gus, Larry and Madelyn, Uncle Eddie and Elsa, Patrick and Henry, and Bob, Larry's musical compatriot. I was on all the losing volleyball teams. Patrick and Henry puttered around, making funny noises and silly remarks. I had to do some homework but I put it off. The night before Karen's mom, Barbara, came in from L.A. on her way to Mexico. Marian and Joey were over for dinner, Larry and Madelyn dropped by and someone miraculously stretched our meal. Everyone ate and drank enough and we laughed all evening at crazy things. Barbara's friend Danny related. The kids were great and gave no trouble.

Tuesday, March 14, 1972

Sometimes driving on the freeway lacks any excitement or moving experience, but yesterday, on my way home, I kept smelling manure. At first I thought I'd gone someplace that had a few cows, but the lingering smell made me wonder.

Then looming before me was a huge cattle truck. Farrell's Cattle from Gonzales, Texas was shipping a truckload of sad and frightened-looking cattle.

There were four barred windows on the back panel, and two levels, an upper and lower compartment where these pitiful animals were squeezed against each other. A head hung over another's back as it pressed against the barred openings. Some isolated tail flapped in the wind.

In the lower berth, one of the faces glared wildly. The exhaust from the truck constantly clouded his face.

I thought of Jews. Somehow it didn't ring true. It was my exit. The truck continued to its fate.

Wednesday

Sunday the Bakers took the boys and me on a family picnic to Sonoita. We drove undaunted in a camper bus mobile through dry grassy hills, patched with green bushy trees and blooming yuccas. It was a warm family atmosphere.

(Undated entry, 1972)

The wind blows gently; my brother's children are playing in the next room. The freeway has its steady roar; a bird singularly chirps a melancholy song. I know Los Angeles, a place full of incongruities; a Rolls Royce passes a barefoot hitchhiker.

The drive from Tucson was uneventful, yet I'm grateful there weren't any accidents. The car performed to its maximum. Lawyers generally friendly and cautious. The old homestead looked a bit sad, overrun with gopher holes and dry weeds. It didn't look like spring.

Smog everywhere. Saw a few old friends, nothing much to say. Asked Lisa Lamelle to visit with kids and later regretted it. The pace seemed too fast for me, glad to return tired.

Hard to return to school and schedule after vacation. Feeling of waiting for unknown something. Things must be getting better. The house looks full with the furniture I brought from old house. It feels happy.

I find I tire easily of any unnecessary conversation and wishy washy, milquetoast people. I'm becoming less tolerant and more outspoken in my feelings. Sometimes it seems unfair and downright hostile.

I want something and I want to give something. And there's this persistent gnawing that I have something to give; not just to one person, but to many. I like that. It excites my blood. I know I can move and touch emotions. I want to find the best way.

The realization that Tucson is the best place for me right now, was finally implanted in my brain during my trip. This is a period of reconstruction, reevaluation, and reexamination of what I am, who I am, and where I'm going. Getting involved might be nice, but not very profitable in my general state.

(Undated entry, 1972)

Another Friday evening, a glass of dry red wine and cigarette; a *Bangladesh* album that skips occasionally, love competing with the network special on Blacks; the kids bouncing around; Henry waving a glass in front of my face wanting juicy, Patrick asking for his after-dinner treat. What does it all mean?

Mother's been in L.A. all week. I guess I'm beginning to miss her. She said over the phone last night, she wondered if her asking me to live here in Tucson was a good idea, because she'd seen a lot of nice-looking young men alone. What a laugh. So I'll continue to drink my wine, smoke my cigarettes, wondering if the kids will go to sleep.

Ahh – for the days when I was married to a rock and roll star; what prestigious friends, who would stab you in the back given the opportunity. Evenings where you were lucky if Roger could get home intact, full of liquor, cocaine, Placidyl, Preludin, and grass. Feelings of inadequacy because everyone around was a virtual genius, at least they had the money and popularity to prove it. Unable ultimately to compete with a nineteen-year-old *Playboy* body. Alas, what does one do?

I read in *Psychology Today* that when one loses his position or money it's a traumatic experience, causing great depression and even suicide. I suppose it isn't that drastic.

At my brother Larry's house the other day, one of his friends sat next to me and said he'd heard I'd met the Beatles. He wanted to know what they were like. I told him it had been five years since I'd met them and I was sure they'd changed – so I really couldn't say much more. We looked at each other blankly and he moved away.

If I get really drunk tonight I'll probably listen to one of Roger's records and mourn my fate. I saw Brando in *The Godfather* and recollected the time at some party when he asked me to run away with him; but I benignly refused because I was with Roger. What true fidelity – what true love. What a dummy.

I ran away with a thirty-three-year-old New York musician when I was eighteen, and his name was Peter.

(Undated entry, 1972)

Today during lunch, I spotted my young Behavioral Science instructor and found myself thinking shockingly lascivious thoughts. I first noticed him in the dining hall, he wiggles his leg back and forth nervously; then Blam. I went back to eating my pressed ham and cheese and reading Vonnegut, after deciding they didn't mix.

Which reminds me of an occasion in the library of Los Angeles City College nine years ago. There I was industriously doing my homework, two seats next to me was a shy, clean-cut young Negro about seventeen years old. As I continued my homework, something in me froze. I happened to look over, and there he was masturbating, in the library, two seats away!

I quickly looked away, stared blankly ahead and hurriedly gathered my books and left.

Starry Stellars stay not forever
Stoney Stoics start to break

Patrick says Angels are bright blue light
By God, I think he's right!

Los Angeles is falling, the cry rang out
Some cursed, some cried, some laughed, some left

A child's world of dreams never ends.
Gladness teaches the lonely heart
Through fear, frustration and emptiness
Wrongs that are never sought,
Never bought, just taught.

(Undated entry, 1972)

Somewhere, things got lost or dissipated. I feel school is passing me by. Things aren't measuring out the way I'd hoped; I feel lethargic and unsettled and indecisive.

When I took Patrick to school there was a sign on the wall, 'Fat Jews.' I was surprised, was that learned? After I dropped him off, I went down to Broadway, outside the school yard of Miles Elementary, two boys, one Black and one White were pushing and scuffling.

The differences in people, we still haven't learned to accept. Is it that we don't want to learn to overcome our fears or pre-conceived ideas? I wonder if wars and fighting are a way of life that we can never rid ourselves of. That whole thing about territorial rights and dominance in apes carries over subtly. Men having to prove they are masculine to cover innumerable insecurities. A society that devalues people's role and self worth.

Feeling rejected and generally unreliable and unworthy. I've come in here to hide. I don't want to see anyone, and I don't want anyone to see me. I missed two days of school last week and it feels as if a week went by.

(Undated entry, 1972)

Today I almost bought a gun. I couldn't believe how scared I got last night. Maybe it's buying trouble, but what should I do alone? Learn Karate?

The dingos are winning
Hooray-hurrah
The rain hasn't fallen
Plunk plunk plink plank
The flowers are blooming
Bluuuum bluuuum
The walls are crashing
KRRASHHHHHhhh

(Undated entry, 1972)

So I said to myself, "Ianthe, old girl, it's not that you're so bad, awful and ugly and unworthy that you don't have anyone. It isn't because you're so good, and cool and groovy and fancy-looking either. It happens to be a fact, man, and you should face it. God wants you to channel all he's given you into something worthwhile."

My physical frustrations are at this point beyond me. Out of control should I want to run my life. No – I've done that, bounced back and now I'm on a one-way track with the kids.

I want to let them channel my feelings into something constructive. I guess I've been trying too hard. I know for sure as I drove down streets that to me, twenty-three years ago, seemed like highways, and the one-bedroom homes that stood on my way to school seemed like mansions. Outside them, the few flowers that the old, wizened Mexican ladies passed over, watering, throwing coffee grounds on the earth, using egg shells ceremoniously for their calcium content, scolding them on occasion, grew meagerly, but with as much strength and fortitude as their benefactors displayed.

Henry and Patrick, 1973

April 28, 1973

This evening I phoned Roger to ask if he was coming to see the kids. He said he hadn't made a decision. So I asked (because he seemed apprehensive and uptight) if it was something secretive, and he said, "No – it's nothing I want to keep from Linda, I don't want to talk to you, fuck you." CLICK–

Well I sigh and still nothing is answered. I know if he were to see me, he would be so critical. A voice harsh and unyielding. He would want to leave. Yet, I know I want communication with him. Yet he doesn't want it with me. Goodnight.

(Undated entry, 1973)

I was utterly surprised to hear Susie White's trembling voice on the other end of the phone. "Clarence is dead," she wept. "He was crushed by a drunk driver... I don't know if you'll be able to come to the funeral. It would be good to see you."

I was speechless, "Susie, I'm so sorry." I told her that I didn't think I'd be going, since I didn't have the money, and I was wary of seeing Roger so soon after our last traumatic experience. Susie said that she and her children would be returning to Kentucky. I felt so awful, realizing the depth of her loss. My image of Clarence's children growing up without knowing him saddened me.

(Undated entry, 1973)

The days pass and I find I'm still with the same thoughts, in relatively the same mood, and essentially doing the same things. My life seems almost at a slow-paced gait. People alienate me, or I them, in obtrusive ways. It seems odd, I always start out on a good foot and eventually, through the relationship, get myself so wrought and involved in their lives until I have to destroy it.

I don't know what people think of me. A lonely, confused person, I presume.

I saw Henry timidly return to a dead bumblebee and a small green plastic car missing its left front tire. The same tire that was crashed in the Porsche. He approached it cautiously at first, then grabbed the green car and cursed the dry bumblebee for being stupid.

(end of journal entries)

One day in late September 1973, Eddie Tickner phoned. "Gram Parsons died of an overdose in Joshua Tree." My heart sank. Gram was so young. He had such vitality and beauty; I was disgusted and saddened to think of his life ending. There was so much for him yet to offer. I thanked Eddie for the news, and cried, thinking of all the humor and joy Gram had brought in my life. A memory came back to me: once, when I was cleaning the house on Alomar, and Roger was on tour, Gram had festively stopped by the house with a bottle of champagne. It wasn't a seduction, he was just a friendly soul with a mischievous spirit. No sooner did he get there, than Bob Hippard arrived, and the both of them started talking and laughing. They decided to go hang out together. The champagne bottle was never opened. I still had the mop in my hand when they left together.

The McGuinns were wonderful grandparents, and Dorothy gave the boys her complete set of L. Frank Baum's 'Oz' book series, that she had owned and read as a child. I would read a chapter with the boys each night before their bedtime. The colorful characters and beautiful illustrations captivated Patrick. Henry was still too young to fully appreciate the books. One of the characters introduced in the second installment, *The Land of Oz,* Jack Pumpkinhead, was a sweet innocent, given life by a mystical powder shaken on him like a jar of pepper, called, 'The Powder of Life.' This possibility fascinated Patrick.

Halloween approached, and the boys were excited to attend a Halloween party with me, given by my new friends, Joey and Marian Kahn, who had a young son, Jaime, all of them friends of Jet Thomas, who had originally told me about Marian's parents, the Bakers. It was a costume party, for grown-ups and kids. Everyone was festive, and I was dressed as Amelia Earhart, wearing jodhpurs, a leather coat, and a silk scarf.

We were all delighted to see Jack Pumpkinhead walk into the room. Lanky and energetic, dressed in white shirt and pants, with a bulky carved pumpkin face, he seemed straight out of the Oz book we'd been reading.

I approached him to compliment his costume.

"You're Jack Pumpkinhead, aren't you?" He was surprised I knew the character. "You're right," he said as he lifted the huge pumpkin off his shoulders, once his entrance was complete. "Most people would say I was a Jack O' Lantern."

The striking, handsome face that emerged was a pleasant surprise. "I'm Macfarland," he said, extending his hand. "What's your real name, Amelia?"

"Ianthe," I said, smiling. "I've been reading the Oz books to my children."

"My mother's a Baum," he said. "She's L. Frank Baum's granddaughter."

"Well, we have the whole collection of books," I said, intrigued by his lineage.

"So you have children, are you married?"

"Divorced," I said, sipping my beer.

"Good!" he smiled with a twinkle in his beautiful blue eyes.

The evening flew by, and Mac and I exchanged phone numbers. He lived on an isolated ranch near the Tortuga Mountains, so the phone number was his parents' house in town, where he stayed on weekends, but he said he would get in touch with me to go out to dinner.

To my surprise and delight, Mac phoned and it seemed like an indication that he had been thinking of me, too. Monday night, I felt as if I was his woman, not withstanding my current of turmoil or distance.

He seemed very essential to my being, and like a security and excitement, no matter what. I'd not felt so strongly about anyone in some time.

The excitement and happiness I felt meeting Macfarland Donaldson after a year and a half of single life was most welcome. It was as if I'd come to an oasis in the desert. He was not in the least bit threatened that I was divorced with two young boys. His kindness and manners were matched by his masculine good looks.

Things moved in a positive direction with Mac. His family was from the East Coast: Duponts on one side, and the Baums on the other. His parents, Janet and John, were genteel and sophisticated. They enjoyed Tucson as a resort, and had made their way west to become cowboys.

John owned a cattle ranch outside of Tucson in the Avra Valley. Mac and his brother, Johnny, lived on the ranch, attempting to breed thoroughbred horses. Polo was their weekend sport in the spring and fall. Mac had an older sister, Bonnie, who was about my age. She and her husband, Murray Hudson, had two sons, Mac and Duncan, who were identical in age to Patrick and Henry. We all became immediate friends.

As we dated, Mac, seeing my Porsche and knowing my history in Los Angeles, realized I wasn't an ordinary Tucson Latina. This intrigued him as well. Mac and I had a tremendous, instant chemistry. We fell in love quickly, and he helped erase my Los Angeles pain. On weekends, Mac and I would have dinner out, and go dancing. The boys would stay with Mac's parents or with Mac and Duncan and their babysitter.

It was easy to love Mac: he was a sensitive, loving and considerate gentleman. He enjoyed the boisterous quality of the boys' play, and I thought Mac might become a good father figure to them.

It was two years into our relationship when Mac suggested we all move in with him at the isolated ranch, fifty miles outside of Tucson. Initially, I thought this might be a bit far for the boys, but it turned out there was a nearby public school they could attend. I thought of the money we'd save, not paying a monthly rent.

About this time, and with a myriad of car troubles, I sold the Porsche to a mechanic who knew its issues intimately. I bought a Volkswagen 'Thing' Jeep, which would adapt to our new lifestyle on the ranch.

I'd visited the ranch house before – it was a small adobe cottage, three rooms, railroad style, with a roofed-in porch. There was running water from a well and electricity, but no phone or television. The nearest neighbor, Mac's brother Johnny, lived a mile away in a narrow mobile home, with his wife and young daughter. They did have a telephone and a television.

This was a fascinating period in my life. I became a cowboy's 'wife.' Mac would spend his days out on the ranch feeding, shoeing and caring for the horses and undertaking other tasks, while I kept the house. I would pick up the boys at their school bus stop, and serve them tea and cookies as an after-school treat.

During the rainy season, the dirt roads became so muddy that Mac and the boys rode horses to the bus stop. Cars got stuck in the muddy roads. I experimented with different foods and we always had good meals. At night, we used hurricane lamps, which seemed appropriate, given our pioneer setting.

Patrick and Henry, without television, became imaginative and creative, putting on nightly puppet shows and drawing with pastels and watercolors continuously.

Sometimes, I would feel very lonely. Luckily, around this time, a new radio program came on National Public Radio, called *All Things Considered*. I felt as if I was connecting to kindred spirits from the East Coast; it was *The New York Times* without a subscription. The latest news was shared, in my mind, through an appropriate angle of journalism. Susan Stamberg became an afternoon friend.

Mac told me that friends of his from Australia were stopping through Tucson, and would be staying with us in a nearby cottage on the ranch. We'd had occasional visitors from the city but these guests were world travelers on tour, who'd stay for at least a month.

The adobe cottage they would inhabit had far less amenities: it was almost a shack with a dirt floor, no electricity or running water. There was an outhouse. They arrived, and they were wonderful, Harley and Jane, new friends that enriched our life on the ranch.

Harley Gale and Mac had met in Sydney, Australia, where Mac lived for a while. Jane McCartney was from Auckland, New Zealand, and she had been with Harley for a few years. Large eyeglasses accented her friendly, pretty face. She became a dear friend; we shared a common sensibility. We cooked meals together in the kitchen, and had a knack for curry, which became a household favorite for all of us.

Harley and Jane had traveled to Thailand and China, where Harley was interested in and had learned more about acupuncture. He gave both Mac and me acupuncture treatments. Harley had also brought his super-8mm movie camera, with which he'd documented their travels. At nightfall, we'd turn out the lights and watch his movies projected on the white stucco wall: New York City, China, Thailand, Tahiti and Las Vegas all came to life through his Kodachrome movies.

The homespun cinema inspired Patrick, and Harley was generous in wanting to make an experimental Tucson film, cast with Patrick and Henry, using the ranch as a backdrop. They filmed in the daylight hours after school, Henry with an assortment of ghoulish rubber masks and costumes, Patrick illustrating backdrops, used in forced perspectives, with live action characters.

The resulting film gave all of us profound amusement – Harley had used special effects photography to create a magical story of a demon in pursuit of an innocent boy. Patrick began his film quest, seeing the power of filmmaking as a storytelling tool.

It was a sad day, many months later, when Harley and Jane had to leave Arizona for Costa Rica, via Mexico. I would not see either of them for a decade. Jane had become my confidante and best friend. It was heartbreaking to see her leave, but I knew we'd see each other again.

Life on the ranch became more difficult: there was the isolation, dust storms, and the question as to whether Mac and I would get married.

On weekends in town, Mac was flirting with other women, and I was reminded of men's nature, having learned from Roger, an expert philanderer. Mac, an increasingly stern disciplinarian, sometimes punished the boys – no different from how Mac himself was raised. I didn't agree with corporal punishment though. Sometimes I felt concerned; we were out in the middle of nowhere, with no phone, no way to let anyone know if trouble fell on us.

Occasionally, illegal Mexican immigrants passed through the property, trying to find a better life. I never felt threatened, but it was disturbing to think who might pass through the wilderness of the property at any given time.

On one hot summer night, Mac and I slept on the roof of the house, under the starlight, to cool down. The boys slept below, with only a hurricane lamp lit as a night light.

Early the next morning, a few Mexican men came to the door. Patrick and Henry were up and dressed in costumes, playing. They offered the Mexicans some food, and they soon left.

When Mac and I awoke, Patrick told me this story. I was amused, and yet thought, what if they'd taken the boys away? Or tried to steal something from the house? My concern grew out of our isolation, and I realized it was time for us to leave the ranch, and move back to the city, so I could continue to pursue my studies.

Mac didn't take the news well. He thought this was the beginning of our breakup. I insisted it wasn't, that it was solely for the boys' education and welfare, and my studies. As it turned out, it did become the reason Mac and I would break up.

Journal entry, May 30, 1975

I didn't know what to say to dear Patrick as he whispered, "Mommy, Roger hates me because he doesn't like you. Does he have another son? He'll really hate me then." I tried explaining that even if Roger doesn't like me, that has nothing to do with their relationship. I told him I was certain Roger loved him.

But it's been over four years since he's seen them. Does that show he loves them? He left us alone and unprotected, expecting me to function as mother and father. How will anyone love them with the abiding, fulfilling love a parent has? Who will help and show them the way? Oh God, help me to be strong, to do what's right by making the correct decisions. Fill the void the boys have because Roger was too scared, too immature, and too selfish.

They are truly wonderful: bright, handsome boys. Everything happens for the best, for a reason. Hopefully they will be healthy and happy. For this grave negative there will be something good happening from it.

Journal entry, June 4, 1975

The boys are finally out of school today. Patrick still has tomorrow but it is such a joy. They will spend Mondays and Tuesdays with the

McGuinns and hopefully we can leave the following week on our much-needed vacation. Going in the car and taking as little, yet as many useful things as needed. Don't know where except beginning in San Diego and ending in Mendocino with the whole summer to putter around.

I've been considering a trip to Chicago and New York, by means of flying of course. Maybe leave the car in L.A. Will have to think more on that.

Mom, after being asked by Patrick whether she knew Cleopatra, replied, "I knew her. She taught me all that I know."

Journal entry, June 17, 1975

In Denny's on Interstate-8 just outside of Yuma on our way to San Diego. Feeling thoughtful and glad to be with the boys. They are inspiration and joy. So many dead animals on the road. The only mistake they made was trying to get from one side to the other.

Journal entry, July 3, 1975

Returned from a two-day stay, longer than expected as far as both Mac and I were concerned. Feeling, however, iciness from Mac. Can't blame him. I wouldn't want him to do that. Nothing to add except there isn't a place.

Journal entry, July 4, 1975

You see, it was all in my mind. Mac wasn't upset to the extent I had imagined. Had a horrible right-sided headache last night. The kind that put me in the hospital four years ago.

Henry found an enormous toad. Green, wet and fat. He's very vocal, especially when Henry picks him up with both hands and peers into his face, meeting bulging yellow eyes with his own fond cow-brown eyes.

Journal entry, July 10, 1975

Drove into town like a mad fiend. Late for an appointment with a nursing counselor, smelling like Pears soap, coffee and Eau de Citrus. They of course made me wait for fifteen minutes, only to let me know the first two years are in Liberal Arts College.

Spoke to Sister Ann about boys' school. Saw D. Johnson about buying a home. Don't know exactly how to approach that situation, buying versus renting. Depends largely on Roger and his financial and contributing aspect. Alas – only fate knows.

Journal entry, July 12, 1975

What a ridiculous state to be in, an invariable predicament each year. Sick of looking for some place to live. Wondering if that house is worth investing in. There are others. Perhaps waiting. No more wait. Please. Tired of it, transient as a hobo, not quite.

The myth of life is fading as age is on the continuum. Lost is the soul-searching light in man. I, so named, is longing as truth shrouded in cloaks of darkness and lean, hungry gapes of people, without. Where are the seekers of wisdom and truth, drowning in their sorrow and drunk in the face of it all?

(end of journal entries)

Just before school started, I found a house in town, near the University of Arizona, a charming Tudor-style chalet with high ceilings, that we could rent. The boys were thrilled to be back in civilization, with neighborhood children and television, the normal things kids want. I enrolled them in a nearby Catholic school, Saints Peter and Paul. Mac visited on the weekends.

It was around this time, in the autumn of 1975, when Dorothy called me. "Roger will be in town in a week, he's performing a show. He'd like to see the boys." I couldn't believe my ears. Four years had gone by since Roger had seen or even communicated with his children in any way. The last Patrick saw of his father was when he was four years old, and now he was about to turn nine. The divorce attorneys had not settled anything – all was at a standstill, apparently, because Roger's career, and money-earning power, was at a low ebb.

I told the boys they'd be seeing their father at their grandparents' on the north side of Tucson. They were fascinated by the impending visit. I was enrolled in the nursing department at Pima College, getting general studies out of the way. Mac learned of Roger's show, and the boys seeing their father. I think he felt threatened. He had grown closer to the boys, but now he felt like we were all pulling away from him.

The McGuinns came to pick up the boys, and took them to see Roger, and his performance, opening for the Eagles at the Tucson Community Center, a three-thousand-seat auditorium.

Mac and I had a quiet dinner together that night. He talked about how difficult things continued to be on the ranch, especially without me. I felt bad, but knew I could not return to that isolation. It must have been at this point that Mac realized our future together was limited, if I couldn't exist in his world of horses, braving the elements, and hard physical labor.

Patrick and Henry returned from the McGuinns' and Roger's concert, carrying large puppets that Roger had given them: Patrick's a clown marionette and Henry's a Cookie Monster hand puppet. Apparently Roger and Linda had separated, and she was the reason he had not stayed in touch with the boys. She had felt threatened.

The boys were shy in conveying what this encounter with their mysterious, illustrious father had been like. They each had an un-opened vinyl record, *Roger McGuinn & Band*, depicting Roger in a control room with knobs and TV monitors everywhere. Mac examined the album and asked Patrick, "Do you still like me?"

Patrick said, "Yes."

I thought of my own fathers, Daddy Gus, and my father Marcus, and the duality of their roles in my life.

It was a sad day when I told Mac that he and I should not remain together, if we were not going to get married. I admit it was an ultimatum. I wanted a future, and more children. Mac didn't think it would work, and we both cried on each other's shoulders.

A few months later, when I was well into my studies, he brought me flowers, but I knew our relationship was over. Part of me felt it was better to leave than to be left, a sorry lesson learned from my heartbreak with Roger. Mac was a wonderful companion and kind man.

1976 - 1989 - The Ties That Bind

Brian, Roger, Dorothy, Patrick and Henry McGuinn, autumn 1975

Journal entry, Sept. 25, 1976

After all these years of knowing and caring for Chris Hillman, wanting to be with him, I'm on my way to meet him in Charlotte, N.C. An innocuous place; means nothing to me, but the South. Mac now living on the ranch with a cowgirl he's met. My inner joy of seeing Chris is swelling inside, old friend, recorder of similar events, shared realities in L.A.

I told mother I was staying with brother Larry in Phoenix, I knew she would be upset on Roger's behalf if she knew about me and Chris.

Chris over the phone: "What if we don't like each other?"

Me: "What a thing to say!"
Airplanes parking, shadow cast on green pastures spotted with cows and cattle, livestock. Misty haze over lush growth hiding – a lot of trees. Chris.
7:00
God – make this last. How do we enjoy this to the fullest? Give me two beers. I am really loaded. Good to see him.
Reality – moment by moment. Take it or leave it. Being on the road never being reality is a misconception. It *is* reality. Then is now accepted by all those present.

Journal entry, Oct. 12, 1976

Boys' birthdays coming soon. I expect nothing from anyone, must motivate myself, be more directed in a positive attitude. Find strength and stop taking negative reinforcing drugs. Admit that we are alone in our lives.

Journal entry, Nov. 15, 1976

Celebrated my 34th birthday in Phoenix with a bottle of champagne and a $30.00 wine – good meal and infantile company. Needless to say, worse news from Mac's end, he's getting married to that cowgirl at the beginning of the year. C'est la vie. The good thing that has happened is that Patrick is taking piano lessons. My grades are very average and depressing; must put my mind to raising them. No word from Roger or Chris.

(end of journal entries)

Jeannie called me one evening. "Dolores, how could you?" She was referring to Chris and me in North Carolina. *Easily*, I thought. They were breaking up, and secrets were being revealed. In reality, it had been a disaster with Chris. I drank too much, and Chris was on cocaine, so neither of us experienced each other in a state of clarity.

Perhaps we both felt guilty about changing the dynamic of our long-standing platonic friendship. The sex was forgettable, if we even had it, which was sad, because in the 1960s there seemed to be a mutual tenderness, an unexplored potential that we both respected, and now was broken.

It was a December evening near Christmas in 1976 when Dorothy and James McGuinn drove up to our house; and who should emerge from their green Lincoln Town Car, but Roger? He wore a white suit and tinted blue aviator glasses, his long hair parted in the middle. I was having a small dinner party for my parents, the McGuinns, my brother, Larry, and his girlfriend. The boys were excited because I had baked my famous chocolate soufflé. Roger's presence was an utter surprise – no one but the McGuinns knew he was coming.

I hadn't seen Roger since the Roman billiard incident in Malibu, five years earlier. It was very strange and surreal to have him in my kitchen and living room, friendly as ever, attempting charm. He and Linda had officially split up. Impossibly, he seemed ready to leave the past behind, and wanted to be my friend. I had held on to this notion as a possibility over the years, because I still loved him. Now that he was here in the flesh, I was in a state of disbelief.

Patrick and Henry seemed to feel a cohesive family unit coming together: seeing Roger and me sitting at the table to dinner with both sets of our parents made sense to them. I served a great meal of prime rib, string beans, Yorkshire pudding, and red wine – there was plenty for everyone. It was a festive, loving atmosphere.

As the night wore on, we all drank and celebrated this impromptu family reunion. Larry and Roger played guitars together in the living room, people sang along with Roger's song from his upcoming *Thunderbyrd* album, 'We Can Do It All Over Again,' which seemed to be the message he was sending me. Gradually, the hour got late, and the McGuinns said thanks and goodnight, leaving the house without Roger.

My mother Hope, Daddy Gus, Larry and his girlfriend also left. I was alone with Roger and my children, in our house as I washed the dinner dishes. It wasn't a dream. It was real. Roger was different, though. Repentant, he said he'd stopped cocaine use and only drank now. He talked about his recent exciting travels with Bob Dylan's tour. He wore a silver medallion, with the logo for the Rolling

Thunder Revue on a chain around his neck, which he carefully removed before coming to bed with me.

The boys were asleep. Roger and I made love. It was like old times. We slept late the next morning, and I prepared French toast with bacon for breakfast, for the four of us. The road to this sweet, tender and familiar breakfast together was hard won. I didn't want to think about any of the ugliness that had preceded this visit with Roger. In a way, I still couldn't believe all of this was really happening.

Roger said that he wanted to see the boys more often. Part of me wondered if there was some financial motive involved... was he trying to get out of a commitment to a trust fund for the boys? I thought the alimony probably wouldn't come through, at this point. But were Roger and I getting back together? I was receiving mixed signals. I was further along in my nursing education, and was starting to get to the point where I might make a living as a nurse.

Roger and I maintained contact over the course of the next year. The new album, *Thunderbyrd*, came out. He sent me a promotional copy in the mail. We still received our monthly payment of $1,125.00 from his accounting firm, and there still had been no legal financial settlement from our divorce.

Journal entry, Jan. 12, 1977

The holidays are over - thankful that everything is still together. Mother was desperately ill in L.A. Roger was here before Christmas and we spent most of our time with him during the holiday. One night he got really drunk and it was as if replaying an old tape. He was mean and arrogant. I felt then that getting together would be out of the question.

Undated Journal entry, 1977

School began yesterday. What a relief to be doing something other than scurrying around. My classes look promising. Everyone looks so dapper in what I suppose is their Christmas finery. Everything will work out - Everything comes to light.

(end of journal entries)

That summer of 1977, the boys and I made our annual summer trip to Los Angeles, to stay with my brother, Marcus, and his family. One night when we were there, I stayed with Roger in his Century City apartment.

I was surprised at how Roger was living his life now, very simply, in a modest one-bedroom urban high-rise. We stayed together, only leaving the apartment to go out to eat. It seemed he was living the bachelor life again.

We made a trip to Disneyland, Roger wearing his white suit. The boys had fun seeing the park through Roger's perspective, since he had inside information on some of the 'Disney magic' in the Pirates of the Caribbean and Haunted Mansion attractions. The boys and I had been to Disneyland a few times before, but this was a special visit, as a family. It all felt right.

That October, Bob Hippard came to Tucson with Roger, to pick up the boys and go on a 'camping trip' to Mount Lemmon, about an hour east of Tucson. I was grateful that Roger was making an effort to be present in his children's lives.

The camping was a bust. It had been rainy, and the ground was far too wet for a campfire. Roger and Bob had sprayed charcoal lighter fluid on wet wood, with no results. It was a sweet gesture.

We drove to Los Angeles for Thanksgiving weekend, 1977. My mother was going to prepare a meal at Marcus' house. I invited Roger, and my good friend Madelyn who had been living in Manhattan Beach. My brother's family was surprised to see Roger after what had been many years. It was an interesting evening. However, the warmth I'd felt with Roger had not been sustained: we were living very different lives in two separate cities.

That December, Roger came to Tucson, this time with a new girlfriend, Season Hubley. She was an actress Roger had probably met in an acting class. This came as no surprise to me that he had someone new. I was disappointed, but knew that it was always in the realm of possibility that Roger would 'fly away' again. He had made no commitment to me. As long as he wanted to see his sons, I was grateful. They were seeing him more now than they'd ever seen him in the last four years combined.

Season and Roger took Patrick, Henry and a neighborhood friend to see *Close Encounters of the Third Kind*. Patrick conveyed how friendly Season was, and how much they all enjoyed the film together. I was grateful that Roger found someone so easygoing who even said to Roger, "You have a nice little family." This must have meant something to him, because he and Season weren't together long. He later made up his mind and said yes, he and I should get back together, to be a family again, with the boys. The logistics were to be determined, but we set a date of Easter, 1978, that he would come to Tucson to figure things out.

Easter approached, and I still had not heard from Roger. I called his Century City apartment, no answer. I was beginning to wonder if he'd slipped back into drug abuse. On Easter Sunday, the boys and I were having dinner at my mother's house in Tucson. The phone rang. It was Roger.

"I've made my decision. I've found the Lord Jesus, and I've gotten married. I'm not coming to Tucson." My head was in a spin. What kind of joke was this? Leave it to Roger to come up with the cruelest humor, when you least expected it. "You're kidding?" I asked. He confirmed that he'd met a young actress in acting class, and had gotten married.

I shook my head in disappointment and disgust, "He's just gotten married," I said, in an aside to my mother, who was looking on, perplexed. My mother immediately scowled and grabbed the phone from me, speaking to Roger directly, "Roger, don't you ever come to this house again!" She slammed the phone on the receiver, hanging up on him.

I never told the boys Roger had planned to reunite with our little family and become a father again to them. Roger had mistreated me in the past and been evasive, and it was now with caution that I accepted any goodwill gestures from him. It was a good thing I had not told them, and didn't get their hopes up.

I started working as an LPN, as I continued classes toward my RN license. I was employed at the University of Arizona Medical Center.

It was rough, going to school and working full time. We were lucky that we lived close to the University, and that the boys and I could eat together on my lunch break.

In 1979, Roger stopped sending monthly payments. It was hard to make ends meet on the salary I was earning as an LPN. My brother Marcus suggested that we move back to Los Angeles, where the salary for nurses was higher than in Tucson.

Before the move, a Subud friend in California told me that one of their friends was moving out of a small house in Sherman Oaks, and that it would be available in July. We made plans to move back to Los Angeles that summer.

That May, Roger brought his new wife, Camilla, to Tucson to meet his parents and the boys. Roger, sporting a new short haircut and wearing white cotton pants and a light blue-collared shirt embroidered with a rainbow across it, stood silently at the door to pick up the boys. I was sitting on the couch, reading a paperback. I didn't look up, or say a word to him.

The boys were ready to leave, and could see my annoyance at Roger. He said, "We'll be back later." When the boys returned that evening, they spoke of Camilla, and how Dorothy thought she resembled Henry.

A day or two later, Camilla stopped by the house while I was preparing dinner. She wanted to break the ice. I was chopping vegetables for a spaghetti Bolognese sauce, as she looked on, and spoke of Roger's desire to see more of his kids. She was a younger woman, and I could see a resemblance to Henry; even their haircuts were similar. I didn't find anything she said particularly enlightening. Feeling hurt about Roger's decision, I couldn't really absorb what she was trying to say. Her words seemed meaningless. Everyone starts out with good intentions, I thought to myself. She would eventually manage Roger and his life.

We moved to Los Angeles as planned, an ordeal in the summertime, with a panting bulldog in the passenger seat, and a bunny rabbit in a cage in the front cab with me as I drove. My nurse friend, Mary Schmazel, took turns driving the U-Haul truck and our Subaru station wagon, across the desert in the merciless July heat.

Mother cried when we left Tucson. I did, too. The boys were growing up, and Los Angeles would provide more opportunities for all of us. They would have closer proximity to their father, and I felt that I could be closer to the divorce attorney to settle the financial aspect of the dissolution, which had dragged on throughout the Seventies.

Los Angeles was no longer the city I remembered. Places in Hollywood that were a part of the Sixties scene were now boarded up or covered in graffiti. The smog had worsened over the years, along with the traffic. It was quite an adjustment from Tucson. L.A. did pay higher salaries for Licensed Practical Nurses, but, as it turned out, my clinical hours were not enough to have an LPN license in California. There was no reciprocity between states, and I ended up working at Sherman Oaks Hospital as a nurse's aide. To make matters worse, costs in Los Angeles were significantly higher. Everything, from groceries to gasoline, cost more, and we were under even more financial stress.

The boys did see a bit more of Roger, but later discovered that he was soon moving to Morro Bay, a five-hour drive up the coast. One day I called him. There was little food in the refrigerator. We were out of money, as I'd just paid rent and utilities. We had no money leftover in our budget for food. Roger had ceased all payments of child support by this time, with the excuse that he was not earning a salary. When he answered the phone, I said, "Roger, can you please send us some money? There's no milk in the refrigerator."

"Call your lawyer," he spat back, and hung up the phone on me. I was furious. I now knew that despite his newfound Christianity, he was still self-centered. He was just as venomous toward me, now with his new bride, as he'd been when married to Linda. I realized the boys and I had to fend for ourselves, yet again. I called my mother and borrowed some money.

About this time, I ran into Eddie Tickner at a bank on Ventura Boulevard in Studio City. He was surprised to see me. I told him we'd moved back to L.A. He said that he and Rita had gotten a divorce. Eddie was managing the career of Emmylou Harris, and he invited me to dinner, to a favorite Chinese Restaurant of his. He said, "Bring the boys."

Eddie arrived one night in his blue Oldsmobile and took the three of us to Ho Toy's, a Polynesian-style Chinese restaurant in the San Fernando Valley. Eddie's wry humor, kindness and good-natured conversation made me feel comfortable. He set the boys at ease. Patrick had remembered Eddie from long ago: Eddie had given him a small bag of salted peanuts when we lived on Alomar. Patrick always remembered that kind gesture. There was a shared history between us that seemed to come full circle.

This was the start of a romantic involvement, which would turn into marriage, years later. I thank God for Eddie. He was so good to all of us, a true gentleman and provider. One of our favorite spots became the Villa Capri, our old haunt with Terry Melcher. Eddie loved fine dining and travel and lavished all of us with his generosity.

Our relationship grew deeper. I wasn't sure, after all of the heartache and escapades, that I could fall in love again, but Eddie won my heart. We moved in together the next year, renting a small house in Sherman Oaks with the boys. I was fortunate enough to return to nursing school at Valley College, where I eventually got my degree in 1982. I found a job at Olive View Hospital in Van Nuys.

One afternoon while I was studying, the phone rang that loud irritating cry. It was Eddie. He had terrible news. Susie White's car had collided with a tractor while she was driving through the winding mountains in Kentucky. She and her young son, Bradley, had been killed. He was exactly Henry's age. I was stunned. I had lost touch with Susie, but always felt such warmth when I thought of our friendship. I had imagined there would be a reunion with her and our children someday. Why was all this tragedy happening to this beautiful family? What would happen to Michelle, her daughter? She and Patrick were the same age and had been playmates. I knew Clarence's brother Roland would be there for Michelle. No words could describe my lament for Susie, Bradley and Clarence. I counted my blessings and cherished my family.

My life with Eddie continued in Los Angeles, complete and fulfilling. His friends and business partners led an active social life, and we were a part of it. It was familiar to be with the people in the music business again, and everyone was doing well, as many of them were involved in some aspect of management or A&R for record labels.

I'll never forget the time Phil Kaufman brought a special wine for Eddie, when he came over for dinner one night. Wrapped in gift paper, Eddie was startled to discover a bottle of Ripple, a cheap swill.

Eddie, being a wine connoisseur, was the butt of Phil's joke. They were great friends.

Patrick and Henry became involved in the burgeoning Los Angeles music scene, forming multiple punk rock bands in the Eighties. We flourished as a family. Henry began playing drums with a group and became a skateboard enthusiast. Patrick continued his film pursuits in high school, and maintained a punk rock band, Carousel of Death, which played a number of shows in Hollywood. I brought along an old friend, Lizzie, a former Franzoni Dancer, to one of Patrick's elaborate shows. She too, had become an RN.

In the spring of 1984, Patrick, Henry and I visited Mother in Tucson. Dorothy was caring for Jim at home through hospice; he was dying of prostate cancer. The four of us went to see them. It was difficult to believe this once robust and athletic man could wither away. He said through a whispered voice, "I'm dying. Dorothy doesn't want to believe it." The tears ran down my face uncontrollably. This was the man who had comforted and supported me when Roger left me. We had kept our secret: Dorothy never knew about that afternoon with Roger, Linda and me. He passed a few days later. I was not invited to the funeral, Roger would be there.

Roger and Camilla, beleaguered by financial duress and guilty consciences, no doubt, eventually offered $10,000 to settle the divorce, out of court. Eddie said, "Why bother? Too little, too late. Don't accept it." I didn't, though I was always sorry that I hadn't set the money aside for the boys. I was now earning a living as an RN, and we were able to provide for ourselves.

Emmylou Harris, who'd been based in Encino, an LA suburb, decided to relocate to Nashville, Tennessee. Eddie, being her manager, wanted to move out of Los Angeles as well. His proposal of marriage was based on Eddie wanting us to join him in Nashville. I accepted, and Eddie and I married in Hawaii, in 1985.

No sooner did we arrive in Nashville than Emmylou's new husband, Paul Kennerly, fired Eddie. This, I believe, was much to Emmy's dismay, but her husband had convinced her that she needed to go with a high-powered management company at this stage in her career, instead of Eddie's personal, one-on-one operation. The termination was a blow to Eddie, since we'd paid out of pocket to relocate. In order to make ends meet, I took a job at a nearby hospital.

This was grueling work, and once the brutally cold winter hit Nashville, I knew I wanted to leave, to return to Arizona.

I missed my mother, and I knew that deep down I belonged in the desert. Eventually, Eddie and I would relocate to Tucson, when he went into partial retirement, maintaining an office in Nashville.

I've been happily working as a registered nurse at St. Mary's Hospital since 1989. Few people there know that I was once a Rock 'n' Roll Star Queen. Sometimes, it all seems like a dream from a hundred years ago.

Epilogue - Forgiveness

It was Thanksgiving, 2008. I was surprised to receive a dinner invitation from Dorothy McGuinn, who had remained in Tucson since 1972. She had just turned ninety-eight years old the previous July. Roger and Camilla were to attend the dinner. I hadn't seen either of them since Henry's wedding in 1995, thirteen years before. Few words had passed between Roger and me on that occasion.

As I walked up the flagstone steps that evening, I was very nervous. I peeked in the window and I saw a thin, little old man stooped over the coffee table. I was shocked when I realized it was Roger. I rang the doorbell and Camilla and Roger rushed to meet me. Camilla, without even saying hello, asked, "Roger wants to know if you'll forgive him." Roger stood beside her, nodding his head, looking at me plaintively.

I was stunned by their request. I'd become a widow since they'd last seen me. It was the urgency of the question, dismissing a greeting: I was lost for words. I heard myself saying, "I don't think I can ever forgive you, Roger."

Camilla scoffed, "You have to forgive him."

I shrugged my shoulders, and said "Only God can forgive you," realizing how awkward my dramatic response made the situation. Seeing their collective disappointment, I then muttered, "Okay. I forgive you." They instantly looked relieved.

Dorothy called out to us, "Hi Ianthe," not knowing what had just transpired. The three of us walked into the sunroom where Dorothy greeted guests and offered us drinks. The subsequent meal went by with mundane conversation sprinkled with awkward moments.

I had never thought to forgive Roger formally for breaking my heart and destroying our family. I had numbed myself to the pain and rejection over the years, knowing his absence had traumatized Patrick and Henry throughout their young lives. He had been a terrible father to them, something Dorothy acknowledged frequently. "Roger is a taker, not a giver," she used to say on hot summer days, when she and I would have beers together. I reflected on those words as I arrived home.

Despite Roger's neglect of his sons during their childhood, his parents, Jim and Dorothy, had always been supportive. I never spoke an unkind word about Roger to the boys, and I found myself even making excuses for his failures. They had grown to know Roger through their grandparents. Dorothy recounted many memorable boyhood stories of Roger. The McGuinns nurtured Patrick and Henry and showed them love where Roger could not. I loved both Jim and Dorothy dearly.

Perhaps I had already forgiven Roger years before. Bitterness and resentment only destroys one's self. I could not have kept my sanity or carried on if I *hadn't* forgiven him.

"If you love deeply, you're going to get hurt badly. But it's still worth it." – *C.S. Lewis*

James, Dorothy and Jimmy (Roger) McGuinn, Chicago, ca 1945

Afterword

Many of my beloved friends and family have died in the years since these events took place. With a heavy heart, I mourned the loss of my mother, Hope, and Daddy Gus in 2003, my father, Marcus, in 1992, and my husband Eddie in 2006.

Henry's sons, James and Ciaron, born in the Nineties, have been a blessing to me. I see their ambitions in life and in music and I remember the days when I first met Roger, then Jim, innocently gazing at a performance in the Ash Grove, the stage light casting a halo around his head. I think the bigger message of life that I have witnessed through all of my adventures is that innocence cannot always survive in a world that seeks to corrupt. Nevertheless, the moments of innocence that exist are pure.

God gave me the courage and strength to continue when Henry, Patrick and I were alone and struggling in the Seventies. My career in nursing has taught me that helping others is the true source of inner peace.

I thank my sons, for in spite of my past misdeeds and failings, they still love me. God knows they kept me going.

I dedicate this book to my grandsons, Ciaron and James, who once said, "Tell me everything about the Byrds and the Sixties, Nana. And don't leave anything out." Well Boys, now you know.

Ianthe McGuinn

Lightning Source UK Ltd.
Milton Keynes UK
UKHW02f1931020318
318807UK00007B/361/P